Essential Software Architecture

Ian Gorton

Essential
Software
Architecture

With 93 Figures and 11 Tables

 Springer

Author

Ian Gorton

National ICT Australia
Bay 15, Locomotive Workshop
Australian Technology Park, Garden St
Eveleigh NSW 1430, Australia
Ian.gorton@nicta.com.au

Library of Congress Control Number: 2006921741

ACM Computing Classification (1998): D.2

ISBN-10 3-540-28713-2 Springer Berlin Heidelberg New York
ISBN-13 978-3-540-28713-1 Springer Berlin Heidelberg New York

Springer is a part of Springer Science+Business Media

springer.com

© Springer-Verlag Berlin Heidelberg 2006
Printed in Germany

Typeset by the author
Production: LE-TEX Jelonek, Schmidt & Vöckler GbR, Leipzig
Cover design: KünkelLopka Werbeagentur, Heidelberg

Printed on acid-free paper   45/3100/YL - 5 4 3 2 1 0

Foreword

Architecture is something of a black art in the IT world. Architects learn on the job, bringing years of experience in design and technology to the business problems they tackle. It's not an easy task to impart architecture knowledge.

So when Ian first spoke to me about the idea of writing this book, I thought "Great! Finally there will be a book that I can recommend to the many developers and students who approach me asking what they have to do to become an IT architect". I knew that from reading the book they would discover many of the essential ingredients of being a good practicing IT architect.

In the years that I have known Ian, he has been an inspirational educator, a pragmatic and decisive software architect, and an idealistic software architecture researcher. On top of all that, he is an excellent communicator, who articulates advanced computing concepts clearly and succinctly irrespective of his audience – the novice or the experienced. Ian is also full of great life stories to tell – all told with a great sense of humor (especially after a few glasses of good wine!).

It is not until Ian handed me drafts of the various chapters that I realized that this is a *must have* book for the experienced IT architects too. As consulting enterprise architects, we are usually working inside an enterprise's boundary, trying to influence the IT directions of the various departments within the enterprise, and designing the next evolution of IT architecture that breaks down the silos within the organization. We are often lone spirits, making important technology acquisition and design decisions without having a reference to look upon for validation of what we are doing. Now, for practicing architects, Ian's book serves this precise purpose – it brings a sense of relief knowing that we are not alone, and that there are many others who also face similar architecture challenges. Ian's book, although by no means a silver bullet to all of our IT architecture challenges, certainly helps us head in the right direction through the various techniques and approaches presented.

So here it is, an essential guide to computer science students as well as practicing developers and IT professionals who aspire to become an IT architect. For the experienced architects, it serves as a reference, a good validation of our thinking, and provides a summary of emerging technologies and practices that will be important in the not-too-distant future.

I hope you will enjoy the read as much as I have.

Dr. Anna Liu
Architect Advisor, Microsoft
Sydney, Australia

Preface

Motivation

In the not too distant past, on a decent sized project I was working on, I convinced a senior developer, a highly skilled and experienced software engineer, to purchase a copy of "Documenting Software Architectures: Views and Beyond". The project was a little sparse in terms of documentation and process, the team was well aware of this, and I was trying to help improve the situation. Soon after the book arrived, a brief corridor conversation saw strong expressions of enthusiasm. So strong, an additional project team meeting was called for the next week.

In the meeting, the senior engineer held up this "wonderful" book, and espoused many of its key messages to the team. I was, of course, pleased that the book I'd recommended had made such an impact. Then the follow line caught my attention:

"I read the first 30 or so pages, which were great, but only skimmed the rest."

I was a little surprised at this statement. Why was the content of this very informative and incredibly useful book mostly "skimmed"? Surely anyone could learn much from investing a little time in reading the more technical chapters? I certainly did. This set me pondering the root cause of this issue, as I really wanted to instill more architectural knowledge in the development teams I was working with.

In my career as a *roving* software architect, I've spent a lot of time consulting on projects, providing architectural design skills and knowledge. These projects have spanned many organizations and different application domains over the last decade.

A common theme though, is that I work mostly in what would be considered general information technology (IT) application domains. The sort of applications that financial institutions, utilities and Government agencies build to manage and deliver information to their customers and trading partners. These are, broadly, *business information systems* that leverage

Commercial-off-the-shelf (COTS) technologies like databases, middleware, packaged applications and web technologies.

I occasionally work on projects in what are considered *more technical* domains, such as military, embedded control and telecommunications applications. I can do this because many of the underlying architectural issues are the same across domains. However, the way these issues manifest themselves, the particular technology solutions that are commonly adopted and the technical vocabularies used are radically different. Hence I specialize in IT systems – this is where I can hopefully add more value.

Sometimes my role involves designing new application architectures, or actually more frequently evaluating existing ones and helping evolve them. In the process, I work closely with the members of projects teams. This is enjoyable. I always learn from them, and I hope they sometimes learn from me.

A strikingly common characteristic of most of these projects is a lack of explicit architectural design. Functional requirements are usually captured, agreed with stakeholders and managed, and designs that address the functional specifications are fleshed out in detail. But the architectural issues, the "how" the application achieves its purpose, the "what" happens when things change and evolve or fail, are frequently implicit (this means they are in somebody's head) at best. At worst, they are simply not addressed in any way that can be described in terms other than accidental. Frequently, when I ask for an overview of the application architecture and the driving non-functional requirements at the first technical meeting, people start drawing on a whiteboard. Or they show me code. Either of these is rarely a good sign.

The problems and risks of poor architectural practices are well known and documented within the software engineering profession. A large body of excellent architectural knowledge is captured in broadly accessible books, journals and reports from members of the Software Engineering Institute (SEI), Siemens and various other renowned industrial and academic institutions.

So, I pondered further, why is this information on best practices and tools not permeating through the IT industry? In response, I can only posit the following.

In general, the many sources of software architecture information are extremely thorough, learned and lengthy, requiring a serious investment of time to fully digest. The SEI books, for example, are based upon many years of experience working in mostly in military applications. These typically comprise large embedded, real-time software systems, with a set of architectural approaches and issues that have a particular emphasis to this application domain. For example, many of the case studies are about avionics, flight simulation, and engine control applications, and present solutions, such as fixed priority scheduling and process distribution, to the problems that are encountered in such systems.

I suspect this emphasis on military and embedded domains makes these materials a difficult read for IT software professionals who are unfamiliar with the problems and solutions described. The vocabularies used tend towards those that are prevalent in academic circles – I still have not heard many IT architects discuss architectural styles, connectors or the merits of formal architecture description languages. They do though discuss architecture and design patterns, middleware and use UML and informal techniques to model aspects of their architectures.

Further, in the software architecture literature, there is little discussion of the types of off-the-shelf technologies that are commonly used to address architectural problems in business information systems. Fixed priority schedulers and embedded operating systems are mostly irrelevant in information systems. Application servers, component technologies and messaging infrastructures are the basic building blocks that are important to an IT architect. These are the foundations of the architectures of modern information systems. It is therefore essential that architects understand how these technologies can be leveraged to effectively provide the architectural mechanisms required by a given application.

This book, then, is an attempt to bridge the gap between the needs of IT professionals and the current body of knowledge in software architecture.

- It attempts to provide clear and concise discussions about the issues, techniques and methods that are at the heart of sound architectural practices.
- It describes and analyzes the general purpose component and middleware technologies that support many of the fundamental architectural patterns used in applications.
- It looks forward to how changes in technologies and practices may affect the next generation of business information systems.
- It uses familiar information systems as examples, taken from the author's experiences in banking, e-commerce and government information systems.
- It also provides pointers and references to existing work on software architecture.

If you work as an architect or senior designer, or you want to one day, this book should be of value to you. And if you're a student who is studying software engineering and need an overview of the field of software architecture, this book should be an approachable and useful first source of information. It certainly won't tell you everything you need to know – that will take a lot more than can be included in a book of such modest length. But it aims to convey the essence of architectural thinking, practices and supporting technologies, and to position the reader to delve more deeply into areas that are pertinent to their professional life and interests.

Outline

The book is structured into three basic sections. The first is introductory in nature, and approachable by a relatively non-technical reader wanting an overview of software architecture.

The second section is the most technical in nature. It describes the essential skills and technical knowledge that an IT architect needs.

The third is forward looking. Six chapters each introduce an emerging area of software practice or technology. These are suitable for existing architects and designers, as well as people who've read the first two sections, and who wish to gain insights into the future influences on their profession.

More specifically:

- **Chapters 1–3:** These chapters provide the introductory material for the rest of the book, and the area of software architecture itself. Chapter 1 discusses the key elements of software architecture, and describes the roles of a software architect. Chapter 2 introduces the requirements for a case study problem, a design for which is presented in Chapter 7.This demonstrates the type of problem and associated description that a software architect typically works on. Chapter 3 analyzes the elements of some key quality attributes like scalability, performance and availability. Architects spend a lot of time addressing the quality attribute requirements for applications. It's therefore essential that these quality attributes are well understood, as they are fundamental elements of the knowledge of an architect.
- **Chapters 4–7:** These chapters are the technical backbone of the book. Chapter 4 introduces a range of middleware technologies that architects commonly leverage in application solutions. Chapter 5 presents a three stage iterative software architecture process. It describes the essential tasks and documents that involve an architect. Chapter 6 discusses architecture documentation, and focuses on the new notations available in the UML version 2.0. Chapter 7 brings together the information in the first 6 chapters, showing how middleware technologies can be used to

address the quality attribute requirements for the case study. It also demonstrates the use of the documentation template described in Chapter 6 for documenting an application architecture.

- **Chapters 8–14:** These chapters each focus on an emerging technique or technology that will likely influence the futures of software architects. These include software product lines, model-driven architecture, aspect-oriented architecture, service-oriented architectures and Web services, the Semantic Web and agent technologies. Each chapter introduces the essential elements of the method or technology, describes the state-or-the-art and speculates about how increasing adoption is likely to affect the required skills and practices of a software architect.

Acknowledgements

First, thanks to the chapter contributors who have helped provide the content on software product lines (Mark Staples), aspect-oriented programming (Jenny Liu), model-driven development (Liming Zhu), Web services (Paul Greenfield) and the Semantic Web (Judi Thomson). Your efforts and patience are greatly appreciated. Contact details for the contributing authors are as follows:

Dr Mark Staples, Empirical Software Engineering, National ICT Australia, email: mark.staples@nicta.com.au

Dr Liming Zhu, Empirical Software Engineering, National ICT Australia, email: liming.zhu@nicta.com.au

Dr Yan Liu, Empirical Software Engineering, National ICT Australia, email: jenny.liu@nicta.com.au

Paul Greenfield, School of IT, University of Sydney, email: p.greenfield@computer.org

Dr Judi McCuaig, University of Guelph, Canada, email: judi@cis.uguelph.ca

I'd also like to thank everyone at Springer who has helped make this book a reality, especially the editor, Ralf Gerstner.

I'd also like to acknowledge the many talented software architects, engineers and researchers who I've worked closely with recently and/or who have helped shape my thinking and experience through long and entertaining geeky discussions. In no particular order these are Anna Liu, Paul Greenfield, Shiping Chen, Paul Brebner, Jenny Liu, John Colton, Dave

Thurman, Jereme Haack, Sven Overhage, John Grundy, Muhammad Ali Babar, Justin Almquist, Rik Littlefield, Kevin Dorow, Steffen Becker, Ranata Johnson, Len Bass, Lei Hu, Jim Thomas, Deb Gracio, Nihar Trivedi, Paula Cowley, Jim Webber, Adrienne Andrew, Dan Adams, Dean Kuo, John Hoskins, Shuping Ran, Doug Palmer, Nick Cramer, Liming Zhu, Ralf Reussner, Mark Hoza, Shijian Lu, Andrew Cowell, Tariq Al Naeem, Wendy Cowley and Alan Fekete.

Ian Gorton
March 2006

Table of Contents

1 Understanding Software Architecture

1.1 What is Software Architecture?

The last decade has seen a tremendous rise in the prominence of a software engineering sub-discipline known as software architecture. *Technical Architects* and *Chief Architects* are job titles that now abound in the software industry. There's a Worldwide Institute of Software Architects[1], and even a certain well-known wealthiest person on earth has architect in his job title. It can't be a bad gig, then?

I have a sneaking suspicion that "architecture" is one of the most overused and least understood terms in professional software development circles. I hear it regularly misused in such diverse forums as project reviews and discussions, academic paper presentations at conferences and product pitches. You know a term is gradually becoming vacuous when it becomes part of the vernacular of the software industry sales force.

This book is about software architecture. Its aim is to concisely describe the essential elements of knowledge and key skills that are required to be a software architect in the software and information technology (IT) industry. Conciseness is a key objective. For this reason, by no means everything an architect needs to know will be covered. If you want or need to know more, each chapter will point you to additional worthy and useful resources that can lead to far greater illumination.

So, without further ado, let's try and figure out what, at least I think, software architecture really is. The remainder of this chapter will address this question, as well as briefly introducing the major tasks of an architect, and the relationship between architecture and technology in IT applications.

---

[1] http://www.wwisa.org/

1.2   Definitions of Software Architecture

Trying to define a term such as software architecture is always a potentially dangerous activity. There really is no widely accepted definition by the industry. To understand the diversity in views, have a browse through the list maintained by the Software Engineering Institute[2]. There's a lot. Reading these reminds me of an anonymous quote I heard on a satirical radio program recently, which went something along the lines of 'the reason academic debate is so vigorous is that there is so little at stake'.

I've no intention of adding to this debate. Instead, let's examine three definitions. As an IEEE member, I of course naturally start with the definition adopted by my professional body:

"Architecture is defined by the recommended practice as the fundamental organization of a system, embodied in its components, their relationships to each other and the environment, and the principles governing its design and evolution."
[ANSI/IEEE Std 1471-2000, *Recommended Practice for Architectural Description of Software-Intensive Systems*]

This lays the foundations for an understanding of the discipline. Architecture captures system structure in terms of components and how they interact. It also defines system-wide design rules and considers how a system may change.

Next, it's always worth getting the latest perspective from some of the leading thinkers in the field.

"The software architecture of a program or computing system is the structure or structures of the system, which comprise software elements, the externally visible properties of those elements, and the relationships among them."
[L.Bass, P.Clements, R.Kazman, *Software Architecture in Practice (2nd edition)*, Addison-Wesley 2003]

This builds somewhat on the above ANSI/IEEE definition, especially as it makes the role of abstraction (i.e. externally visible properties) in an architecture and multiple architecture views (structures of the system) explicit. Compare this with another, from Garlan and Shaw's early influential work:

---

[2] http://www.sei.cmu.edu/architecture/definitions.html

"[Software architecture goes] beyond the algorithms and data structures of the computation; designing and specifying the overall system structure emerges as a new kind of problem. Structural issues include gross organization and global control structure; protocols for communication, synchronization, and data access; assignment of functionality to design elements; physical distribution; composition of design elements; scaling and performance; and selection among design alternatives."
[D. Garlan, M. Shaw, *An Introduction to Software Architecture,* Advances in Software Engineering and Knowledge Engineering, Volume I, World Scientific, 1993]

It's interesting to look at these, as there is much commonality. I include the third mainly as it's again explicit about certain issues, such as scalability and distribution, which are implicit in the first two. Regardless, analyzing these a little makes it possible to draw out some of the fundamental characteristics of software architectures. These, along with some key approaches, are described below.

1.2.1 Architecture Defines Structure

Much of an architect's time is concerned with how to sensibly partition an application into a set of inter-related components, modules, objects or whatever unit of software partitioning works for you[3]. Different application requirements and constraints will define the precise meaning of "sensibly" in the previous sentence – an architecture must be designed to meet the specific requirements and constraints of the application it is intended for.

For example, a requirement for an information management system may be that the application is distributed across multiple sites, and a constraint is that certain functionality and data must reside at each site. Or, an application's functionality must be accessible from a web browser. Both these impose some structural constraints (site-specific, web server hosted), and simultaneously open up avenues for considerable design creativity in partitioning functionality across a collection of related components.

In partitioning an application, the architect assigns responsibilities to each constituent component. These responsibilities define the tasks a component can be relied upon to perform within the application. In this man-

---

[3] *Component* here and in the remainder of this book is used very loosely to mean a recognizable "chunk" of software, and not in the sense of the more strict definition in *Szyperski C. (1998) Component Software: Beyond Object-Oriented Programming, Addison-Wesley*

ner, each component plays a specific role in the application, and the overall component ensemble that comprises the architecture collaborates to provide the required functionality.

Responsibility-driven design (see *Wirfs-Brock* in Further Reading) is a technique from object-orientation that can be used effectively to help define the key components in an architecture. It provides a method based on informal tools and techniques that emphasize behavioral modeling using objects, responsibilities and collaborations. I've found this extremely helpful in past projects for structuring components at an architectural level.

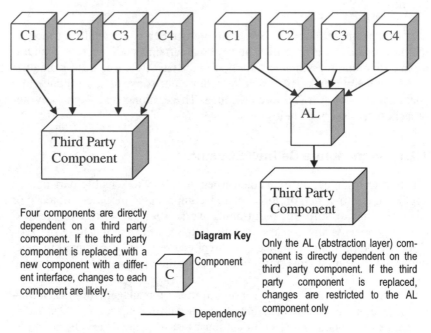

Four components are directly dependent on a third party component. If the third party component is replaced with a new component with a different interface, changes to each component are likely.

Diagram Key

Only the AL (abstraction layer) component is directly dependent on the third party component. If the third party component is replaced, changes are restricted to the AL component only

Fig. 1. Two examples of component dependencies

A key structural issue for nearly all applications is minimizing dependencies between components, creating a loosely coupled architecture from a set of highly cohesive components. A dependency exists between components when a change in one potentially forces a change in others. By eliminating unnecessary dependencies, changes are localized and do not propagate throughout an architecture (see Fig. 1).

Excessive dependencies are simply a bad thing. They make it difficult to make changes to systems, more expensive to test changes, they increase build times, and they make concurrent, team-based development harder.

1.2.2 Architecture Specifies Component Communication

When an application is divided into a set of components, it becomes necessary to think about how these components communicate data and control information. The components in an application may exist in the same address space, and communicate via straightforward method calls. They may execute in different threads or processes, and communicate through synchronization mechanisms. Or multiple components may need to be simultaneously informed when an event occurs in the application's environment. There are many possibilities.

A body of work known collectively as architectural patterns or styles[4] has catalogued a number of successfully used structures that facilitate certain kinds of component communication [see *Patterns* in Further Reading]. These patterns are essentially reusable architectural blueprints that describe the structure and interaction between collections of participating components.

Each pattern has well-known characteristics that make it appropriate to use to satisfy particular types of requirements. For example, the client-server pattern has several useful characteristics, such as synchronous request-reply communications from client to server, and servers supporting one or more clients through a published interface. Optionally, clients may establish sessions with servers, which may maintain state about their connected clients. Client-server architectures must also provide a mechanism for clients to locate servers, handle errors, and optionally provide security on server access. All these issues are addressed in the client-server architecture pattern.

The power of architecture patterns stems from their utility, and ability to convey design information. Patterns are proven to work. If used appropriately in an architecture, you leverage existing design knowledge by using patterns.

Large systems tend to use multiple patterns, combined in ways that satisfy the architecture requirements. When an architecture is based around patterns, it also becomes easy for team members to understand a design, as the pattern infers component structure, communications and abstract mechanisms that must be provided. When someone tells me their system is based on a three-tier client-server architecture, I know immediately a considerable amount about their design. This is a very powerful communication mechanism indeed.

---

[4] Patterns and styles are essentially the same thing, but as a leading software architecture author told me recently, "the patterns people won". This book will therefore use patterns instead of styles!

1.2.3   Architecture Addresses Non-functional Requirements

Non-functional requirements are the ones that don't appear in use cases. Rather than define *what* the application does, they are concerned with *how* the application provides the required functionality.

There are three distinct areas of non-functional requirements:

- **Technical constraints:** These will be familiar to everyone. They constrain design options by specifying certain technologies that the application must use. "We only have Java developers, so we must develop in Java." "The existing database runs on Windows XP only." These are usually non-negotiable.
- **Business constraints:** These too constraint design options, but for business, not technical reasons. For example, "In order to widen our potential customer base, we must interface with XYZ tools." Another example is "The supplier of our middleware has raised prices prohibitively, so we're moving to an open source version." Most of the time, these too are non-negotiable.
- **Quality attributes** These define an application's requirements in terms of scalability, availability, ease of change, portability, usability, performance, and so on. Quality attributes address issues of concern to application users, as well as other stakeholders like the project team itself or the project sponsor. Chapter 3 discusses quality attributes in some detail.

An application architecture must therefore explicitly address these aspects of the design. Architects need to understand the functional requirements, and create a platform that supports these and simultaneously satisfies the non-functional requirements.

1.2.4   Architecture is an Abstraction

One of the most useful, but often non-existent, descriptions from an architectural perspective is something that is colloquially known as a *marketecture*. This is one page, typically informal depiction of the system's structure and interactions. It shows the major components, their relationships and has a few well chosen labels and text boxes that portray the design philosophies embodied in the architecture. A *marketecture* is an excellent vehicle for facilitating discussion by stakeholders during design, build, review, and of course the sales process. It's easy to understand and explain, and serves as a starting point for deeper analysis.

A thoughtfully crafted *marketecture* is particularly useful because it is an abstract description of the application. In reality, any architectural description must employ abstraction in order to be understandable by the team members and project stakeholders. This means that unnecessary details are suppressed or ignored in order to focus attention and analysis on the salient architectural issues. This is typically done by describing the components in the architecture as black boxes, specifying only their *externally visible properties*. Of course, describing system structure and behavior as collections of communicating black box abstractions is normal for practitioners who use object-oriented design techniques.

One of the most powerful mechanisms for describing an architecture is hierarchical decomposition. Components that appear in one level of description are decomposed in more detail in accompanying design documentation. As an example, Fig. 2 depicts a very simple two level hierarchy using an informal notation, with two of the components in the top-level diagram decomposed further.

Different levels of description in the hierarchy tend to be of interest to different developers in a project. In Fig. 2 it's likely that the three components in the top level description will be designed and built by different teams working on the application. The architecture clearly partitions the responsibilities of each team, defining the dependencies between them.

In this hypothetical example, the architect has refined the design of two of the components, presumably because some non-functional requirements dictate that further definition is necessary. Perhaps an existing security service must be used, or the *Broker* must provide a specific message routing function requiring a directory service that has a known level of throughput. Regardless, this further refinement creates a structure that defines and constrains the detailed design of these components.

The simple architecture in Fig. 2 doesn't decompose the *Client* component. This is, again presumably, because the internal structure and behavior of the client is not significant in achieving the application's overall non-functional requirements. How the *Client* gets the information that is sent to the *Broker* is not an issue that concerns the architect, and consequently the detailed design is left open to the component's development team. Of course, the *Client* component could possibly be the most complex in the application. It might have an internal architecture defined by its design team, which meets specific quality goals for the *Client* component. These are, however, localized concerns. It's not necessary for the architect to complicate the application architecture with such issues, as they can be safely left to the *Client* design team to resolve.

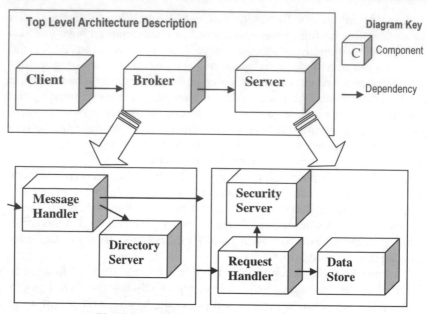

Fig. 2. Describing an architecture hierarchically

1.2.5 Architecture Views

A software architecture represents a complex design artifact. Not surprisingly then, like most complex artifacts, there are a number of ways of looking at and understanding an architecture. The term "architecture views" rose to prominence in Philippe Krutchen's 1995[5] paper on the *4+1 View Model*. This presented a way of describing and understanding an architecture based on the following four views:

- **Logical view:** This describes the architecturally significant elements of the architecture and the relationships between them. The logical view essentially captures the structure of the application using class diagrams or equivalents.
- **Process view:** This focuses on describing the concurrency and communications elements of an architecture. In IT applications, the main concerns are describing multi-threaded or replicated components, and the synchronous or asynchronous communication mechanisms used.

---

[5] P.Krutchen, *Architectural Blueprints–The "4+1" View Model of Software Architecture*, IEEE Software, 12(6) Nov. 1995.

- **Physical view:** This depicts how the major processes and components are mapped on to the applications hardware. It might show, for example, how the database and web servers for an application are distributed across a number of server machines.
- **Development view:** This captures the internal organization of the software components, typically as they are held in a development environment or configuration management tool. For example, the depiction of a nested package and class hierarchy for a Java application would represent the development view of an architecture.

These views are tied together by the architecturally significant use cases (often called scenarios). These basically capture the requirements for the architecture, and hence are related to more than one particular view. By working through the steps in a particular use case, the architecture can be "tested", by explaining how the design elements in the architecture respond to the behavior required in the use case. We'll explore how to do this 'architecture testing' in Chapter 5.

Since Krutchen's paper, there's been much thinking, experience and development in the area of architecture views. Mostly notably is the work from the SEI, colloquially known as the "Views and Beyond" approach (see Further Reading). This recommends capturing an architecture model using three different views:

- **Module:** This is a structural view of the architecture, comprising the code modules such as classes, packages and subsystems in the design. It also captures module decomposition, inheritance, associations and aggregations.
- **Component and Connector:** This view describes the behavioral aspects of the architecture. Components are typically objects, threads or processes, and the connectors describe how the components interact. Common connectors are sockets, middleware like CORBA or shared memory.
- **Allocation:** This view shows how the processes in the architecture are mapped to hardware, and how they communicate using networks and/or databases. It also captures a view of the source code in the configuration management systems, and who in the development group has responsibility for each modules.

The terminology used in "Views and Beyond" is strongly influenced by the architecture description language (ADL) research community. This community has been influential in the world of software architecture, but has had limited impact on mainstream information technology. So while this book will concentrate on two of these views, we'll refer to them as the structural view and the behavioral view. Discerning readers should be able to work out the mapping between terminologies.

1.3   What Does a Software Architect Do?

The environment that a software architect works in tends to define their exact roles and responsibilities. A good general description of the architect's role is maintained by the SEI on their web site[6]. Instead of summarizing this, I'll briefly describe, in no particular order, four essential skills for a software architect, regardless of their professional environment.

- **Liaison:** Architects play many liaison roles. They liaise between the customers or clients of the application and the technical team, often in conjunction with the business and requirements analysts. They liaise between the various engineering teams on a project, as the architecture is central to each of these. They liaise with management, justifying designs, decisions and costs. They liaise with the sales force, to help promote a system to potential purchasers or investors. Much of the time, this liaison takes the form of simply translating and explaining different terminology between different stakeholders.
- **Software Engineering:** Excellent design skills are what get a software engineer to the position of architect. They are an essential pre-requisite for the role. More broadly though, architects must promote good software engineering practices. Their designs must be adequately documented and communicated and their plans must be explicit and justified. They must understand the downstream impact of their decisions, working appropriately with the application testing, documentation and release teams.
- **Technology Knowledge:** Architects have a deep understanding of the technology domains that are relevant to the types of applications they work on. They are influential in evaluating and choosing third party components and technologies. They track technology developments, and understand how new standards, features and products might be usefully exploited in their projects. Just as importantly, good architects know what they don't know.

---

[6] http://www.sei.cmu.edu/ata/arch_duties.html

- **Risk Management** Good architects tend to be cautious. They are constantly enumerating and evaluating the risks associated with the design
  and technology choices they make. They document and manage these
  risks in conjunction with project sponsors and management. They develop and instigate risk mitigation strategies, and communicate these to
  the relevant engineering teams. They try to make sure no unexpected
  disasters occur.

Look for these skills in the architects you work with or hire. Architects
play a central role in software development, and must be multi-skilled in
software engineering, technology, management and communications.

1.4 Architectures and Technologies

Architects must make design decisions early in a project lifecycle. Many
of these are difficult, if not impossible, to validate and test until parts of
the system are actually built. Judicious prototyping of key architectural
components can help increase confidence in a design approach, but sometimes it's still hard to be certain of the success of a particular design choice
in a given application context.

Due to the difficulty of validating early design decisions, architects sensibly rely on tried and tested approaches for solving certain classes of
problems. This is one of the great values of architectural patterns. They
enable architects to reduce risk by leveraging successful designs with
known engineering attributes.

Patterns are an abstract representation of an architecture, in the sense
that they can be realized in multiple concrete forms. For example, the publish-subscribe architecture pattern describes an abstract mechanism for
loosely coupled, many-to-many communications between publishers of
messages and subscribers who wish to receive messages. It doesn't however specify how publications and subscriptions are managed, what communication protocols are used, what types of messages can be sent, and so
on. These are all considered implementation details.

Unfortunately, abstract descriptions of architectures don't yet execute
on computers, either directly or through rigorous transformation. Until
they do, abstract architectures must be reified by software engineers as
concrete software implementations.

Fortunately, software products vendors have come to the rescue. Widely
utilized architectural patterns are supported in a variety of commercial off-
the-shelf (COTS) technologies. If a design calls for publish-subscribe mes-

saging, or a message broker, or a three-tier architecture, then the choices of available technology are many and varied indeed. This is an example of software technologies providing reusable, application-independent software infrastructures that implement proven architectural approaches.

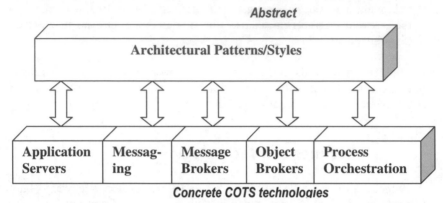

Fig. 3. Mapping between logical architectural patterns and concrete technologies

As Fig. 3 depicts, several classes of COTS technologies are used in practice to provide packaged implementations of architectural patterns for use in IT systems. Within each class, competing commercial and open source products exist. Although these products are superficially similar, they will have differing feature sets, be implemented differently and have varying constraints on their use.

Architects are somewhat simultaneously blessed and cursed with this diversity of product choice. Competition between product vendors drives innovation, better feature sets and implementations, and lower prices, but it also places a burden on the architect to select a product that has quality attributes that satisfy the application requirements. All applications are different in some ways, and there is rarely, if ever, a *one-size-fits-all* product match. Different COTS technology implementations have different sets of strengths and weaknesses and costs, and consequently will be better suited to some types of applications than others.

The difficulty for architects is in understanding these strengths and weaknesses early in the development cycle for a project, and choosing an appropriate reification of the architectural patterns they need. Unfortunately, this is not an easy task, and the risks and costs associated with selecting an inappropriate technology are high. The history of the software industry is littered with poor choices and subsequent failed projects.

Chapter 4 provides a detailed description and analysis of these infrastructural technologies.

1.5 Summary

Software architecture is a fairly well defined and understood design discipline. However, just because we know what it is and more or less what needs doing, this doesn't mean it's mechanical or easy. Designing and validating an architecture for a complex system is a creative exercise, requiring considerable knowledge, experience and discipline. The difficulties are exacerbated by the early lifecycle nature of much of the work of an architect. To my mind, the following quote from Philippe Krutchen sums up an architect's role perfectly:

"The life of a software architect is a long (and sometimes painful) succession of sub-optimal decisions made partly in the dark"

The remainder of this book will describe methods and techniques that can help you to shed at least some light on architectural design decisions. Much of this light comes from understanding and leveraging design principles and supporting technologies that have proven to work in the past. Armed with this knowledge, you'll be able to tackle complex architecture problems with more confidence, and after a while, perhaps even a little panache.

1.6 Further Reading

There are lots of good books, reports and papers available in the software architecture world. Below are some I'd especially recommend. These expand on the information and messages covered in this chapter.

1.6.1 General Architecture

In terms of defining the landscape of software architecture, and describing their project experiences, mostly with defense projects, it's difficult to go past the following books from members of the Software Engineering Institute.

L. Bass, P. Clements, R Kazman. Software Architecture in Practice, Second Edition. Addison-Wesley, 2003.

P. Clements, F. Bachmann, L. Bass, D. Garlan, J. Ivers, R. Little, R. Nord, J. Stafford. *Documenting Software Architectures: Views and Beyond.* Addison-Wesley, 2002.

P. Clements, R. Kazman, M. Klein. *Evaluating Software Architectures: Methods and Case Studies.* Addison-Wesley, 2002.

For a description of the 'Decomposition Style', see *Documenting Software Architecture*, page 53. And for an excellent discussion of the *uses* relationship and its implications, see the same book, page 68.

1.6.2   Architecture Requirements

The original book describing use-cases is:

I. Jacobson, M. Christerson, P. Jonsson, G. Overgaard. *Object-Oriented Software Engineering: A Use Case Driven Approach.* Addison-Wesley, 1992.

Responsibility-driven design is an incredibly useful technique for allocating functionality to components and sub-systems in an architecture. The following should be compulsory reading for architects.

R. Wirfs-Brock, A. McKean. Object Design: Roles, Responsibilities, and Collaborations. Addison-Wesley, 2002.

1.6.3   Architecture Patterns

There's a number of fine books on architecture patterns. Buschmann's work is an excellent introduction.

F. Buschmann, R. Meunier, H. Rohnert, P. Sommerlad, M. Stal,. *Pattern-Oriented Software Architecture, Volume 1: A System of Patterns.* John Wiley & Sons, 1996.
D. Schmidt, M. Stal, H. Rohnert, F. Buschmann. *Pattern-Oriented Software Architecture, Volume 2, Patterns for Concurrent and Networked Objects.* John Wiley & Sons, 2000.

Two recent books that focus more on patterns for enterprise systems, especially enterprise application integrations, are well worth a read.

M. Fowler. Patterns of Enterprise Application Architecture. Addison-Wesley, 2002.
G. Hohpe, B. Woolf. Enterprise Integration Patterns: Designing, Building, and Deploying Messaging Solutions. Addison-Wesley, 2003

1.6.4 Technology Comparisons

A number of papers that emerged from the Middleware Technology Evaluation (MTE) project give a good introduction into the issues and complexities of technology comparisons.

P.Tran, J.Gosper, I.Gorton. *Evaluating the Sustained Performance of COTS-based Messaging Systems.* in Software Testing, Verification and Reliability, vol 13, pp 229-240, Wiley and Sons, 2003.

I.Gorton, A Liu. *Performance Evaluation of Alternative Component Architectures for Enterprise JavaBean Applications,* in IEEE Internet Computing, vol.7, no. 3, pages 18-23, 2003.

A.Liu, I. Gorton. *Accelerating COTS Middleware Technology Acquisition: the i-MATE Process.* in IEEE Software, pages 72-79,volume 20, no. 2, March/April 2003.

2 Introducing the Case Study

2.1 Requirements Overview

This chapter introduces a case study that will be used in subsequent chapters to illustrate some of the design principles in this book[7]. The Information Capture and Dissemination Environment (ICDE) is part of a suite of software systems for providing intelligent assistance to professionals such as financial analysts, scientific researchers and intelligence analysts. To this end, ICDE automatically captures and stores data that records a range of actions performed by a user when operating a workstation. For example, when a user performs a Google search, the ICDE system will transparently store in a database:

- the search query string
- copies of the web pages returned by Google that the user displays in their browser

This data can be used subsequently retrieved from the ICDE database and used by third-party software tools that attempt to offer intelligent help to the user. These tools might interpret a sequence of user inputs, and try to find additional information to help the user with their current task. Other tools may crawl the links in the returned search results that the user does not click on, attempting to find potentially useful details that the user overlooks.

A use case diagram for the ICDE system is shown in Fig. 4. The three major use cases incorporate the capture of user actions, the querying of

---

[7] The case study project is based on an actual system that is operational at the time of writing. Some creative license has been exploited to simplify the functional requirements, so that these don't overwhelm the reader with unnecessary detail. Also, the events, technical details and context described do not always conform to reality, as reality can be far too messy for illustration purposes.

data from the data store, and the interaction of the third party tools with the user.

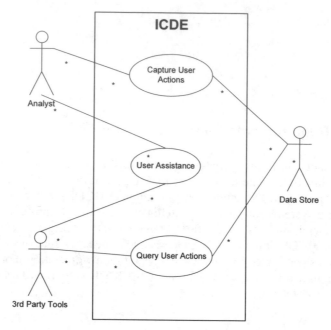

Fig. 4. ICDE system use cases

2.2   Project Context

Few real projects are green-field efforts, allowing the design team to start with a clean and mostly unconstrained piece of paper. The ICDE system certainly isn't one of these.

An initial production version (v1.0) of ICDE was implemented by a small development team. Their main aim was to implement the *Capture User Actions* use case. This allowed several low-level technical issues to be solved, and forced the design and implementation of the data store to be carried out. This was important as the data store was an integral part of the rest of the system's functionality, and its design had to be suitable to support a fairly high transaction rate.

ICDE v1.0 was only deployed in a small user trial involving a few users. This deployment successfully tested the software functionality and demonstrated the concepts of data capture and storage. The design of v1.0 was based upon a simple 2-tier architecture, with all components executing on the user's workstation. This design is shown as a UML v1.X component diagram in Fig. 5. The collection and analysis components were written in Java and access the data store directly using the JDBC[8] API. The complete ICDE application executed on Microsoft Windows XP.

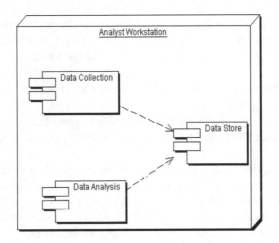

Fig. 5. ICDE Version 1.0 application architecture

The role of each component is as follows:

- **Data Collection:** The collection component comprises a number of loosely coupled processes that transparently track the user's relevant activities and store them in the *Data Store*. The captured events relate to Internet accesses, documents that are opened and browsed, edits made to documents, and some basic windowing information about when the user opens and closes applications on the desktop.
- **Data Store:** This component comprises a commercial-off-the-shelf (COTS) relational database. The relational database stores information in various tables regarding the user activities, with timestamps added so that the order of events can be reconstructed. Large objects such as images on web pages and binary documents are stored as Binary Large Object Fields (BLOBS) using the native database facilities.

---

[8] Java Database Connectivity

- **Data Analysis**: A graphical user interface (GUI) based tool supports a set of queries on the data store. This was useful for testing purposes, and to give the third party tool creators an initial look at the data that was being captured, and was hence available to them for analysis.

2.3 Business Goals

ICDE v2.0 had much more ambitious aims. Having proven that the system worked well in trial deployments, the project sponsors had two major business objectives for the next version. These were:

- Encourage third party tool developers to write applications for the ICDE system.
- Promote the ICDE concept and tools to potential customers, in order to enhance their analytical working environment.

Clearly, both these objectives are focused on fostering a growing business around the ICDE technology, by creating an attractive market for third party tools and an advanced advisory environment for users. Achieving these goals requires detailed technical and business plans to be drawn up and followed through. From a purely technical perspective, leaving out such activities as sales and marketing, the following major objectives were identified – see Table 1:

Table 1. ICDE v2.0 business goals

Business Goal	Supporting Technical Objective
Encourage third party tool developers	Simple and reliable programmatic access to data store for third party tools
	Heterogeneous (i.e. non-Windows) platform support for running third party tools
	Allow third party tools to communicate with ICDE users from a remote machine
Promote the ICDE concept to users	Scale the data collection and data store components to support up to 150 users at a single site
	Low-cost deployment for each ICDE user workstation

In order to attract third party tool developers, it is essential that the environment has a powerful and easy-to-use application programming interface (API) that could be accessed from Windows as well as Linux and Unix platforms. This would give tool developers flexibility in choosing their deployment platform, and make porting existing tools simpler. Surveys of existing tools also raised the issue that powerful analytical tools might require high-end cluster machines to run on. Hence they'd need the capability to communicate with ICDE deployments over local (and eventually wide) area networks.

Another survey of likely ICDE clients showed that potential user organizations had groups of 10 to 150 analysts. It was consequently important that the software could be easily scaled to support such numbers. There should also be no inherent design features that inhibit the technology from supporting larger deployments which may appear in the future.

Equally important, to keep the base cost of a deployment as low as possible, expensive COTS technologies should be avoided wherever possible. This in turn will make the product more attractive in terms of price for clients.

2.4 Constraints

A time horizon of twelve months was set for ICDE v2.0. An interim release after six months was planned to expose tool developers to the API, and allow them to develop their tools at the same time that ICDE v2.0 was being productized and enhanced.

As well as having a fixed schedule, the development budget was also fixed. This meant the development resources available would constrain the features that could be included in the v2.0 release. These budget constraints also influence the possible implementation choices, given that the number of developers, their skills and time available was essentially fixed.

2.5 Summary

The ICDE application makes an interesting case study. It requires the architecture of an existing application to be extended and enhanced to create a platform for new features and capabilities. Time and budget constraints restrict the possible options. Certainly a redevelopment of the existing ICDE v1.0 is completely out of the question.

In the next chapter, we'll explore from a general perspective the spectrum of architectural requirements that arise in projects like ICDE. These requirements are fundamental in driving the design of application architectures, and a hence an understanding of their nature and complex trade-offs is a key part of an architect's arsenal.

3 Software Quality Attributes

3.1 Quality Attributes

Much of a software architect's life is spent designing software systems to meet a set of quality attribute requirements. General software quality attributes include scalability, security, performance and reliability. These are often informally called an application's "-ilities" (though of course many, like performance, don't quite fit this lexical specification).

Quality attribute requirements are part of an application's non-functional requirements, which capture the many facets of *how* the functional requirements of an application are achieved. All but the most trivial application will have non-functional requirements that can be expressed in terms of quality attribute requirements.

To be meaningful, quality attribute requirements must be specific about how an application should achieve a given need. A common problem I regularly encounter in architectural documents is a general statement such as "The application must be scalable".

This is far too imprecise and really not much use to anyone. As is discussed later in this chapter, scalability requirements are many and varied, and each relates to different application characteristics. So, must this hypothetical application scale to handle increased simultaneous user connections? Or increased data volumes? Or deployment to a larger user base? Or all of these?

Defining which of these scalability measures must be supported by the system is crucial from an architectural perspective, as solutions for each differ. It's vital therefore to define concrete quality attribute requirements, such as:

"It must be possible to scale the deployment from an initial 100 geographically dispersed user desktops to 10,000 without an increase in effort/cost for installation and configuration."

This is precise and meaningful. As an architect, this points me down a path to a set of solutions and concrete technologies that facilitate zero-effort installation and deployment.

Note however, that many quality attributes are actually somewhat difficult to validate and test. In this example, it'd be unlikely that in testing for the initial release, a test case would install and configure the application on 10,000 desktops. I just can't see a project manager signing off on that test somehow.

This is where common sense and experience come in. The adopted solution must obviously function for the initial 100-user deployment. Based on the exact mechanisms used in the solution (perhaps Internet download, corporate desktop management software, etc), we can then only analyze it to the best of our ability to assess whether the concrete scalability requirement can be met. If there are no obvious flaws or issues, it's probably safe to assume the solution will scale. But will it scale to 10,000? As always with software, there's only one way to be absolutely, 100% sure, as "it is all talk until the code runs". [9]

There are many general quality attributes, and describing them all in detail could alone fill a book or two. What follows is a description of some of the most relevant quality attributes for general IT applications, and some discussion on architectural mechanisms that are widely used to provide the required quality attributes. These will give you a good place to start when thinking about the qualities an application that you're working on must possess.

3.2 Performance

Although for many IT applications, performance is not a really big problem, it gets all the spotlight in the crowded quality attribute community. I suspect this is because it is one of the qualities of an application that can often be readily quantified and validated. Whatever the reason, when performance matters, it *really* does matter. Applications that perform poorly in some critical aspect of their behavior often become road kill on the software engineering highway.

A performance quality requirement defines a metric that states the amount of work an application must perform in a given time, and/or deadlines that must be met for correct operation. Few IT applications have *hard real-time* constraints like those found in military or robotics systems,

---

[9] Ward Cunningham at his finest!

where if some output is produced a millisecond or three too late, really nasty and undesirable things can happen (I'll let the reader use their imagination here). But applications needing to process hundreds, sometimes thousands and tens of thousands of transactions every second are found in many large organizations, especially in the worlds of finance, telecommunications and government.

Performance usually manifests itself in the following measures.

3.2.1 Throughput

Throughput is a measure of the amount of work an application must perform in unit time. Work is typically measured in transactions per second (tps), or messages processed per second (mps). For example, an on-line banking application might have to guarantee it can execute 1000 transactions per second from Internet banking customers. An inventory management system for a large warehouse might need to process 50 messages per second from trading partners.

It's important to understand precisely what is meant by a throughput requirement. Is it average throughput over a given time period (e.g. a business day), or peak throughput? This is a crucial distinction.

A stark illustration of this is an application for placing bets on events such as horse racing. For most of the time, an application of this ilk does very little work, and hence has a low and easily achievable average throughput requirement. However, every time there is a racing event, perhaps every evening, the five or so minute period before each race sees hundreds of bets being placed every second. If the application is not able to process these bets as they are placed, then the business loses money, and users become very disgruntled (and denying gamblers the opportunity to lose money is not a good thing for anyone). Hence for this scenario, the application must be designed to meet anticipated *peak* throughput, not average. In fact, supporting only average throughput would likely be a disaster.

3.2.2 Response Time

This is a measure of the latency an application exhibits in processing a business transaction. Response time is most often (but not exclusively) associated with the time an application takes to respond to some input. A rapid response time allows users to work more effectively, and consequently is good for business. An excellent example is a point-of-sale application supporting a large store. When an item is scanned at the checkout, a fast, second or less response from the system with the item's price means a customer can be served quickly. This makes the customer and the store happy, and that's a good thing for all involved stakeholders.

Again, it's often important to distinguish between guaranteed and average response times. Some applications may need *all* requests to be serviced within a specified time limit. This is a guaranteed response time. Others may specify an average response time, allowing larger latencies when the application is extremely busy. It's also widespread in the latter case for an upper bound response time requirement to be specified. For example, 95% of all requests must be processed in less than four seconds, and no requests must take more than 15 seconds.

3.2.3   Deadlines

Everyone has probably heard of the weather forecasting system that took 36 hours to produce the forecast for the next day! I'm not sure if this is apocryphal, but it's an excellent example of the requirement to meet a performance deadline. Deadlines in the IT world are commonly associated with batch systems. A social security payment system must complete in time to deposit claimant's payments in their accounts on a given day. If it finishes late, claimants don't get paid when they expect, and this can cause severe disruptions and pain, and not just for claimants. In general, any application that has a limited window of time to complete will have a performance deadline requirement.

These three performance attributes can all be clearly specified and validated. Still, there's a common pitfall to avoid. It lies in the definition of a transaction, request or message, all of which are used very imprecisely in the above. Essentially this is the definition of an application's workload. The amount of processing required for a given business transaction is an *application specific* measure. Even within an application, there will likely be many different types of requests or transactions, varying perhaps from fast database read operations, to complex updates to multiple distributed databases.

Simply, there is no generic workload measure, it depends entirely on what work the application is doing. So, when agreeing to meet a given performance measure, be precise about the exact workload or *transaction mix*, defined in application-specific terms, that you're signing up for.

3.2.4   Performance for the ICDE System

Performance in the ICDE system is an important quality attribute. The key performance requirement pertains to the interactive nature of ICDE. As user's perform their work tasks, the client portion of the ICDE application traps key actions and sends these to the ICDE server for storage. It is consequently exteremely important that ICDE users don't experience any delays in using their applications while the ICDE software traps and stores events.

Trapping user and application generated events in the GUI relies on exploiting platform-specifc system API calls. The APIs provide hooks into the underlying GUI and operating system event handling mechanisms. Implementing this functionality is an ICDE client application concern, and hence it is the responsibility of the ICDE client team to ensure this is carried out as efficiently and fast as possible.

Once an event is trapped, the ICDE client must call the server to store the event in the data store. It's vital therefore that this operation does not contribute any delay that the user might experience. For this reason, when an event is detected, it is written to an in-memory queue in the ICDE client. Once the event is in the queue, the event detection thread returns and waits to capture the next event. Another thread pulls events from the queue and calls the ICDE server.

This solution within the ICDE client decouples event capture and storage. A delayed write to the server cannot delay the GUI code. From the ICDE server's perspective, this is crucial. The server must be designed to store events in the data store as quickly as possible. But the design can be guaranteed that there will only ever be one client request per user workstation outstanding at any instant.

So for the ICDE server, its key performance requirements were easy to specify. It should provide sub-second average response times to ICDE client requests.

3.3   Scalability

Let's start with a representative definition of scalability[10]:

"How well a solution to some problem will work when the size of the prob-lem increases."

---

[10] From www.hyperdictionary.com

This is useful in an architectural context. It tells us that scalability is about how a design can cope with some aspect of the application's requirements increasing in size. To become a concrete quality attribute requirement, we need to understand exactly what is expected to get bigger. Here are some examples:

3.3.1 Request Load

Based on some defined mix of requests on a given hardware platform, an architecture for a server application may be designed to support 100 tps at peak load, with an average one second response time. If this request load were to grow by ten times, can the architecture support this increased load?

In the perfect world and without additional hardware capacity, as the load increases, application throughput should remain constant (i.e. 100 tps), and response time per request should increase only linearly (i.e. 10 seconds). A scalable solution will then permit additional processing capacity to be deployed to increase throughput and decrease response time. This additional capacity may be deployed in two different ways, one adding more CPUs[11] (and likely memory) to the machine the applications runs on (scale up), the other from distributing the application on multiple machines (scale out). This is illustrated in Fig. 6.

Scale up works well if an application is multi-threaded, or multiple single threaded process instances can be executed together on the same machine. The latter will of course consume additional memory and associated resources, as processes are heavyweight, resource hungry vehicles for achieving concurrency.

Scale out works well if there is little or ideally no additional work required managing the distribution of requests amongst the multiple machines. The aim is to keep each machine equally busy, as the investment in more hardware is wasted if one machine is fully loaded and others idle away. Distributing load evenly amongst multiple machines is known as load-balancing.

Importantly, for either approach, scalability should be achieved without modifications to the underlying architecture (apart from inevitable configuration changes if multiple servers are used). In reality, as load increases, applications will exhibit a decrease in throughput and a subsequent exponential increase in response time. This happens for two reasons. First, the increased load causes increased contention for resources such as CPU and memory by the processes and threads in the server architecture.

---

[11] Adding faster CPUs is never a bad idea either. This is especially true if an application has components or calculations that are inherently single-threaded.

Second, each request consumes some additional resource (buffer space, locks, and so on) in the application, and eventually this resource becomes exhausted and limits scalability.

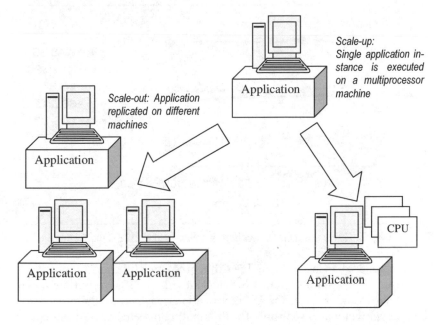

Fig. 6. Scale out versus scale up

As an illustration, Fig. 7 shows how six different versions of the same application implemented using different J2EE application servers perform as their load increases from 100 to 1000 clients.[12]

3.3.2 Simultaneous Connections

An architecture may be designed to support 1000 concurrent users. How does the architecture respond if this number grows significantly? If a con-

---

[12] The full context for these figures is described in: I.Gorton, A Liu, *Performance Evaluation of Alternative Component Architectures for Enterprise JavaBean Applications, in IEEE Internet Computing, vol.7, no. 3, pages 18-23, 2003.* Bear in mind, these results are a snapshot in time and are meant for illustrative purposes. Absolutely no conclusions about the performance of the current versions of these technologies can or should be drawn.

nected user consumes some resources, then there will likely be a limit to
the number of connections that can be effectively supported.

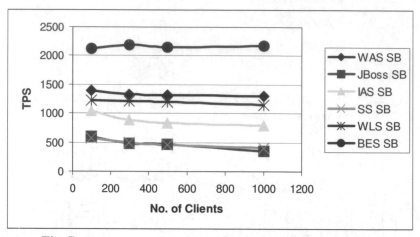

Fig. 7. Effects of increasing client request load on J2EE platforms.

I encountered a classic example of this problem while performing an architecture review for an Internet Service Provider (ISP). Every time a user
connected to the service, the ISP application spawned a new process on
their server that was responsible for distributing targeted advertisements to
the user. This worked beautifully, but each process consumed considerable
memory and processing resources, even when the user simply connected
and did nothing. Testing quickly revealed that the ISP's server machines
could only support about 2000 connections before their virtual memory
was exhausted and the machines effectively ground to a halt in a disk
thrashing frenzy. This made scaling the ISP's operations to support
100,000 users a prohibitively expensive proposition, and eventually, despite frantic redesign efforts, this was a root cause of the ISP going out of
business.

3.3.3 Data Size

In a nutshell, how does an application behave as the data it processes increases in size? For example, a message broker application, perhaps a chat
room, may be designed to process messages of an expected average size.
How well will the architecture react if the size of messages grows significantly? In a slightly different vein, an information management solution
may be designed to search and retrieve data from a repository of a speci-

fied size. How will the application behave if the size of the repository grows, in terms of raw size and/or number of items?

3.3.4 Deployment

How does the effort involved in deploying or modifying an application to an increasing user base grow? This would include effort for distribution, configuration and updating with new versions. An ideal solution would provide automated mechanisms that can dynamically deploy and configure an application to a new user, capturing registration information in the process. This is in fact exactly how many applications are today distributed on the Internet.

3.3.5 Some Thoughts on Scalability

Designing scalable architectures is not easy. In many cases, the need for scalability early in the design just isn't apparent and is not specified as part of the quality attribute requirements. It takes a savvy architect to ensure inherently non-scalable approaches are not introduced as core architectural components. Even if scalability is a required quality attribute, validating that it is satisfied by a proposed solution often just isn't practical in terms of schedule or cost. That's why its important for an architect to rely on tried and tested designs and technologies whenever practical.

3.3.6 Scalability for the ICDE Application

The major scalability requirement for the ICDE system is to support the number of users expected in the largest anticipated ICDE deployment. The requirements specify this as approximately 150 users. The ICDE server application should therefore be capable of handling a peak load of 150 concurrent requests from ICDE clients.

3.4 Modifiability

All capable software architects know that along with death and taxes, modifications to a software system during its lifetime are simply a fact of life. That's why taking into account likely changes to the application is a good practice during architecture formulation. The more flexibility that can be built into a design upfront, then the less painful and expensive subsequent changes will be. That's the theory anyway.

The modifiability quality attribute is a measure of how easy it may be to change an application to cater for new functional and non-functional requirements. Note the use of "may" in the previous sentence. Predicting modifiability requires an *estimate* of effort and/or cost to make a change. You only know for sure what a change will cost after it has been made. Then you find out how good your estimate was.

Modifiability measures are only relevant in the context of a given architectural solution. This solution must be expressed at least structurally as a collection of components, the component relationships and a description of how the components interact with the environment. Then, assessing modifiability requires the architect to assert likely change scenarios that capture how the requirements may evolve. Sometimes these will be known with a fair degree of certainty. In fact the changes may even be specified in the project plan for subsequent releases. Much of the time though, possible modifications will need to be elicited from application stakeholders, and drawn from the architect's experience. There's definitely an element of crystal ball gazing involved.

Illustrative change scenarios are:

- Provide access to the application through firewalls in addition to existing "behind the firewall" access.
- Incorporate new features for self-service check-out kiosks.
- The COTS speech recognition software vendor goes out of business and we need to replace this component.
- The application needs to be ported from Linux to the Microsoft Windows platform.

For each change scenario, the impact of the anticipated change on the architecture can be assessed. This impact is rarely easy to quantify, as more often than not the solution under assessment does not exist. In many cases, the best that can be achieved is a convincing impact analysis of the components in the architecture that will need modification, or a demonstration of how the solution can accommodate the modification without change.

Finally, based on cost, size or effort estimates for the affected components, some useful quantification of the cost of a change can be made. Changes isolated to single components or loosely-coupled subsystems are likely to be less expensive to make than those that cause ripple effects across the architecture. If a likely change appears difficult and complex to make, this may highlight a weakness in the architecture that might justify further consideration and re-design.

3.4.1 Modifiability for the ICDE Application

Modifiability for the ICDE application is a difficult one to specify. A likely requirement would be for the range of events trapped and stored by the ICDE client to be expanded. This would have implication on the design of both the ICDE cleint and the ICDE server and data store.

Another would be for third party tools to want to communicate new message types. This would have implications on the message exchange mechanisms that the ICDE server supported. Hence both these modifiability scenarios could be used to test the resulting design for ease of modification.

3.5 Security

Security is a complex technical topic that can only be treated somewhat superficially here. At the architectural level, security boils down to understanding the precise security requirements for an application, and devising mechanisms to support them. The most common security-related requirements are:

- **Authentication:** Applications can verify the identity of their users and other applications with which they communicate.
- **Authorization:** Authenticated users and applications have defined access rights to the resources of the system. For example, some users may have read-only access to the application's data, while others have read-write.
- **Encryption:** The messages sent to/from the application are encrypted.
- **Integrity:** This ensures the contents of a message are not altered in transit.
- **Non-repudiation:** The sender of a message has proof of delivery and the receiver is assured of the sender's identity. This means neither can subsequently refute their participation in the message exchange.

There are well known and widely used technologies that support these elements of application security. The Secure Socket Layer (SSL) and Public Key Infrastructures (PKI) are commonly used in Internet applications to provide authentication, encryption and non-repudiation. Authentication and authorization is supported in Java technologies using the Java Authentication and Authorization Service (JAAS). Operating systems and databases provide login-based security for authentication and authorization.

Hopefully you're getting the picture. There are many ways, in fact sometimes too many, to support the required security attributes for an application. Databases want to impose their security model on the world. .NET designers happily leverage the Windows operating security features. Java applications can leverage JAAS without any great problems. If an application only needs to execute in one of these security domains, then solutions are readily available. If an application comprises several components that all wish to manage security, appropriate solutions must be designed that typically localize security management in a single component that leverages the most appropriate technology for satisfying the requirements.

3.5.1 Security for the ICDE Application

Authentication of ICDE users and third party ICDE tools is the main security requirements for the ICDE system. In v1.0, users supply a login name and password which is authenticated by the database. This gives them access to the data in the data store associated with their activities. ICDE v2.0 will need to support similar authentication for users, and extend this to handle third party tools. Also, as third party tools may be executing remotely and access the ICDE data over an insecure network, the in-transit data should be encrypted.

3.6 Availability

Availability is related to an application's reliability. If an application isn't available for use when needed, then it's unlikely to be fulfilling its functional requirements. Availability is relatively easy to specify and measure. In terms of specification, many IT applications must be available at least during normal business hours. Most Internet sites desire 100% availability, as there are no regular business hours on-line. For a live system, availability can be measured by the proportion of the required time it is useable.

Failures in applications cause them to be unavailable. Failures impact on an application's reliability, which is usually measured by the mean time between failures. The length of time any period of unavailability lasts is determined by the amount of time it takes to detect failure and restart the system. Consequently, applications that require high availability minimize or preferably eliminate single points of failure, and institute mechanisms that automatically detect failure and restart the failed components.

Replicating components is a tried and tested strategy for high availability. When a replicated component fails, the application can continue executing using replicas that are still functioning. This may lead to degraded performance while the failed component is down, but availability is not compromised.

Recoverability is closely related to availability. An application is recoverable if it has the capability to reestablish required performance levels and recover affected data after an application or system failure. A database system is the classic example of a recoverable system. When a database server fails, it is unavailable until it has recovered. This means restarting the server application, and resolving any transactions that were in-flight when the failure occurred. Interesting issues for recoverable applications are how failures are detected and recovery commences (preferably automatically), and how long it takes to recover before full service is re-established. During the recovery process, the application is unavailable, and hence the mean time to recover is an important metric to consider.

3.6.1   Availability for the ICDE Application

While high availability for the ICDE application is desirable, it is only crucial that it be available during the business hours of the office environment it is deployed in. This leaves plenty of scope for downtime for such needs as system upgrade, backup and maintenance. The solution should however include mechanisms such as component replication to ensure as close to 100% availability as possible during business hours.

3.7   Integration

Integration is concerned with the ease with which an application can be usefully incorporated into a broader application context. The value of an application or component can frequently be greatly increased if its functionality or data can be used in ways that the designer did not originally anticipate. The most widespread strategies for providing integration are through data integration or providing an application programming interface (API).

Data integration involves storing the data an application manipulates in ways that other applications can access. This may be as simple as using a standard relational database for data storage, or perhaps implementing mechanisms to extract the data into a known format such as XML or a comma-separated text file that other applications can ingest.

With data integration, the ways in which the data is used (or abused) by other applications is pretty much out of control of the original data owner. This is because the data integrity and business rules imposed by the application logic are by-passed. The alternative is for interoperability to be achieved through an API (see Fig. 8). In this case, the raw data the application owns is hidden behind a set of functions that facilitate controlled external access to the data. In this manner, business rules and security can be enforced in the API implementation. The only way to access the data and integrate with the application is by using the supplied API.

The choice of integration strategy is not simple. Data integration is flexible and simple. Applications written in any language can process text, or access relational databases using SQL. Building an API requires more effort, but provides a much more controlled environment, in terms of correctness and security, for integration. It is also much more robust from an integration perspective, as the API clients are insulated from many of the changes in the underlying data structures. They don't break every time the format is modified, as the data formats are not directly exposed and accessed. As always, the best choice of strategy depends on what you want to achieve, and what constraints exist.

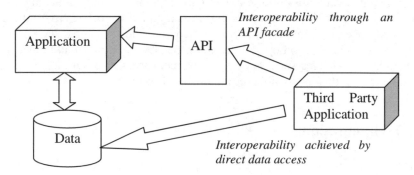

Fig. 8. Integration options

3.7.1   Integration for the ICDE Application

The integration requirements for ICDE revolve around the need to support third party analysis tools. There must be a well-defined and understood mechanism for third party tools to access data in the ICDE data store. As third party tools will often execute remotely from an ICDE data store, integration at the data level, by allowing tools direct access to the data store, seems unlikely to be viable. Hence integration is likely to be facilitated through an API supported by the ICDE application.

3.8 Other Quality Attributes

There are numerous other quality attributes that are important in various application contexts. Some of these are:

- **Portability:** Can an application be easily executed on a different software/hardware platform to the one it has been developed for? Portability depends on the choices of software technology used to implement the application, and the characteristics of the platforms that it needs to execute on. Easily portable code bases will have their platform dependencies isolated and encapsulated in a small set of components that can be replaced without affecting the rest of the application.
- **Testability:** How easy or difficult is an application to test? Early design decisions can greatly affect the amount of test cases that are required. As a rule of thumb, the more complex a design, the more difficult it is to thoroughly test. Simplicity tends to promote ease of testing.[13] Likewise, writing less of your own code by incorporating pre-tested components reduces test effort.
- **Supportability:** This is a measure of how easy an application is to support once it is deployed. Support typically involves diagnosing and fixing problems that occur during application use. Supportable systems tend to provide explicit facilities for diagnosis, such as application error logs that record the causes of failures. They are also built in a modular fashion so that code fixes can be deployed without severely inconveniencing application use.

---

[13] "There are two ways of constructing a software design: One way is to make it so simple that there are obviously no deficiencies, and the other way is to make it so complicated that there are no obvious deficiencies. The first method is far more difficult.", C.A.R. Hoare

3.9   Design Trade-Offs

If an architect's life were simple, design would merely involve building
policies and mechanisms into an architecture to satisfy the required quality
attributes for a given application. Pick a required quality attribute, and
provide mechanisms to support it.

Unfortunately, this isn't the case. Quality attributes are not orthogonal.
They interact in subtle ways, meaning a design that satisfies one quality attribute requirement may have a detrimental effect on another. For example,
a highly secure system may be difficult or impossible to integrate in an
open environment. A highly available application may trade-off lower performance for greater availability. An application that requires high performance may be tied to a particular platform, and hence not be easily
portable.

Understanding trade-offs between quality attribute requirements, and
designing a solution that makes sensible compromises is one of the tough-
est parts of the architect role. It's simply not possible to fully satisfy all
competing requirements. It's the architect's job to tease out these tensions,
make them explicit to the system's stakeholders, prioritize as necessary,
and explicitly document the design decisions.

Does this sound easy? If only this were the case. That's why they pay
you the big bucks.

3.10 Summary

Architects must expend a lot of effort precisely understanding quality attributes, so that a design can be conceived to address them. Part of the difficulty is that quality attributes are not always explicitly stated in the requirements, or adequately captured by the requirements engineering team.
That's why an architect must be associated with the requirements gathering exercise for system, so that they can ask the right questions to expose
and nail down the quality attributes that must be addressed.

Of course, understanding the quality attribute requirements is merely a
necessary prerequisite to designing a solution to satisfy them. Conflicting
quality attributes are a reality in every application of even mediocre complexity. Creating solutions that choose a point in the design space that adequately satisfies these requirements is remarkably difficult, both technically and socially. The latter involves communications with stakeholders
to discuss design tolerances, discovering scenarios when certain quality
requirements can be safely relaxed, and clearly communicating design

compromises so that the stakeholders understand what they are signing up for.

3.11 Further Reading

The broad topic of non-functional requirements is covered extremely thoroughly in:

L. Chung, B. Nixon, E. Yu, J. Mylopoulos, (Editors). Non-Functional Requirements in Software Engineering Series: The Kluwer International Series in Software Engineering. Vol. 5, Kluwer Academic Publishers. 1999.

An excellent general reference on security and the techniques and technologies an architect needs to consider is:

J. Ramachandran. Designing Security Architecture Solutions. Wiley & Sons, 2002.

An interesting and practical approach to assessing the modifiability of an architecture using architecture reconstruction tools and impact analysis metrics is described in:

I.Gorton, L. Zhu. *Tool Support for Just-in-Time Architecture Reconstruction and Evaluation: An Experience Report.* International Conference on Software Engineering (ICSE) 2005, St Loius, USA, ACM Press

4 A Guide to Middleware Architectures and Technologies

4.1 Introduction

I'm not really a great enthusiast for drawing strong analogies between the role of a software architect and that of a traditional building architect. There are similarities, but also lots of profound differences.[14] But let's ignore those differences for a second, in order to illustrate the role of middleware in software architecture.

When an architect designs a building, they create drawings, essentially a design that shows, from various angles, the structure and geometric properties of the building. This design is based on the building's requirements, such as the available space, function (office, church, shopping center, home), desired aesthetic and functional qualities and budget. These drawings are an abstract representation of the intended concrete (sic) artifact.

There's obviously an awful lot of design effort still required to turn the architectural drawings into something that people can actually start to build. There's detailed design of walls, floor layouts, staircases, electrical systems, water and piping to name just a few. And as each of these elements of a building is designed in detail, suitable materials and components for constructing each are selected.

These materials and components are the basic construction blocks for buildings. They've been created so that they can fulfill the same essential needs in many types of buildings, whether they are office towers, railway stations or humble family homes.

Although perhaps it's not the most glamorous analogy, I like to think of middleware as the equivalent of the plumbing or piping or wiring for software applications. The reasons are:

---

[14] The following paper discusses of issues: J. Baragry and K. Reed. *Why We Need a Different View of Software Architecture*. The Working IEEE/IFIP Conference on Software Architecture (WICSA), Amsterdam, The Netherlands, 2001

- Middleware provides proven ways to connect the various software components in an application so they can exchange information using relatively easy-to-use mechanisms. Middleware provides the pipes for shipping data between components, and can be used in a wide range of different application domains.
- Middleware can be used to wire together numerous components in useful, well-understood topologies. Connections can be one-to-one, one to many or many-to-many.
- From the application user's perspective, middleware is completely hidden. Users interact with the application, and don't care how information is exchanged internally. As long as it works, and works well, middleware is *invisible* infrastructure.
- The only time application users are ever aware of the role middleware plays is when it fails. This is of course very like real plumbing and wiring systems!

It's probably not wise to push the plumbing analogy any further. But hopefully it has served its purpose. Middleware provides ready-to-use infrastructure for connecting software components. It can be used in a whole variety of different application domains, as it has been designed to be general and configurable to meet the common needs of software applications.

4.2 Technology Classification

Middleware got its label because it was conceived as a layer of software "plumbing-like" infrastructure that sat between the application and the operating system, that is, the middle of application architectures. Of course in reality middleware is much more complex than plumbing or a simple layer insulating an application from the underlying operating system services.

Different application domains tend to regard different technologies as middleware. This book is about mainstream IT applications, and in that domain there's a fairly well-understood collection that is typically known as middleware. Fig. 9 provides a classification of these technologies, and names some example products/technologies that represent each category. Brief explanations of the categories are below, and the remainder of this chapter then goes on to describe each in detail:

- The transport layer represents the basic pipes for sending requests and moving data between software components. These pipes provide simple facilities and mechanisms that make exchanging data straightforward in distributed application architectures.

- Application servers are typically built on top of the basic transport services. They provide additional capabilities such as transaction, security and directory services. They also support a programming model for building multi-threaded server-based applications that exploit these additional services.
- Message brokers exploit either a basic transport service and/or application servers and add a specialized message processing engine. This engine provides features for fast message transformation and high-level programming features for defining how to exchange, manipulate and route messages between the various components of an application.
- Business process orchestrators (BPOs) augment message broker features to support workflow-style applications. In such applications, business processes may take many hours or days to complete due to the need for people to perform certain tasks. BPOs provide the tools to describe such business processes, execute them and manage the intermediate states while each step in the process is executed.

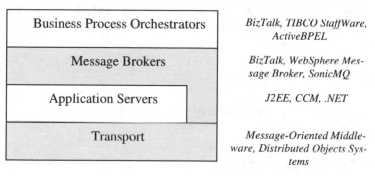

Fig. 9. Classifying middleware technologies

4.3 Distributed Objects

Distributed object technology is a venerable member of the middleware family. Best characterized by CORBA[15], distributed object-based middleware has been in use since the earlier 1990's. As many readers will be fa-

---

[15] Common Object Request Broker Architecture

miliar with CORBA and the like, only the basics are briefly covered in this section for completeness.

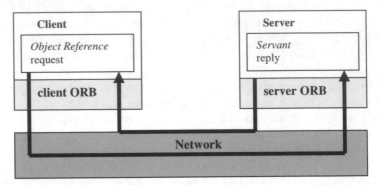

Fig. 10. Distributed objects using CORBA

A simple scenario of a client sending a request to a server across an object request broker (ORB) is shown in Fig. 10. In CORBA, servant objects support interfaces that are specified using CORBA's IDL (interface description language). IDL interfaces define the methods that a server object supports, along with the parameter and return types. A trivial IDL example is:

```
module ServerExample {
    interface MyObject
    {
        string isAlive();
    };
};
```

This IDL interface defines a CORBA object that supports a single method, isAlive, which returns a string and takes no parameters. An IDL compiler is used to process interface definitions. The compiler generates an object skeleton in a target programming languages (typically, but not necessarily, C++ or Java). The object skeleton provides the mechanisms to call the servant implementation's methods. The programmer must then write the code to implement each servant method in a native programming language:

```
class MyServant extends _MyObjectImplBase {
  public String isAlive()    {
    return "\nLooks like it…\n";
    }
}
```

The server process must create an instance of the servant and make it callable through the ORB:

```
ORB orb = ORB.init(args, null);
MyServant objRef = new MyServant();
orb.connect(objRef);
```

A client process can now initialize a client ORB and get a reference to the servant that resides within the server process. Servants typically store a reference to themselves in a directory. Clients query the directory using a simple logical name, and it returns a reference to a servant that includes its network location and process identity.

```
ORB orb = ORB.init(args, null);
// Lookup is a wrapper that actually access the CORBA Naming
// Service directory - details omitted for simplicity
MyServant servantRef = lookup("Myservant")
String reply = servantRef.isAlive();
```

The servant call looks like a synchronous call to a local object. However, the ORB mechanisms transmit, or marshal, the request and associated parameters across the network to the servant. The method code executes, and the result is marshaled back to the waiting client.

This is a very simplistic description of distributed object technology. There's much more detail that must be addressed to build real systems, issues like exceptions, locating servants and multi-threading to name just a few. From an architect's perspective though, the following are some essential design concerns that must be addressed in applications:

• Requests to servants are remote calls, and hence relatively expensive (slow) as they traverse the ORB and network. This has a performance impact. It's always wise to design interfaces so that remote calls can be minimized, and performance is enhanced.
• Like any distributed application, servers may intermittently or permanently be unavailable due to network or process or machine failure. Applications need strategies to cope with failure and mechanisms to restart failed servers.
• If a servant holds state concerning an interaction with a client (e.g. a customer object stores the name/address), and the servant fails, the state is lost. Mechanisms for state recovery must consequently be designed.

4.4   Message-Oriented Middleware

Message-oriented middleware (MOM) is one of the key technologies for
building large-scale enterprise systems. It is the glue that binds together
otherwise independent and autonomous applications and turns them into a
single, integrated system. These applications can be built using diverse
technologies and run on different platforms. Users are not required to re-
write their existing applications or make substantial (and risky) changes
just to have them play a part in an enterprise-wide application. This is
achieved by placing a queue between senders and receivers, providing a
level of indirection during communications.

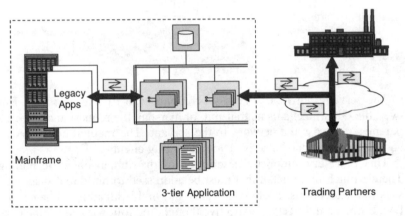

Fig. 11. Integration through messaging

How message-oriented middleware can be used within an organization
is illustrated in Fig. 11. The MOM creates a *software bus* for integrating
home grown applications with legacy applications, and connecting local
applications with the business systems provided by business partners.

4.4.1   Message-Oriented Middleware Basics

Message-oriented middleware is an inherently loosely-coupled, asynchronous technology. This means the sender and receiver of a message are not
tightly coupled, unlike synchronous middleware technologies such as
CORBA. Synchronous middleware technologies have many strengths, but
can lead to fragile designs if all of the components and network links always have to be working at the same time for the whole system to successfully operate.

A messaging infrastructure decouples senders and receivers using an intermediate message queue. The sender can send a message to a receiver and know that it will be eventually delivered, even if the network link is down or the receiver is not available. The sender just tells the MOM technology to deliver the message and then continues on with its work. Senders are unaware of which application or process eventually processes the request. Fig. 12 depicts this basic send-receive mechanism.

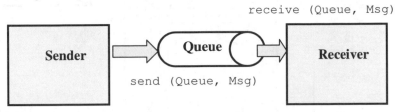

Fig. 12. MOM basics

MOM is often implemented as a server that can handle messages from multiple concurrent clients.[16] In order to decouple senders and receivers, the MOM provides message queues that senders place messages on and receivers remove messages from. A MOM server can create and manage multiple messages queues, and can handle multiple messages being sent from queues simultaneously using threads organized in a thread pool. One or more processes can send messages to a message queue, and each queue can have one or many receivers. Each queue has a name which senders and receivers specify when they perform send and receive operations. This architecture is illustrated in Fig. 13.

A MOM server has a number of basic responsibilities. First, it must accept a message from the sending application, and send an acknowledgement that the message has been received. Next, it must place the message at the end of the queue that was specified by the sender. A sender may send many messages to a queue before any receivers remove them. Hence the MOM must be prepared to hold messages in a queue for an extended period of time.

Messages are delivered to receivers in a First-In-First-Out (FIFO) manner, namely the order they arrive at the queue. When a receiver requests a message, the message at the head of the queue is delivered to the receiver, and upon successful receipt, the message is deleted from the queue.

---

[16] MOM can also be simply implemented in a point-to-point fashion without a centralized message queue server. In this style of implementation, 'send' and 'receive' queues are maintained on the communicating systems themselves.

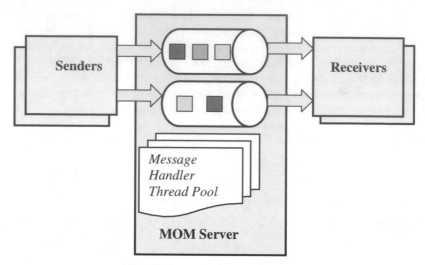

Fig. 13. Anatomy of a MOM server

The asynchronous, decoupled nature of messaging technology makes it an extremely useful tool for solving many common application design problems. These include scenarios in which:

- The sender doesn't need a reply to a message. It just wants to send the message to another application and continue on with its own work. This is known as *send-and-forget* messaging.
- The sender doesn't need an immediate reply to a request message. The receiver may take perhaps several minutes to process a request and the sender can be doing useful work in the meantime rather than just waiting.
- The receiver, or the network connection between the sender and receiver, may not operate continuously. The sender relies on the MOM to deliver the message when a connection is next established. The MOM layer must be capable of storing messages for later delivery, and possibly recovering unsent messages after system failures.

4.4.2   Exploiting Message Oriented Middleware Advanced Features

The basic features of MOM technology are rarely sufficient in enterprise applications. Mission critical systems need much stronger guarantees of message delivery and performance than can be provided by a basic MOM server. Commercial-off-the-shelf (COTS) MOM products therefore supply additional advanced features to increase the reliability, usability and scalability of MOM servers. These features are explained in the following sections.

4.4.2.1   Message Delivery

MOM technologies are about delivering messages between applications. In many enterprise applications, this delivery must be done reliably, giving the sender guarantees that the message will eventually be processed. For example, an application processing a credit card transaction may place the transaction details on a queue for later processing, to add the transaction total to the customer's account. If this message is lost due the MOM server crashing – such things do happen – then the customer may be happy, but the store where the purchase was made and the credit card company will lose money. Such scenarios obviously cannot tolerate message loss, and must ensure reliable delivery of messages.

Reliable message delivery however comes at the expense of performance. MOM servers normally offer a range of quality of service (QoS) options that let an architect balance performance against the possibility of losing messages. Three levels of delivery guarantee (or QoS) are typically available, with higher reliability levels always coming at the cost of reduced performance. These QoS options are:

- **Best effort:** The MOM server will do its best to deliver the message. Undelivered messages are only kept in memory on the server and can be lost if a system fails before a message is delivered. Network outages or unavailable receiving applications may also cause messages to time out and be discarded.
- **Persistent:** The MOM layer guarantees to deliver messages despite system and network failures. Undelivered messages are logged to disk as well as being kept in memory and so can be recovered and subsequently delivered after a system failure. This is depicted in Fig. 14. Messages are kept in a disk log for the queue until they have been delivered to a receiver.
- **Transactional:** Messages can be bunched into "all or nothing" units for delivery. Also, message delivery can be coordinated with an external resource manager such as a database. More on transactional delivery is explained in the following sections.

Various studies have been undertaken to explore the performance differences between these three QoS levels. All of these by their very nature are specific to a particular benchmark application, test environment and

MOM product. Drawing some very general conclusions, you can expect to see between 30%–80% performance reduction when moving from best-effort to persistent messaging, depending on message size and disk speed. Transactional will be slower than persistent, but often not by a great deal, as this depends mostly on how many transaction participants are involved. See the further reading section at the end of this chapter for some pointers to these studies.

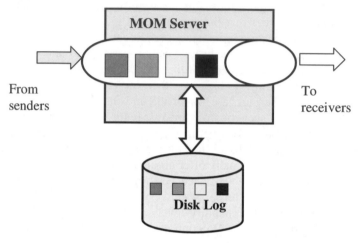

Fig. 14. Guaranteed message delivery in message oriented middleware

4.4.2.2   Transactions

Transactional messaging typically builds upon persistent messages. It tightly integrates messaging operations with application code, not allowing transactional messages to be sent until the sending application commits their enclosing transaction. Basic MOM transactional functionality allows applications to construct batches of messages that are sent as a single atomic unit when the application commits.

Receivers must also create a transaction scope and ask to receive complete batches of messages. If the transaction is committed by the receivers, these transactional messages will be received together in the order they were sent, and then removed from the queue. If the receiver aborts the transaction, any messages already read will be put back on the queue, ready for the next attempt to handle the same transaction. In addition, consecutive transactions sent from the same system to the same queue will arrive in the order they were committed, and each message will be delivered to the application exactly once for each committed transaction.

Transactional messaging also allows message sends and receives to be coordinated with other transactional operations, such as database updates. For example, an application can start a transaction, send a message, update a database and then commit the transaction. The MOM layer will not make the message available on the queue until the transaction commits, ensuring either that the message is sent and the database is updated, or that both operations are rolled back and appear never to have happened.

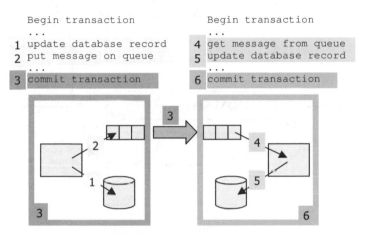

Fig. 15. Transactional messaging

A pseudo-code example of integrating messaging and database updates is shown in Fig. 15. The sender application code uses transaction demarcation statements (the exact form varies between MOM systems) to specify the scope of the transaction. All statements between the *begin* and *commit* transaction statements are considered to be part of the transaction. Note we have two, independent transactions occurring in this example. The sender and receiver transactions are separate and commit (or abort) individually.

4.4.2.3 Clustering
MOM servers are the primary message exchange mechanism in many enterprise applications. If a MOM server becomes unavailable due to server or machine failure, then applications can't communicate. Not surprisingly then, industrial strength MOM technologies make it possible to cluster MOM servers, running instances of the server on multiple machines (see Fig. 16).

Exactly how clustering works is product dependent. However, the scheme in Fig. 16 is typical. Multiple instances of MOM servers are configured in a logical cluster. Each server supports the same set of queues, and the distribution of these queues across servers is transparent to the MOM clients. MOM clients behave exactly the same as if there was one physical server and queue instance.

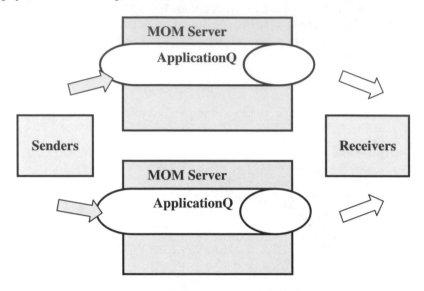

Fig. 16. Clustering MOM servers for reliability and scalability

When a client sends a message, one of the queue instances is selected and the message stored on the queue. Likewise, when a receiver requests a message, one of the queue instances is selected and a message removed. The MOM server clustering implementation is responsible for directing client requests to individual queue instances. This may be done statically, when a client opens a connection to the server, or dynamically, for every request.[17]

A cluster has two benefits. First, if one MOM server fails, the other queue instances are still available for clients to use. Applications can consequently keep communicating. Second, the request load from the clients can be spread across the individual servers. Each server only sees a fraction (ideally 1/[number of servers] in the cluster) of the overall traffic. This helps distribute the messaging load across multiple machines, and can provide much higher application performance.

---

[17] An application that needs to receive messages in the order they are sent is not suitable for operating in this a clustering mode.

4.4.2.4   Two-way Messaging

Although MOM technology is inherently asynchronous and decouples senders and receivers, it can also be used for synchronous communications and building more tightly coupled systems. In this case, the sender simply uses the MOM layer to send a request message to a receiver on a request queue. The message contains the name of the queue to which a reply message should be sent. The sender then waits until the receiver sends back a reply message on a reply queue, as shown in Fig. 17.

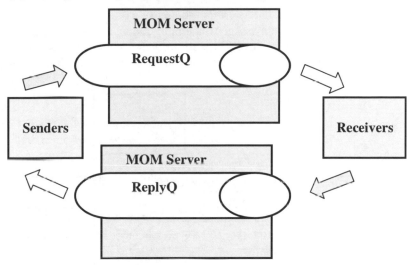

Fig. 17. Request-Reply messaging

This synchronous style of messaging using MOM is frequently used in enterprise systems, replacing conventional synchronous technology such as CORBA. There are a number of pragmatic reasons why architects might choose to use messaging technology in this way, including:

- Messaging technology can be used with existing applications at low cost and with minimal risk. *Adapters* are available, or can be easily written to interface between commonly used messaging technologies and applications. Applications do not have to be rewritten or ported before they can be integrated into a larger system.
- Messaging technologies tend to be available on a very wide range of platforms, making it easier to integrate legacy applications or business systems being run by business partners.

- Organizations may already have purchased, and gained experience in using, a messaging technology and they may not need the additional features of an application server technology.

4.4.3   Publish-Subscribe

Message oriented middleware is a proven and effective approach for building loosely-coupled enterprise systems. But, like everything, it has its limitations. The major one is that MOM is inherently a one-to-one technology. One sender sends a single message to a single queue, and one receiver retrieves that message for the queue. Not all problems are so easily solved by a 1-1 messaging style. This is where publish-subscribe architectures enter the picture.

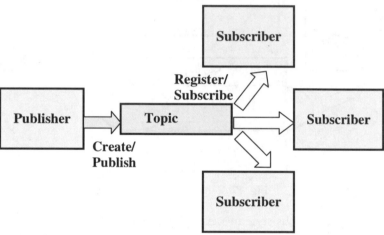

Fig. 18. Publish-Subscribe messaging

Publish-subscribe messaging extends the basic MOM mechanisms to support *1 to many*, *many to many*, and *many to 1* style communications. Publishers send a single copy of a message addressed to a named *topic*, or *subject*. Topics are a logical name for the publish-subscribe equivalent of a queue in basic MOM technology. Subscribers listen for messages that are sent to topics that interest them. The publish-subscribe server then distributes each message sent on a topic to every subscriber who is listening on that topic. This basic scheme is depicted in Fig. 18.

In terms of loose coupling, publish-subscribe has some attractive properties. Senders and receivers are decoupled, each respectively unaware of which applications will receive a message, and who actually sent the message. Each topic may also have more than one publisher, and the publishers may appear and disappear dynamically. This gives considerable flexibility over static configuration regimes. Likewise, subscribers can dynamically subscribe and unsubscribe to a topic. Hence the subscriber set for a topic can change at any time, and this is transparent to the application code.

In publish-subscribe technologies, the messaging layer has the responsibility for managing topics, and knowing which subscribers are listening to which topics. It also has the responsibility for delivering every message sent to all active current subscribers. Topics can be persistent or nonpersistent, with the same effects on reliable message delivery as in basic point-to-point MOM (explained in the previous section). Messages can also be published with an optional "time-to-live" setting. This tells the publish-subscribe server to attempt to deliver a message to all active subscribers for the time-to-live period, and after that delete the message from the queue.

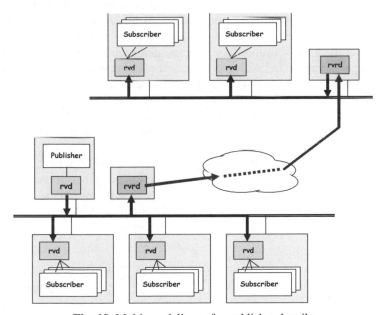

Fig. 19. Multicast delivery for publish-subscribe

The underlying protocol a MOM technology uses for message delivery can profoundly affect performance. By default, most use straightforward point-to-point TCP/IP sockets. Implementations of publish-subscribe built on point-to-point messaging technology duplicate each message send operation from the server for every subscriber. In contrast, some MOM technologies support multicast or broadcast protocols, which send each message only once on the wire, and the network layer handles delivery to multiple destinations.

In Fig. 19, the multicast architecture used in TIBCO's Rendezvous publish-subscribe technology is illustrated. Each node in the publish-subscribe network runs a daemon process known as *rvd*. When a new topic is created, it is assigned a multicast IP address.

When a publisher sends a message, its local *rvd* daemon intercepts the message and multicasts a single copy of the message on the network to the address associated with the topic. The listening daemons on the network receive the message, and each checks if it has any local subscribers to the message's topic on its node. If so, it delivers the message to the subscriber(s), otherwise it ignores the message. If a message has subscribers on a remote network,[18] an *rvrd* daemon intercepts the message and sends a copy to each remote network using standard IP protocols. Each receiving *rvrd* daemon then multicasts the message to all subscribers on its local network.

Not surprisingly, solutions based on multicast tend to provide much better raw performance and scalability for best effort messaging. Not too long ago, I was involved in a project to quantify the expected performance difference between multicast and point-to-point solutions. We investigated this by writing and running some benchmarks to compare the relative performance of three publish-subscribe technologies, and Fig. 20 shows the benchmark results.

It shows the average time for delivery from a single publisher to between 10 and 50 concurrent subscribers when the publisher outputs a burst of messages as fast as possible. The results clearly show that multicast publish-subscribe is ideally suited to applications with demands for low message latencies and hence very high throughput.

4.4.3.1   Understanding Topics

Topics are the publish-subscribe equivalent of queues. Topic names are simply strings, and are specified administratively or programmatically when the topic is created. Each topic has a logical name which is specified by all applications which wish to publish or subscribe using the topic.

---

[18] And the wide area network doesn't support multicast.

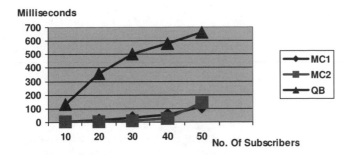

Fig. 20. Publish-subscribe best effort messaging performance: Comparing 2 multicast technologies (MC1, MC2) with a queue-based (QB) publish-subscribe technology

Some publish-subscribe technologies support hierarchical topic naming. The details of exactly how the mechanisms explained below work are product dependent, but the concepts are generic and work similarly across implementations. Let's use the slightly facetious example shown in Fig. 21 of a topic naming tree.

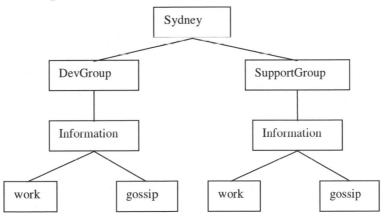

Fig. 21. An example of hierarchical topic naming

Each box represents a topic name that can be used to publish messages. The unique name for each topic is a fully qualified string, with a "/" used as separator between levels in the tree. For example, the following are all valid topic names:

```
Sydney
Sydney/DevGroup
Sydney/DevGroup/Information
Sydney/DevGroup/Information/work
Sydney/DevGroup/Information/gossip
Sydney/SupportGroup
Sydney/SupportGroup/Information
Sydney/SupportGroup/Information/work
Sydney/SupportGroup/Information/gossip
```

Hierarchical topic names become really useful when combined with topic wildcards. In our example, an "*" is used as a wildcard that matches zero or more characters in a topic name. Subscribers can use wildcards to receive messages from more than one topic when they subscribe. For example:

```
Sydney/*/Information
```

This matches both `Sydney/DevGroup/Information` and `Sydney/SupportGroup/Information`. Similarly, a subscriber that specifies the following topic:

```
Sydney/DevGroup/*/*
```

This will receive messages published on all three topics within the `Sydney/DevGroup` tree branch. As subscribing to whole branches of a topic tree is very useful, some products support a shorthand for the above, using another wildcard character such as "**", i.e.:

```
Sydney/DevGroup/**
```

The "**" wildcards also matches all topics that are in `Sydney/DevGroup` branch. Such a wildcard is powerful as it is naturally extensible. If new topics are added within this branch of the topic hierarchy, subscribers do not have to change the topic name in their subscription request in order to receive messages on the new topics.

Carefully crafted topic name hierarchies combined with wildcarding make it possible to create some very flexible messaging infrastructures. Consider how applications might want to subscribe to multiple topics, and organize your design to support these.

4.5 Application Servers

There are many definitions for application servers, but all pretty much agree on the core elements. Namely, an application server is a component-based server technology that resides in the middle-tier of an N-tier architecture, and provides distributed communications, security, transactions and persistence.

Application servers are widely used to build internet-facing applications. Fig. 22 shows a block diagram of the classic N-tier architecture adopted by many web sites.

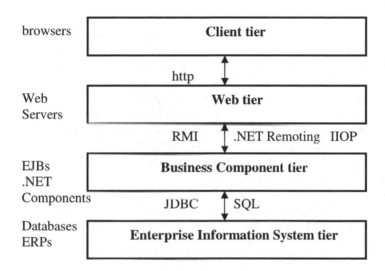

Fig. 22. N-Tier architecture for web applications

An explanation of each tier is below:

- **Client Tier:** In a web application, the client tier typically comprises an Internet browser that submits HTTP requests and downloads HTML pages from a web server. This is commodity technology, not an element of the application server.
- **Web Tier:** The web tier runs a web server to handle client requests. When a request arrives, the web server invokes web server-hosted components such as servlets, Java Server Pages (JSPs) or Active Server Pages (ASPs) depending on the flavor of web server being used. The incoming request identifies the exact web component to call. This component processes the request parameters, and uses these to call the business

logic tier to get the required information to satisfy the request. The web component then formats the results for return to the user as HTML via the web server.

- **Business Component Tier:** The business components comprise the core business logic for the application. The business components are realized by for example Enterprise JavaBeans (EJB) in J2EE, .NET components or CORBA objects. The business components receive requests from the web tier, and satisfy requests usually by accessing one or more databases, returning the results to the web tier. A run-time environment known as a *container* accommodates the components. The container supplies a number of services to the components it hosts. These varying depending on the container type (e.g. EJB, .NET, CORBA), but include transaction and component lifecycle management, state management; security, multithreading and resource pooling. The components specify, in files external to their code, the type of behavior they require from the container at run-time, and then rely on the container to provide the services. This frees the application programmer from cluttering the business logic with code to handle system and environmental issues.

- **Enterprise Information Systems Tier:** This typically consists of one or more databases and back-end applications like mainframes and other legacy systems. The business components must query and interact with these data stores to process requests.

The core of an application server is the business component container and the support it provides for implementing business logic using a software component model. As the details vary between application server technologies, let's just look at the widely used EJB model supported by J2EE. This is a representative example of application server technology.

4.5.1   Enterprise JavaBeans

The Enterprise JavaBeans (EJB) architecture defines a standard programming model for constructing server-side Java applications. A J2EE-compliant application server provides an EJB container to manage the execution of application components. In practical terms, the container provides an operating system process (in fact a Java virtual machine) that hosts EJB components. Fig. 23 shows the relationship between an application server, a container and the services provided. When an EJB client invokes a server component, the container allocates a thread and invokes an instance of the EJB component. The container manages all resources on behalf of the component and all interactions between the component and the external systems.

4.5.2 EJB Component Model

The EJB component model defines the basic architecture of an EJB component. It specifies the structure of the component interfaces and the mechanisms by which it interacts with its container and with other components.

The EJB version 1.1 specifications defines two main types of EJB components, namely *session beans* and *entity beans*.

Session beans are typically used for executing business logic and to provide services for clients to call. Session beans correspond to the controller in a model-view-controller architecture because they encapsulate the business logic of a three-tier architecture.

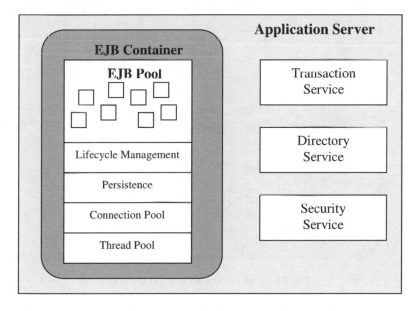

Fig. 23. J2EE application server, EJB container and associated services

Entity beans are typically used for representing business data objects. The data members in an entity bean map directly to some data items stored in an associated database. Entity beans are usually accessed by a session bean that provides the business level services to the client.

Further, there are two types of session beans, known as *stateless* session beans and *stateful* session beans. The difference between these is depicted in Fig. 24.

A stateless session bean is defined as not being *conversational* with respect to its calling process. This means that it does not keep any state information on behalf of any client that calls it. A client will get a reference to a stateless session bean in a container, and can use this reference to make many calls on an instance of the bean. However, between each successive bean invocation, a client is not guaranteed to bind to any particular stateless session bean instance. The EJB container delegates client calls to stateless session beans on *an as needed* basis, so the client can never be certain which bean instance they will actually talk to. This makes it meaningless to store client related state information in a stateless session bean.

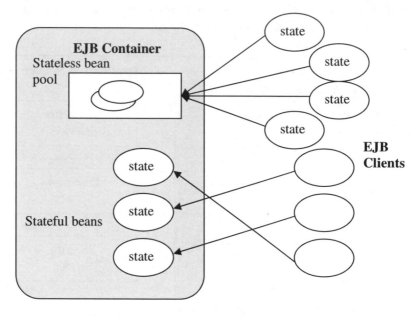

Fig. 24. Stateless versus stateful session beans

On the other hand, a stateful session bean is said to be conversational with respect to its calling process; therefore it can maintain state information about a conversation with a client. Once a client gets a reference to a stateful session bean, all subsequent calls to the bean using this reference are guaranteed to go to the same bean instance. The container creates a new, dedicated stateful session bean for each client that creates a bean instance. Clients may store any state information they wish in the bean, and can be assured it will still be there next time they access the bean.

EJB containers assume responsibility for managing the lifecycle of stateful session beans. The container will write out a bean's state to disk if it has not been used for a while, and will automatically restore the state when the client makes a subsequent call on the bean. This is known as *passivation* and *activation* of the stateful bean. Containers can also be configured to destroy a stateful session bean and its associated resources if a bean is not used for a specified period of time.

There are also two types of entity beans, called *Container Managed Persistence* (CMP) entity beans and *Bean Managed Persistence* (BMP) entity beans. Persistence in this context refers to the way in which the data (usually a row in a relational database table) associated with the entity bean is read and written.

In the CMP entity bean case, the data that the bean represents is mapped automatically to the associated persistent data store (e.g. database) by the container. The container is responsible for loading the data into the bean instance, and writing changes back to the persistent data store at appropriate times, such as the start and end of a transaction. CMP relies on container-provided services and requires no application code as the container automatically generates the data access code. CMP is hence easy to implement, and supported for relational databases accessed using SQL.

In the case of a BMP entity bean, the bean code itself is responsible for accessing the persistent data it represents. This is typically done using handcrafted JDBC calls, or calls to a proprietary database or application API. Bean-managed persistence gives the bean developer the flexibility to perform persistence operations that are too complicated for the container to generate, or to use a data source that is not supported by the container, for example a custom or legacy database or an FTP site. While BMP requires more effort on the programmer's behalf to implement, it can sometimes provide opportunities to optimize data access, and in such cases may provide better performance than CMP.

4.5.3   EJB Programming

An EJB depends on the EJB container for everything it needs. If an EJB needs to access a JDBC connection or another bean, it uses the container services to achieve this.

To create an EJB component, the developer must provide two interfaces that define a bean's business and lifecycle management methods, plus the actual bean implementation class. The two interfaces are called the *remote* and *home* interfaces, and have different purposes.

The *home* interface contains the lifecycle methods of the EJB. These provide clients with services to create, destroy and find bean instances. In contrast, the *remote* interface contains the business methods offered by the bean. These are of course application specific. In order to use the methods in the bean's *remote* interface, clients must use the bean's *home* interface to obtain a reference to the remote interface.

A simple *home* interface is shown below. The *home* interface must inherit from *EJBHome*, and in this example, the interface contains a method to create an EJB of type *Broker*.

```
public interface BrokerHome extends EJBHome {
/*
* This method creates the EJB Object.
* @return The newly created EJB Object.
*/
    Broker create()
            throws RemoteException, CreateException;
}
```

The (cut down) remote interface for this EJB looks like this:

```
public interface Broker extends EJBObject {
    public int newAccount(String name, String address,
        int credit)
        throws RemoteException, SQLException;

    public void buyStock(int accno, int stock_id, int amount)
        throws RemoteException, SQLException,
        TransDenyException;

    public void updateAccount(int accno, int credit)
        throws RemoteException, SQLException;
}
```

An EJB client uses a bean's public interfaces to create and call an instance of the EJB. One instantiated by the client, the EJB implementation class, normally known as the bean class, becomes an accessible distributed Java object. Some example, rather simplified, client code is shown below:

```
Broker broker = null;
// find the home interface
Object _h = ctx.lookup("EntityStock.BrokerHome");
BrokerHome home =
    (BrokerHome)javax.rmi.PortableRemoteObject.narrow(_h,
```

```
      BrokerHome.class);

// Use the home interface to create the Broker EJB Object
broker = home.create();
// execute requests at the broker EJB
broker.updateAccount(accountNo, 200000);
broker.buyStock(accountNo, stockID, 5000);

//we're finished...
broker.remove();
```

EJB clients may be standalone Java applications, servlets, applets, or even other EJBs. All clients use the server bean's *home* interface to obtain a reference to an instance of the server bean. This reference is associated with the class type of the server bean's *remote* interface. Therefore the client interacts with the server bean entirely through the methods defined in the bean's *remote* interface.

In this example, the *Broker* bean is a stateless session bean that handles client requests. Internally, it actually uses the services of a number of entity beans to perform the data access logic. An example of one of the *Broker* methods, the *updateAccount* method, is included below:

```
public void updateAccount(int accno, int credit)
throws RemoteException {
   try {
      Account account = accountHome.findByPrimaryKey
         (new AccountPK(accno));
      account.update(credit);
   }
   catch (Exception e) {
         throw new RemoteException(e.toString());
   }
}
```

This method uses an entity bean called *Account*. The entity bean encapsulates all the detailed manipulation of the application's data, in this case, exactly how an account record is updated. The code in the *updateAccount* method uses an entity bean *finder* method called *findByPrimaryKey*, which is provided by the *Account* bean in its *home* interface. The finder method takes the primary key for the account, and accesses the underlying database. If an account record is found in the database with this primary key, the EJB container creates an *Account* entity bean. The entity bean methods, in this example the *update* method, can then be used to access the data in the account record.

The *home* and *remote* interface for *Account* look like this:

```
public interface AccountHome extends EJBHome
{
public Account create(String name, String address,
   int credit) throws CreateException, RemoteException;

/**
* Finds an Account by its primary Key (Account ID)
*/
public Account findByPrimaryKey(AccountPK key)
   throws FinderException, RemoteException;
}
public interface Account extends EJBObject
{ // many methods missing for brevity
   public void deposit(int amount) throws RemoteException;
   public int withdraw(int amount)
       throws AccountException, RemoteException;
   // Getter/setter methods on Entity Bean fields
   public String getSubName() throws RemoteException;
   public void setSubName(String name) throws RemoteException;
}
```

The bean class for the entity bean contains the implementation of the remote methods. The code for the *update* method is included below. Note it is very simple, in fact a single line of Java.

```
public class AccountBean implements EntityBean {
   // Container-managed state fields
   public int     sub_accno;
   public String sub_name;
   public String sub_address;
   public int     sub_credit;
   // lots missing….
   public void update(int amount) {
     sub_credit = amount;
   }
}
```

This simplicity is due to the fact that the entity bean is using "container managed persistence". The EJB container *knows* (we'll see how it knows soon) that there is a correspondence between the data members in the *Account* bean and the fields in an account table in the database the application is using.

Using this information, the container tools can generate the SQL statements needed to implement the finder method, and the queries needed to automatically read/write the data from/to the entity bean at the beginning/end of a transaction.

In this example, at the end of the *Broker* session bean's *updateAccount* method, the data items in the *Account* entity bean will be written back to the database, making the changes to the *sub_credit* persistent field. All this is done transparently, without explicit control from the programmer.

4.5.4 Deployment Descriptors

One of the major attractions of the EJB component model is the way in which it achieves a *separation of concerns* between business logic and infrastructure code. This separation of concerns refers to the fact that EJB's are mostly concerned with executing pure business logic. The EJB container becomes responsible for handling environmental and infrastructure issues like transactions, bean lifecycle management and security. This makes the code in the bean components simpler, as they aren't littered with code to handle all these additional complexities.

Beans inform the container of the services they require through deployment descriptors. A deployment descriptor is an XML document associated with an EJB. When a bean is deployed into a container, the container reads the deployment descriptor to find out how transactions, persistence (for entity beans), and access control should be handled. Hence deployment descriptors provide a declarative mechanism describing how these issues are handled.

The beauty of this mechanism is that the same EJB component can be deployed with different deployment descriptors suited to different application environments. If security is an issue, the component can specify its access control needs. If security is not an issue, no access control is specified in the deployment descriptor. In both cases the code in the EJB is identical. From a software engineering perspective, this is really nice to have.

The deployment descriptor example below is specified in an XML Document Type Definition (DTD). The deployment descriptor describes the type of bean (session or entity) and the classes used for the *remote*, *home*, and bean class. It also specifies the transactional attributes of every method in the bean, which security roles can access each method (access control), and whether persistence in the entity beans is handled automatically by the container or is performed explicitly by the bean code.

The deployment descriptor for the *Broker* bean used in the example above is shown below. In addition to the attributes described above, the deployment descriptor specifies that this bean is stateless session bean, and that a container managed transaction is required to execute each method in the bean (these attributes are in boldface for ease of reading). As an example, we could simply change the *<session-type>* field in the XML to read *Stateful*, and the container would manage the bean very differently indeed.

```
<ejb-jar>
  <enterprise-beans>
    <session>
        <ejb-name>EntityStock.BrokerHome</ejb-name>
        <home>db.entitystock.BrokerHome</home>
        <remote>db.entitystock.Broker</remote>
        <ejb-class>db.entitystock.BrokerBean</ejb-class>
        <session-type>Stateless</session-type>
        <transaction-type>Container</transaction-type>
    </session>
  </enterprise-beans>
  <assembly-descriptor>
    <container-transaction>
      <method>
        <ejb-name>EntityStock.BrokerHome</ejb-name>
        <method-intf>Remote</method-intf>
        <method-name>*</method-name>
      </method>
      <trans-attribute>Required</trans-attribute>
    </container-transaction>
  </assembly-descriptor>
</ejb-jar>
```

As another example, let's look at the deployment descriptor for the *Account* entity bean. It looks like this:

```
<ejb-jar>
  <enterprise-beans>
    <entity>
      <ejb-name>EntityStock.AccountHome</ejb-name>
      <home>db.entitystock.AccountHome</home>
      <remote>db.entitystock.Account</remote>
      <ejb-class>db.entitystock.AccountBean</ejb-class>
      <persistence-type>Container</persistence-type>
      <prim-key-class>db.entitystock.AccPK</prim-key-class>
      <reentrant>False</reentrant>
      <cmp-field>
        <field-name>sub_accno</field-name>
      </cmp-field>
      <cmp-field>
        <field-name>sub_name</field-name>
      </cmp-field>
      <cmp-field>
        <field-name>sub_address</field-name>
      </cmp-field>
      <cmp-field>
        <field-name>sub_credit</field-name>
      </cmp-field>
      <resource-ref>
        <res-ref-name>jdbc/sqlStock_nkPool</res-ref-name>
```

```
    <res-type>javax.sql.DataSource</res-type>
      <res-auth>Container</res-auth>
    </resource-ref>
  </entity>
 </enterprise-beans>
 <assembly-descriptor>
   <container-transaction>
     <method>
       <ejb-name>EntityStock.AccountHome</ejb-name>
       <method-intf>Remote</method-intf>
       <method-name>*</method-name>
     </method>
     <trans-attribute>Required</trans-attribute>
   </container-transaction>
 </assembly-descriptor>
</ejb-jar>
```

As well as the deployment attributes we've already seen, the above tells the container the following (bolded in the XML):

- it must manage persistence for beans of this type
- where to find the JDBC data source for the database
- what the primary key and data items are that must be mapped between the database and the entity bean

4.5.5 Responsibilities of the EJB Container

It should be pretty obvious at this stage that the EJB container is a fairly complex piece of software. It's therefore worth covering exactly what the role of the container is in running an EJB application.

In general, a container provides EJB components with a number of services. These are:

- It provides bean lifecycle management and bean instance pooling, including creation, activation, passivation, and bean destruction.
- It intercepts client calls on the remote interface of beans to enforce transaction and security constraints. It also provides notification callbacks at the start and end of each transaction involving a bean instance.
- It manages the persistence of selected fields of CMP entity beans.

In order to intercept client calls, the tools associated with a container must generate additional classes for an EJB at deployment time. These tools use Java's introspection mechanism to dynamically generate classes to implement the *home* and *remote* interfaces of each bean. These classes enable the container to intercept all client calls on a bean, and enforce the policies specified in the bean's deployment descriptor.

The container also provides a number of other key run-time features for EJBs. These typically include:

- **Threading:** EJB's should not explicitly create and manipulate Java threads. They must rely on the container to allocate threads to active beans in order to provide a concurrent, high performance execution environment. This makes EJBs simpler to write, as the application programmer does not have to implement a threading scheme to handle concurrent client requests.
- **Caching:** The container can maintain caches of the entity bean instances it manages. Typically the size of the caches can be specified in deployment descriptors.
- **Connection Pooling:** The container can manage a pool of database connections to enable efficient access to external resource managers by reusing connections once transactions are complete.

4.5.6 Some Thoughts

This section has given a brief overview of J2EE and EJB technology. The EJB component model is widely used and has proven a powerful way of constructing server-side applications. And although the interactions between the different parts of the code are at first a little daunting, with some exposure and experience with the model, it becomes relatively straightforward to construct EJB applications. Also, EJB version 3.0[19] is attempting to simplify a lot of the housekeeping code that is required, so when this version is widely available, building EJB applications should be even easier.

Still, while the code construction is not difficult, a number of complexities remain. These are:

- The EJB model makes it possible to combine components in an application using many different architectural patterns. This gives the architect a range of design options for an application. Which option is *best* is often open to debate, along with what does *best* mean in a given application? These are not always simple questions, and requires the consideration of complex design trade-offs.

---

[19] http://java.sun.com/products/ejb/docs.html

- The way beans interact with the container is complex, and can have a significant effect of the performance of an application. In the same vein, all EJB server containers are not equal. Product selection and product specific configuration is an important aspect of the application development lifecycle.

For references discussing both these issues, see the further reading section at the end of this chapter.

4.6 Message Brokers

Basic messaging using MOM and publish-subscribe technologies suffices for many applications. It's a simple, effective and proven approach that can deliver high levels of performance and reliability.

MOM deployments start to get a little more complex though when message formats are not totally agreed amongst the various applications that communicate using the MOM. This problem occurs commonly in the domain of enterprise integration, where the basic problem is building business applications from large, complex legacy business systems that were never designed to work together and exchange information.

Enterprise integration is a whole field of study in itself (see Further Reading). From the perspective of this book however, enterprise integration has spawned an interesting and widely used class of middleware technologies, known as message brokers.

Let's introduce message brokers by way of a motivating example. Assume an organization has four different legacy business systems that each hold information about customers.[20] Each of these four stores some common data about customers, as well as some unique data fields that others do not maintain. In addition, each of the applications has a different format for a customer record, and the individual field names are different across each (e.g. one uses ADDRESS, another LOCATION, as a field name for customer address data). To update customer data, a proprietary API is available for each legacy system.

Whilst this is conceptually pretty simple, it's a problem that many organizations have. So, let's assume keeping the data consistent in each of these four applications is a problem for our hypothetical organization. Hence they decide to implement a web site that allows customers to update

---

[20] Duplicate data holdings like this are very common in enterprises. For example, my bank still manages to send my credit card statement and credit card rewards points statement to different addresses

their own details online. When this occurs, the data entered into the web page is passed to a web component in the web server (e.g. a servlet or ASP.NET page). The role of this component is to pass the updated data to each of the four legacy applications, so they can update their own customer data correctly.

The organization uses MOM to communicate between applications. Consequently, the web component formats a message with the new customer data, and uses the MOM to send the message to each legacy system[21]. The message format, labeled *In-format* in Fig. 25, is an agreed format that the web component and all the legacy applications understand.

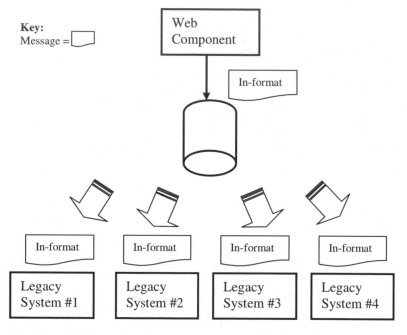

Fig. 25. Using MOM to communicate a customer data update to 4 legacy systems.

Each legacy system has a queue interface component that can read messages from the queue, and using the data in the message, create a call to the customer data update API that the legacy system supports. In this example, the interface component would read the message from the queue, extract the specific data fields from the message that it needs to call its legacy system's API, and finally issue the API call. As shown in Fig. 26, the inter-

---

[21] The MOM may deploy a different queue for each legacy application or a single queue and include a 'destination' field in each message.

face component is basically performing a transformation from the *In-format* to a format suitable for its associated legacy system.

So, for each legacy application, there is a dedicated component that executes the logic to transform the incoming message into a correctly formatted legacy system API call. The transformation is implemented in the program code of the component.

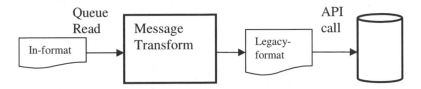

Fig. 26. Message transformation from common to a legacy-specific format.

This solution has some interesting implications:

- If the common *In-format* message format changes, then the web component and every legacy system component that executes the transformation must be modified and tested.
- If any legacy system API changes, then only the transformation for that system must be modified and tested.
- Modifying any of the transformations most likely requires coordinating with the development team who are responsible for the upkeep of the legacy system(s). These development teams are the ones who know the intimate details of how to access the legacy system API.

Hence, there is a tight coupling between all the components in this architecture. This is caused by the need for them to agree on the message format that is communicated. In addition, in large organizations (or even harder, across organizational boundaries), communicating and coordinating changes to the common message format can be slow and painful. It's the sort of thing you'd like to avoid if possible.

The obvious alternative solution is to move the responsibility for the message format transformation to the web component. This would guarantee that messages are sent to each legacy system interface component in the format they need to simply call the legacy API. The transformation complexity is now all in one place, the web component, and the legacy system interface component becomes simple. It basically reads message from the queue and calls the associated API using the data in the message. Changes to the *In-format* message do not cause changes in legacy interface components, as only the web component needs modifying and testing. Changes to any legacy API though require the specific legacy system development team to request a new message format from the web component development team.

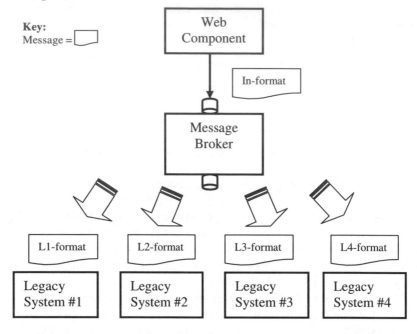

Fig. 27. Decoupling Clients and Servers with a Message Broker.

The major downside of this solution is the complexity of the web component. The transformation for each legacy system is embedded in its program code, making it prone to modification as it is effectively coupled to the message formats of every legacy system it communicates with.

This is where message brokers enter the fray, offering a potential third solution. Architecturally, a broker is a known architecture pattern[22] incorporating a component that decouples clients and servers by mediating the communications between them. Similarly, message broker middleware augments the capabilities of a MOM platform so that business logic can be executed within the broker. In our example, using a broker we could embed the message transformation rules for each legacy system within the broker, giving a solution as in Fig. 27.

---

[22] See Buschmann reference in Further Reading, Chapter 1

A message broker solution is attractive because it completely decouples the web component and the legacy interface components. The web component simply assembles and emits a message, and the broker transforms the message into the necessary format for each legacy system. It then sends an output message to the legacy system interface components in the precise format they desire.

A further attraction is the simplification of all the components in the system, as they now do not have to be concerned with message format transformation. The message transformation logic is localized within the message broker, and becomes the responsibility of the middleware development group to maintain. Consequently, if changes are needed in the web or legacy system message formats, the development team responsible only need liaise with the middleware development group, whose job it is to correctly update the transformations.

It's not a massive job to implement the broker pattern in conjunction with a standard MOM platform[23]. Such a solution would still have the disadvantage of defining the transformation logic in the program code. For simple transformations, this is no big deal, but many such applications involve complex transformations with fiddly string formatting and concatenations, formulas to calculate composite values, and so on. Nothing too difficult to write, but if there were a better solution that made creating complex transformations simple, I doubt many people would complain.

Message broker technologies begin to excel at this stage, because they provide specialized tools for:

- Graphically describing complex message transformations between input formats and output formats. Transformations can be simple in terms of moving an input field value to an output field, or they can be defined using scripting languages (typically product specific) that can perform various formatting, data conversions and mathematical transforms.
- High performance message transformation engines that can handle multiple simultaneous transformation requests.
- Describing and executing message flows, in which an incoming message can be routed to different transformations and outputs depending on the values in the incoming message.

An example of a message mapping tool is shown in Fig. 28. This is Microsoft's BizTalk Mapper, and is typical of the class of mapping technologies. In BizTalk, the mapper can generate the transformations necessary to move data between two XML schemas, with the lines depicting the mapping between source and destination schemas. Scripts (not shown in the

---

[23] The solution is left as an exercise to the reader!

figure) can be associated with any mapping to define more complex mappings.

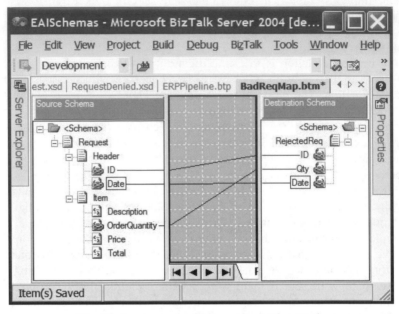

Fig. 28. A message broker mapping tool example

An example of a typical message routing definition tool is shown in Fig. **29**. This is IBM's WebSphere MQSI technology. It shows how an incoming message, delivered on a queue, can be processed according to some data value in the message. In the example, a *Filter* component inspects the incoming message field values, and based on specified conditions, executes one of two computations, or sends the message to one of two output queues. The message flow also defines exception handling logic, which is invoked when, for example, invalidly formatted messages are received.

Hence, message brokers are essentially highly specialized message transformation and routing engines. With their associated customized development tools, they make it simpler to define message transformations that can be:

- Easily understood and modified without changing the participating applications.

- Managed centrally, allowing a team responsible for application integration to coordinate and test changes.
- Executed by a high performance, multi-threaded transformation engine.

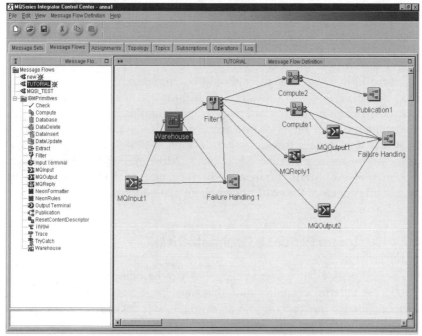

Fig. 29. Message routing and processing

Importantly, message brokers operate on a per message level. They receive an input message, transform it according to the message routing rules and logic, and output the resulting message or messages to their destinations. Brokers work best when these transformations are short-lived and execute quickly, in for example a few milliseconds. This is because they are typically optimized for performance, and hence try to avoid overheads that would slow down transformations. Consequently, if a broker or its host machine crashes, it relies on the fact that failed transformation can simply be executed again from the beginning, meaning expensive state and transaction management is not needed.[24]

---

[24] Many message brokers do optionally support transactional messaging, and even allow the broker to modify databases during transformation execution. These transactions are coordinated by an ACID transaction manager, such as the one supplied with the underlying MOM technology.

For a large class of application integration scenarios, high-speed transformation is all that's required. However, many business integration problems require the definition of a series of requests flowing between different applications. Each request may involve several message transformations, reads and updates to external database systems, and complex logic to control the flow of messages between applications and potentially even humans for off-line decision-making. For such problems, message brokers are insufficient and well, you guessed it, even more technology is required. This is described in the next section.

Before moving on though, it should be emphasized that message brokers, like everything in software architecture and technologies, do have their downsides. First, they are proprietary technologies, and this leads to vendor lock-in. It's the price you pay for all those sophisticated development and deployment tools. Second, in high volume messaging applications, the broker can become a bottleneck. Most message broker products support broker clustering to increase performance, scalability and reliability, but this comes at the costs of complexity and dollars.

4.7   Business Process Orchestration

Business processes in modern enterprises can be complex in terms of the number of enterprise applications that must be accessed and updated to complete the business service. As an example, Fig. 30 is a simple depiction of a sales order business process, in which the following sequence of events occurs.

A customer places an order through a call center. Customer data is stored in a customer relationship management package (Siebel). Once the order is placed, the customer's credit is validated using an external credit service, and the accounts payable database in updated to record the order and send an invoice to the customer.

Placing an order causes a message to be sent to Shipping, who update their inventory system and ship the order to the customer. When the customer receives the order, they pay for the goods and the payment is recorded in the accounts received system. All financial data is periodically extracted from the accounts systems and stored in an Oracle data warehouse for management reporting and archiving.

Implementing such business processes has two major challenges. First, from the time an order is placed to when the payment is received might take several days or weeks, or even longer. Somewhere then, the current state of the business process for a given order, representing exactly what stage it is up to, must be stored, potentially for a long time. Losing this state, and hence the status of the order, is not a desirable option.

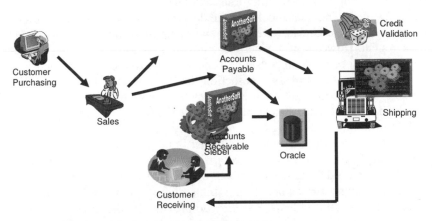

Fig. 30. A typical business process

Second, exceptions in the order process can cause the state of the order to fail and rollback. For example, an order is taken for some stock item. Let's assume this stock is not available in the warehouse, and when it is re-ordered, the supplier tells the warehouse that the old stock is now obsolete, and that a newer, more expensive model will replace it. The customer is informed of this, and they decide to cancel the order. Canceling requires the order data to be removed from the warehouse, accounts payable and Siebel systems. This is potentially a complex task to reliably and correctly perform.

This style of rollback behavior can be defined by the process designer using a facility known as a compensating transaction. Compensating transactions allow the process designer to explicitly define the logic required to undo a failed transaction that partially completed.

In long-running business processes such as sales order processing, standard ACID transactions, which lock all resources until the transaction completes, are not feasible. This is because they lock data in the business systems for potentially minutes, hours or even weeks in order to achieve transaction isolation. Locked data cannot be accessed by concurrent transactions, and hence lock contention will cause these to wait (or more likely fail through timing out) until the locks are released. Such a situation is not likely to produce high-performance and scalable business process implementations for long running business processes.

Transactional behavior for long running processes is therefore usually handled by grouping a number of process activities into a long-running transaction scope. Long-running transactions comprise of multiple process activities that do not place locks on the data items they touch in the various business systems. Updates are made and committed locally at each business system. However, if any activity in the transaction scope fails, the designer must specify a compensating function. The role of the compensator is to undo the effects of the transaction that have already committed. Essentially this means undoing any changes the transaction had made, leaving the data in the same state as it was before the transaction commenced.

Long-running transactions are notoriously difficult to implement correctly. And sometimes they are somewhat impossible to implement sensibly – how do you compensate for a business process that has sent an email confirming an order has been shipped, or has mailed an invoice? So, technology solutions for compensating transactions don't eradicate any of these fundamental problems. But they do provide the designer with a tool to make the existence of a long running transaction explicit, and an execution framework that automatically calls the compensator when failures occur. For many problems this is sufficient for building a workable solution.

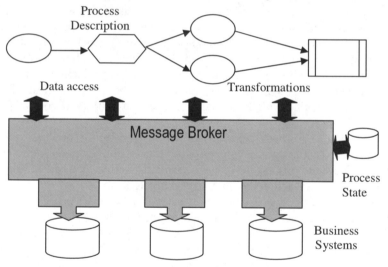

Fig. 31. Anatomy of a business process orchestration platform

As Fig. 31 illustrates, business process orchestration (BPO) platforms are designed to make implementing these long running, highly integrated business processes relatively straightforward.

BPO platforms are commonly built as a layer on top of a message broker. They extend message brokers by adding:

- **State management:** the state of an executing business process is stored
  persistently in a database. This makes it resilient to BPO server failure.
  Also, once the process state is stored in the database, it does not consume any resources in the BPO engine.
- **Development tools:** visual process definition tools are provided for defining business processes.
- **Deployment tools:** these enable developers to easily link logical business process steps to the underlying business systems using various
  types of connectivity, including message queues, web protocols and file
  systems.

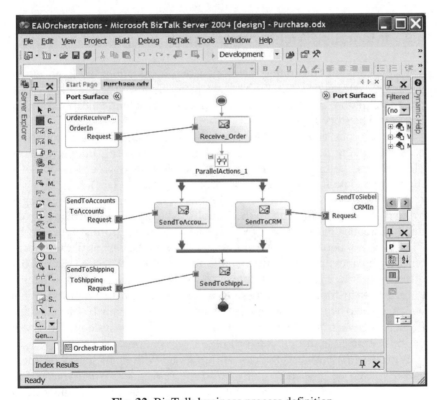

Fig. 32. BizTalk business process definition

An example from Microsoft's BizTalk technology is shown in Fig. 32.
This shows the design of a simple business process for the ordering exam-

ple in Fig. 30. Messages are sent and received by activities in the process using ports. Ports basically connect to the business systems using a port-defined transport mechanism, for example HTTP, a message queue or a file. All messages handled inside an orchestration must be defined by XML schemas. Activities can be carried out in sequence, or in parallel as shown in the example.

BPO engines are the most recent addition to the IT middleware stack. The need for their functionality has been driven by the desire to automate more and more business processes that must access numerous independent business applications. There seems little doubt that this trend will continue as enterprises drive down costs by better integrating and coordinating their internal applications, and seamlessly connecting to external business partners.

4.8   Integration Architecture Issues

The difficulty of integrating heterogeneous applications in large enterprises is a serious one. While there are many issues to deal with in enterprise integration, at the core is an architectural problem concerning modifiability. The story goes like this.

Assume your enterprise has five different business applications that need integrating to support some new business processes. Like any sensible architect, you decide to implement these business processes one at a time (as you know a "big bang" approach is doomed to fail!).

The first process requires one of the business systems to send messages to each of the other four, using their published messaging interfaces. To do this, the sender must create a message payload in the format required by each business application. Assuming one-way messages only, this means our first business process must be able to transform its source data into 4 different message formats. Of course, if the other business systems decide to change their formats, then these transformations must be updated. What we've created with this design is a tight coupling, namely the message formats, between the source and destination business systems. This scenario is depicted in the left-side of Fig. 33.

With the first business process working, and with many happy business users, you go on to incrementally build the remainder. When you've finished, you find you've created an architecture like that in the right-side of Fig. 33. Each application sends messages to each of the other four, creating 20 interfaces, or dependencies, that need to be maintained. When one business application is modified, it's possible that each of the others will need to update their message transformations to send messages in a newly required format.

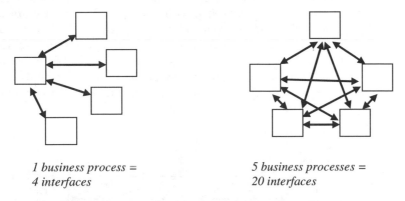

1 business process =
4 interfaces

5 business processes =
20 interfaces

Fig. 33. Integrating applications in a point-to-point architecture

This is a small scale illustration of a problem that exists in thousands of organizations. I've seen enterprise architectures that have three hundred point-to-point interfaces between forty or so standalone business applications. Changing an application's message interface becomes a scary exercise in such enterprises, as so many other systems are dependent on it. Sometimes making changes is so scary, development teams just won't do it. It's simply too risky.

In the general case, the number of interfaces between N applications is (N^2-N). So as N grows, the number of possible interfaces grows exponentially, making such point-to-point architectures non-scalable in terms of modifiability.

Now it's true that very few enterprises have a fully connected point-to-point architecture such as that on the right-side of Fig. 33. But it's also true that many interfaces between two applications are two-way, requiring two transformations. And most applications have more than one interface, so in reality the number of interfaces between two tightly coupled applications can be considerably greater than one.

Another name for a point-to-point architecture is a "spaghetti architecture", hopefully for obvious reasons. When using this term, very few people are referring to spaghetti with the positive connotations usually associated with tasty Italian food. In fact, as the discipline of enterprise integration blossomed in the late 1990's, the emerging dogma was that spaghetti architectures should be avoided at all costs. The solution promoted, for good reasons, was to use a message broker, as explained earlier in this chapter.

Let's analyze exactly what happens when a spaghetti architecture is transformed using a message broker, as illustrated in Fig. 34. Complexity in the end points, the business applications, is greatly reduced as they just send messages using their native formats to the broker, and these are transformed inside the broker to the required destination format. If you need to change an end point, then you just need to modify the message transformations within the broker that are dependent on that end point. No other business applications know or care.

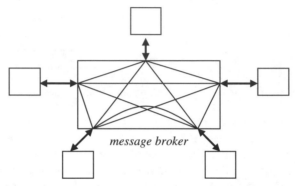

Fig. 34. Eliminating a point-to-point architecture with a message broker.

Despite all these advantages to introducing a message broker, the *no free lunch*[25] principle, as always, applies. The downsides are:

- The spaghetti architecture really still exists. It's now resident inside the message broker, where complex dependencies between message formats are captured in broker-defined message transformations.
- Brokers are a potentially a performance bottleneck, as all the messages between applications must pass through the broker. Good brokers support replication and clustered deployments to scale their performance. But of course, this increases deployment and management complexity, and more than likely the license costs associated with a solution. Message broker vendors, perhaps not surprisingly, rarely see this last point as a disadvantage.

So message brokers are very useful, but not a panacea by any means for integration architectures. There is however a design approach that can be

---

[25] http://en.wikipedia.org/wiki/Tanstaafl

utilized that possesses the scalability of a point-to-point architecture with the modifiability characteristics of broker-based solution.

The solution is to define an enterprise data model (also known as a canonical data model) that becomes the target format for all message transformations between applications. For example, a common issue is that all your business systems have different data formats to define customer information. When one application integrates with another, it (or a message broker) must transform its customer message format to the target message format.

Now let's assume we define a canonical message format for customer information. This can be used as the target format for any business application that needs to exchange customer-related data. Using this canonical message format, a message exchange is now reduced to the following steps:

- Source application transforms local customer data in to canonical customer information format.
- Source sends message to target with canonical message format as payload.
- Target receives message and transforms the canonical format into its own local customer data representation.

This means that each end point (business application) must know:

- how to transform all messages it receives from the canonical format to its local format
- how to transform all messages it sends from its local format to the canonical format

As Fig. 35 illustrates, by using the enterprise data model to exchange messages, we get the best of both worlds. The number of transformations is reduced to 2*N (assuming a single interface between each end point). This gives us much better modifiability characteristics. Also, as there are now considerably fewer and less complex transformations to build, the transformations can be executed in the end points themselves. We have no need for a centralized, broker-style architecture. This scales well, as there's inherently no bottleneck in the design. And there's no need for additional hardware for the broker, and additional license costs for our chosen broker solution.

I suspect some of you might be thinking that this is too good to be true. Perhaps there is at least a low cost lunch option here?

I'm sorry to disappoint you, but there are real reasons why this architecture is not ubiquitous in enterprise integration. The main one is the sheer difficulty of designing, and then getting agreement on, an enterprise data model in a large organization. In a green field site, the enterprise data model is something that can be designed upfront and all end points mandated to adhere to. But green field sites are rare, and most organization's enterprise systems have grown organically over many years, and rarely in a planned and coordinated manner. This is why broker-based solutions are successful. They recognize the reality of enterprise systems and the need for building many ad hoc transformations between systems in a maintainable way.

There are other impediments to establishing canonical data formats. If your systems integrate with a business partner's applications over which you have no control, then it's likely impossible to establish a single, agreed set of message formats. This problem has to be addressed on a much wider scale, where whole industry groups get together to define common message formats. A good example is RosettaNet[26] that has defined protocols for automating supply chains in the semiconductor industry. As I'm sure you can imagine, none of this happens quickly.[27]

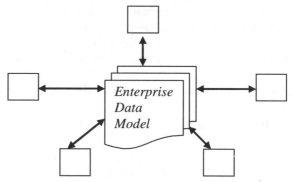

Fig. 35. Integration using an enterprise data model

For many organizations, the advantages of using an enterprise data model can only be incrementally exploited. For example, a new business systems installation might present opportunities to start defining elements of an enterprise data model, and to build point-to-point architectures that exploit end point transformations to canonical formats. Or your broker

---

[26] www.rosettanet.org

[27] See http://www.ebxml.org/ for examples of initiatives in this area.

might be about to be deprecated and require you to upgrade your transformation logic? I'd recommend taking any chance you get.

4.9 Summary

It's taken the best part of fifteen years to build, but now IT architects have a powerful toolkit of middleware technologies to leverage in designing and implementing their applications. These technologies have evolved for two main reasons:

1. They help make building complex, distributed, concurrent applications simpler.
2. They institutionalize proven design practices by supporting them in off-the-shelf middleware technologies.

With all this infrastructure technology available, the skill of the architect lies in how they select, mix and match architectures and technologies in a way that meets their application's requirements and constraints. This requires not only advanced design skills, but also deep knowledge of the technologies involved, understanding what they can be reliably called on to do, and equally importantly, what they cannot sensibly do. Many applications fail or are delivered late because perfectly good quality and well built middleware technology is used in a way in which it was never intended to be used. This is not the technology's fault – it's the designers'. Hence middleware knowledge, and more importantly experience with the technologies in demanding applications, is simply a pre-requisite for becoming a skilled architect in the information technology world.

To make life more complex, it's rare that just a single architecture and technology solution makes sense for any given application. For example, simple messaging or a message broker might make sense for a particular problem. And these logical design alternatives typically have multiple implementation options in terms of candidate middleware products for building the solution.

In such situations, the architect has to analyze the various trade-offs between different solutions and technologies, and choose an alternative (or perhaps nominate a set of competing alternatives) that meets the application requirements. To be honest, I'm always a little suspicious of architects who, in such circumstances, always come up with the same architectural and technology answer (unless they work for a technology vendor – in that case, it's their job).

The cause of this "I have a hammer, everything is a nail" style behavior is often a fervent belief that a particular design, and more often a favored technology, can solve any problems that arise. As it's the end of the chapter, I won't get on my soap box. But I'll simply say that open-minded, experienced and technologically agnostic architects are more likely to consider a wider range of design alternatives. They're also likely to propose solutions most appropriate to the quirks and constraints of the problem at hand, rather than enthusiastically promoting a particular solution that demonstrates the eternal "goodness" of their favorite piece of technology over its "evil" competitors.

4.10 Further Reading

There's an enormous volume of potential reading on the subject matter covered in this chapter. The references that follow should give you a good starting point to delve more deeply.

4.10.1 CORBA

The best place to start for all CORBA related information is the Object Management Group's web site, namely:

www.omg.org

Navigate from here, and you'll find information on everything to do with CORBA, including specifications, tutorials and many books. For specific recommendations, in my experience, anything written by Doug Schmidt, Steve Vinosky or Michi Henning is always informative and revealing.

4.10.2 Message-Oriented Middleware

The best place to look for MOM information is probably the product vendor's documentation and white papers. Use your favorite search engine to look for information on IBM WebSphere MQ, Microsoft Message Queue (MSMQ), Sonic MQ, and many more. If you'd like to peruse the Java Messaging Service specification, it can be downloaded from:

http://java.sun.com/products/jms/docs.html

If you're interested in a very readable and recent analysis of some publish-subscribe technology performance, including a JMS, the following is well worth downloading:

Piyush Maheshwari and Michael Pang, *Benchmarking Message-Oriented Middleware: TIB/RV versus SonicMQ*, Concurrency and Computation: Practice and Experience, volume 17, pages 1507-1526, 2005

4.10.3 Application Servers

Again, the Internet is probably the best source of general information on applications servers. Leading product include WebLogic (BEA), WebSphere (IBM), .NET application server (Microsoft), and for a high quality open source implementation, JBoss.

There's lots of good design knowledge about EJB applications in:

F. Marinescu. EJB Design Patterns: Advanced Patterns, Processes, and Idioms. Wiley, 2002
D. Alur, D. Malks, J. Crupi. Core J2EE Patterns: Best Practices and Design Strategies. Second Edition, Prentice Hall, 2003

The following discusses how to compare middleware and application server features:

I. Gorton, A. Liu, P. Brebner. *Rigorous Evaluation of COTS Middleware Technology.* IEEE Computer, vol. 36, no. 3, pages 50-55, March 2003

4.10.4 Integration Middleware

An excellent book by one of the leaders in enterprise integration is:

D. S. Linthicum. Next Generation Application Integration: From Simple Information to Web Services. Addison-Wesley, 2003

The following three books have broad and informative coverage of design patterns for enterprise integration and messaging.

M. Fowler. Patterns of Enterprise Application Architecture. Addison-Wesley, 2002.

G. Hohpe, B. Woolf. Enterprise Integration Patterns: Designing, Building, and Deploying Messaging Solutions. Addison-Wesley, 2003

C. Bussler, B2B Integration Concepts and Architecture, Springer-Verlag 2003

5 A Software Architecture Process

5.1 Process Outline

The role of an architect is much more than simply carrying out a software design activity. The architect must typically:

- **Work with the requirements team:** The requirements team will be focused on eliciting the functional requirements from the application stakeholders. The architect plays an important role in requirements gathering by understanding the overall systems needs and ensuring that the appropriate quality attributes are explicit and understood.
- **Work with various application stakeholders:** Architects play a pivotal liaison role by making sure all the application's stakeholder needs are understood and incorporated into the design. For example, in addition to the business user requirements for an application, system administrators will require that the application can be easily installed, monitored, managed and upgraded.
- **Lead the technical design team:** Defining the application architecture is a design activity. The architect leads a design team, comprising system designers (or on large projects, other architects) and technical leads in order to produce the architecture blueprint.
- **Work with the project management:** The architect works closely with project management, helping with project planning, estimation and task allocation and scheduling.

In order to guide an architect through the definition of the application architecture, it's useful to follow a defined software engineering process. Fig. 36 shows a simple, three-step iterative architecture process that can be used to guide activities during the design. Briefly, the three steps are:

1. **Define architecture requirements:** This involves creating a statement or model of the requirements that will drive the architecture design.
2. **Architecture design:** This involves defining the structure and responsibilities of the components that will comprise the architecture.
3. **Validation:** This involves "testing" the architecture, typically by walking through the design, against existing requirements and any known or possible future requirements.

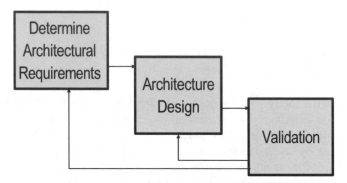

Fig. 36. A three step architecture design process

This architecture process is inherently iterative. Once a design is proposed, validating it may show that the design needs modification, or that certain requirements need to be further defined and understood. Both these lead to enhancements to the design, subsequent validation, and so on, until the design team is satisfied that the requirements are met.

The rest of this chapter explains each of these steps in more detail.

5.1.1   Determine Architectural Requirements

Before an architectural solution can be designed, it's necessary to have a pretty good idea of the requirements for the application architecture. Architecture requirements, sometimes also called architecturally significant requirements or architecture use cases, are essentially the quality and non-functional requirements for the application.

5.1.2 Identifying Architecture Requirements

As Fig. 37 shows, the main sources of architecture requirements are the functional requirements document, and other documents that capture various stakeholder needs. The output of this step is a document that states the architecture requirements for the application.

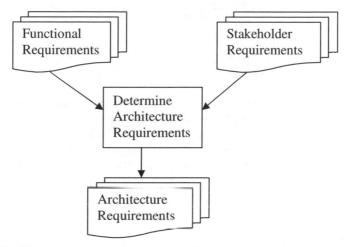

Fig. 37. Inputs and outputs for determining architecture requirements

Let's look at some examples. A typical architecture requirement concerning reliability of communications is:

"Communications between components must be guaranteed to succeed with no message loss"

Some architecture requirements are really constraints, for example:

"The system must use the existing IIS-based web server and use Active Server Page to process web requests"

Constraints impose restrictions on the architecture and are (almost always) non-negotiable. They limit the range of design choices an architect can make. Sometimes this makes an architect's life easier, and sometimes it doesn't. Table 2 lists some example architecture requirements along with the quality attribute they address.

Table 2. Some example architecture requirements

Quality Attribute	Architecture Requirement
Performance	Application performance must provide sub-four second response times for 90% of requests.
Security	All communications must be authenticated and encrypted using certificates.
Resource Management	The server component must run on a low end office-based server with 512MB memory.
Usability	The user interface component must run in an Internet browser to support remote users.
Availability	The system must run 24x7x365, with overall availability of 0.99.
Reliability	No message loss is allowed, and all message delivery outcomes must be known with 30 seconds
Scalability	The application must be able to handle a peak load of 500 concurrent users during the enrollment period.
Modifiability	The architecture must support a phased migration from the current Forth Generation Language (4GL) version to a .NET systems technology solution.

Table 3 gives some typical examples of constraints, along with the source of each constraint.

Table 3. Some example constraints

Constraint	Architecture Requirement
Business	The technology must run as a plug-in for MS BizTalk, as we want to sell this to Microsoft.
Development	The system must be written in Java so that we can use existing development staff.
Schedule	The first version of this product must be delivered within six months.
Business	We want to work closely with and get more development funding from *MegaHugeTech Corp*, so we need to use their technology in our application.

5.1.3   Prioritizing Architecture Requirements

It's a rare thing when all architecture requirements for an application are equal. Often the list of architecture requirements contains items that are of low priority, or "this would be good to have, but not necessary" type features. It's consequently important to explicitly identify these, and rank the architecture requirements using priorities. Initially, it's usually sufficient to allocate each requirement to one of three categories, namely:

1. **High:** the application must support this requirement. These requirements drive the architecture design;
2. **Medium:** this requirement will need to be supported at some stage, but not necessarily in the first/next release;
3. **Low:** this is part of the requirements wish list. Solutions that can accommodate these requirements are desired, but they are not the drivers of the design;

Prioritization gets trickier in the face of conflicting requirements. Common examples are:

- Reusability of components in the solution versus rapid time-to-market. Making components generalized and reusable always takes more time and effort.
- Minimal expenditure on COTS products versus reduced development effort/cost. COTS products mean you have to develop less code, but they cost money.

There's no simple solution to these conflicts. It's part of the architect's job to discuss these with the relevant stakeholders, and come up with possible solution scenarios to enable the issues to be thoroughly understood. Conflicting requirements may even end up as the same priority. It is then the responsibility of the solution to consider appropriate trade-offs, and to try to find that "fine line" that adequately satisfies both requirements without upsetting anyone or having major undesirable consequences on the application. Remember, good architects know how to say "no".

In a project with many stakeholders, it's usually a good idea to get each set of stakeholders to sign off on this prioritization. This is especially true in the face of conflicting requirements. Once this is agreed, the architecture design can commence.

5.2 Architecture Design

While all the tasks an architect performs are important, it's the quality of the architecture design that really matters. Wonderful requirement documents and attentive networking with stakeholders mean nothing if a poor design is produced.

Not surprisingly, design is typically the most difficult task an architect undertakes. Good architects draw on several years of software engineering and design experience. There's no substitute for this experience, so all this chapter can do is try to help readers gain some of the necessary knowledge as quickly as possible.

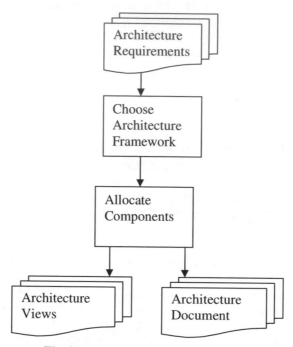

Fig. 38. Inputs and outputs of architecture design

As Fig. 38 shows, the inputs to the design step are the architecture requirements. The design stage itself has two steps, which are iterative in nature. The first involves choosing an overall strategy for the architecture, based around proven architecture patterns. The second involves specifying the individual components that make up the application, showing how they fit into the overall framework and allocating them responsibilities. The output is a set of architecture views that capture the architecture design, and a design document that explains the design, the key reasons for some of the major design decisions, and identifies the risks involved in taking the design forward.

5.2.1   Choosing the Architecture Framework

Most of the IT applications I've worked on in the last ten years are based around a small number of well understood, proven architectures. There's a good reason for this – they work. Leveraging known solutions minimizes the risks that an application will fail due to an inappropriate architecture.

So the initial design step involves selecting an architecture framework that seems likely to satisfy the key requirements. For small applications, a single architecture pattern like *n-tier client-server* may suffice. For more complex applications, the design will incorporate one or more known patterns, with the architect specifying how these patterns integrate to form the overall architecture.

There's no magic formula for designing the architecture framework. A pre-requisite, however, is to understand how each of the main architecture patterns addresses certain quality attributes. The following sub-sections briefly cover some of the major patterns used, and describe how they address common quality requirements.

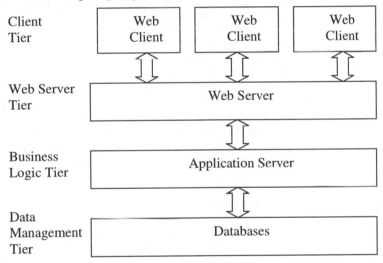

Fig. 39. N-tier client-server example

5.2.1.1   N-Tier Client Server

In Fig. 39 the anatomy of this pattern for a web application is illustrated. The key properties of this pattern are:

- **Separation of concerns:** Presentation, business and data handling logic are clearly partitioned in different tiers.
- **Synchronous communications:** Communications between tiers is synchronous request-reply. Requests emanate in a single direction from the client tier, through the web and business logic tiers to the EIS tier. Each tier waits for a response from the other tier before proceeding.
- **Flexible deployment:** There are no restrictions on how a multi-tier application is deployed. All tiers could run on the same machine, or at the other extreme, each tier may be deployed on its own machine. In web applications, the client tier is usually a browser running on a user's desktop, communicating remotely over the Internet with a web tier components.

Table 4. Quality attributes for the N-Tier Client Server pattern

Quality Attribute	Issues
Availability	Servers in each tier can be replicated, so that if one fails, others remain available. Overall the application will provide a lower quality of service until the failed server is restored.
Failure handling	If a client is communicating with a server that fails, most web and application servers implement transparent failover. This means a client request is, without its knowledge, redirected to a live replica server that can satisfy the request.
Modifiability	Separation of concerns enhances modifiability, as the presentation, business and data management logic are all clearly encapsulated. Each can have its internal logic modified in many cases without changes rippling into other tiers.
Performance	This architecture has proven high performance. Key issues to consider are the amount of concurrent threads supported in each server, the speed of connections between tiers and the amount of data that is transferred. As always with distributed systems, it makes sense to minimize the calls needed between tiers to fulfill each request.
Scalability	As servers in each tier can be replicated, and multiple server instances run on the same or different servers, the architecture scales out and up well. In practice, the data management tier often becomes a bottleneck on the capacity of a system.

Table 4 shows how common quality attributes can be addressed with this pattern. Precisely how each quality attribute is addressed depends on the actual web and application server technology used to implement the application. .NET, each implementation of J2EE, and other proprietary application servers all have different concrete features. These need to be understood during architecture design so that no unpleasant surprises are encountered much later in the project, when fixes are much more expensive to perform.

The N-Tier Client-Server pattern is commonly used and the direct support from application server technologies for this pattern makes it relatively easy to implement applications using the pattern. It's generally appropriate when an application must support a potentially large number of clients and concurrent requests, and each request takes a relatively short interval (a few milliseconds to a few seconds) to process.

5.2.1.2 Messaging

In Fig. 40 the basic components of the messaging pattern are shown. The key properties of this pattern are:

- **Asynchronous communications:** Clients send requests to the queue, where the message is stored until an application removes it. After the client has written the message to the queue, it continues without waiting for the message to be removed.
- **Configurable QoS:** The queue can be configured for high-speed, non-reliable or slower, reliable delivery. Queue operations can be coordinated with database transactions.
- **Loose coupling:** There is no direct binding between clients and servers. The client is oblivious to which server receives the message. The server is oblivious as to which client the message came from.

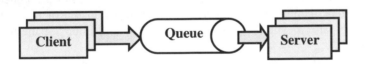

Fig. 40. Anatomy of the messaging pattern

Table 5 shows how common quality attributes are addressed by messaging. Again, bear in mind, exact support for these quality attributes is messaging product dependent.

Messaging is especially appropriate when the client does not need an immediate response directly after sending a request. For example, a client may format an email, and place it on a queue in a message for processing. The server will at some stage in the future remove the message and send the email using a mail server. The client really doesn't need to know when the server processes the message.

Table 5. Quality attributes for the Messaging Pattern

Quality Attribute	Issues
Availability	Physical queues with the same logical name can be replicated across different messaging server instances. When one fails, clients can send messages to replica queues.
Failure handling	If a client is communicating with a queue that fails, it can find a replica queue and post the message there.
Modifiability	Messaging is inherently loosely coupled, and this promotes high modifiability as clients and servers are not directly bound through an interface. Changes to the format of messages sent by clients may cause changes to the server implementations. Self-describing, discoverable message formats can help reduce this dependency on message formats.
Performance	Message queuing technology can deliver thousands of messages per second. Non-reliable messaging is faster than reliable, with the difference dependent of the quality of the messaging technology used.
Scalability	Queues can be hosted on the communicating endpoints, or be replicated across clusters of messaging servers hosted on a single or multiple server machines. This makes messaging a highly scalable solution.

Applications that can divide processing of a request into a number of discrete steps, connected by queues, are a basic extension of the simple messaging pattern. This is identical to the "Pipe and Filter" pattern (see *Buschmann*).

Messaging also provides a resilient solution for applications in which connectivity to a server application is transient, either due to network or server unreliability. In such cases, the messages are held in the queue until the server connects and removes messages. Finally, as Chapter 4 explains, messaging can be used to implement synchronous request-response using a request-reply queue pair.

5.2.1.3   Publish-Subscribe

The essential elements of the Publish-Subscribe pattern are depicted in Fig. 41. The key properties of this pattern are:

- **Many-to-Many messaging:** Published messages are sent to all subscribers who are registered with the topic. Many publishers can publish on the same topic, and many subscribers can listen to the same topic.
- **Configurable QoS:** In addition to non-reliable and reliable messaging, the underlying communication mechanism may be point-to-point or broadcast/multicast. The former sends a distinct message for every subscriber on a topic, the latter sends one message which every subscriber receives.
- **Loose Coupling:** As with messaging, there is no direct binding between publishers and subscribers. Publishers do not know who receives their message, and subscribers do not know which publisher sent the message.

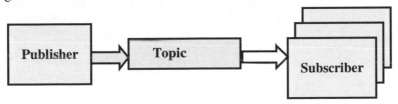

Fig. 41. The Publish-Subscribe pattern

Table 6 explains how publish-subscribe supports common quality attributes.

Architectures based on publish-subscribe are highly flexible and suited to applications which require asynchronous one-many, many-one or many-to-many messaging amongst components. Like messaging, two-way communications is possible using request-reply topic pairs.

Table 6. Quality attributes for the Publish-Subscribe pattern

Quality Attribute	Issues
Availability	Topics with the same logical name can be replicated across different server instances managed as a cluster. When one fails, publishers send messages to replica queues.
Failure handling	If a publisher is communicating with a topic hosted by a server that fails, it can find a live replica server and send the message there.
Modifiability	Publish-subscribe is inherently loosely coupled, and this promotes high modifiability. New publishers and subscribers can be added to the system without change to the architecture or configuration. Changes to the format of messages published may cause changes to the subscriber implementations.
Performance	Publish-subscribe can deliver thousands of messages per second, with non-reliable messaging faster than reliable. If a publish-subscribe broker supports multicast/broadcast, it will deliver multiple messages in a more uniform time to each subscriber.
Scalability	Topics can be replicated across clusters of servers hosted on a single or multiple server machines. Clusters of server can scale to provide very high message volume throughput. Also, multicast/broadcast solutions scale better than their point-to-point counterparts.

5.2.1.4   Broker

The major elements of the Broker pattern are shown in Fig. 42. The properties of a broker-based solution are:

- **Hub-and-spoke architecture:** The broker acts as a messaging hub, and senders and receivers connect as spokes. Connections to the broker are via ports that are associated with a specific message format.
- **Performs message routing:** The broker embeds processing logic to deliver a message received on an input port to an output port. The delivery path can be hard coded or depend on values in the input message.
- **Performs message transformation:** The broker logic transforms the source message type received on the input port to the destination message type required on the output port.

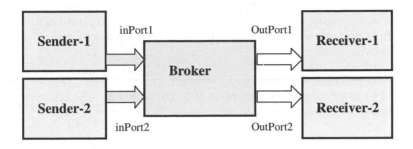

Fig. 42. Elements of the Broker pattern

Table 7 shows the pattern's support for common quality attributes.

Table 7. Quality attributes for the Broker pattern

Quality Attribute	Issues
Availability	To build high availability architectures, brokers must be replicated. This is typically supported using similar mechanisms to messaging and publish-subscribe server clustering.
Failure handling	As brokers have typed input ports, they validate and discard any messages that are sent in the wrong format. With replicated brokers, senders can fail over to a live broker should one of the replicas fail.
Modifiability	Brokers separate the transformation and message routing logic from the senders and receivers. This enhances modifiability, as changes to transformation and routing logic can be made without affecting senders or receivers.
Performance	Brokers can potentially become a bottleneck, especially if they must service high message volumes and execute complex transformation logic. Their throughput is typically lower than simple messaging with reliable delivery.
Scalability	Clustering broker instances makes it possible to construct systems scale to handle high request loads.

Brokers are suited to applications in which components exchange messages that require extensive transformation between source and destination formats. The broker decouples the sender and receiver, allowing them to produce or consume their native message format, and centralizes the definition of the transformation logic in the broker for ease of understanding and modification.

5.2.1.5   Process Coordinator

The Process Coordinator pattern is illustrated in Fig. 43. The essential elements of this pattern are:

- **Process encapsulation:** The process coordinator encapsulates the sequence of steps needed to fulfill the business process. The sequence can be arbitrarily complex. The coordinator is a single point of definition for the business process, making it easier to understand and modify. It receives a process initiation request, calls the servers in the order defined by the process, and emits the results.
- **Loose coupling:** The server components are unaware of their role in the overall business process, and of the order of the steps in the process. The servers simply define a set of services which they can perform, and the coordinator calls them as necessary as part of the business process.
- **Flexible communications:** Communications between the coordinator and servers can be synchronous or asynchronous. For synchronous communications, the coordinator waits until the server responds. For asynchronous communications, the coordinator provides a callback or reply queue/topic, and waits until the server responds using the defined mechanism.

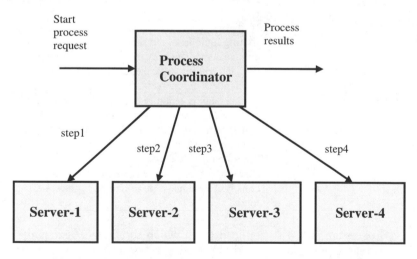

Fig. 43. Components of the Process Coordinator pattern

Table 8 shows how this pattern addresses quality requirements.

Table 8. Quality attributes for the Process Coordinator Pattern

Quality Attribute	Issues
Availability	The coordinator is a single point of failure. Hence it needs to be replicated to create a high availability solution.
Failure handling	Failure handling is complex, as it can occur at any stage in the business process coordination. Failure of a later step in the process may require earlier steps to be undone using compensating transactions. Handling failures needs careful design to ensure the data maintained by the servers remains consistent.
Modifiability	Process modifiability is enhanced because the process definition is encapsulated in the coordinator process. Servers can change their implementation without affecting the coordinator or other servers, as long as their external service definition doesn't change.
Performance	To achieve high performance, the coordinator must be able to handle multiple concurrent requests and manage the state of each as they progress through the process. Also, the performance of any process will be limited by the slowest step, namely the slowest server in the process.
Scalability	The coordinator can be replicated to scale the application both up and out.

The Process Coordinator pattern is commonly used to implement complex business processes that must issue requests to several different server components. By encapsulating the process logic in one place, it is easier to change, manage and monitor process performance. Message broker and Business Process Orchestrator technologies are designed specifically to support this pattern, the former for short lived requests, the latter for processes that may take several minutes or hours or days to complete. In less complex applications, the pattern is also relatively simple to implement without sophisticated technology support, although failure handling is an issue that requires careful attention.

5.2.2 Allocate Components

Once an overall architecture framework has been selected, based on one or more architecture patterns, the next task is to define the major components that will comprise the design. The framework defines the overall communication patterns for the components. This must be augmented by the following:

- Identifying the major application components, and how they plug into the framework.
- Identifying the interface or services that each component supports.
- Identifying the responsibilities of the component, stating what it can be relied upon to do when it receives a request.
- Identifying dependencies between components.
- Identifying partitions in the architecture that are candidates for distribution over servers in a network.

The components in the architecture are the major abstractions that will exist in the application. Hence, it's probably no surprise that component design has much in common with widely used object-oriented design techniques. In fact, class and package diagrams are often used to depict components in an architecture.

Some guidelines for component design are:

- Minimize dependencies between components. Strive for a loosely coupled solution in which changes to one component do not ripple through the architecture, propagating across many components. Remember, every time you change something, you have to re-test it.
- Design components that encapsulate a highly "cohesive" set of responsibilities. Cohesion is a measure of how well the parts of a component fit together. Highly cohesive components tend to have a small set of well-defined responsibilities that implement a single logical function. For example, an *EnrollmentReports* component encapsulates all the functions required to produce reports on a student enrollments in courses. If changes to report format or type are needed, then it's likely the changes will be made in this component. Hence, strong cohesion limits many types of changes to a single component, minimizing maintenance and testing efforts.
- Isolate dependencies on middleware and any COTS infrastructure technologies. The fewer components that are dependent on specific middleware and COTS components API calls, the easier it is to change or up-

grade the middleware or other infrastructure services. Of course this takes more effort to build, and introduces a performance penalty.

- Use decomposition to structure components hierarchically. The outermost level component defines the publicly available interface to the composite component. Internally, calls to this interface are delegated to the locally defined components, whose interfaces are not visible externally.

- Minimize calls between components, as these can prove costly if the components are distributed. Try to aggregate sequences of calls between components into a single call that can perform the necessary processing in a single request. This creates coarser grain methods or services in interfaces that do more work per request.

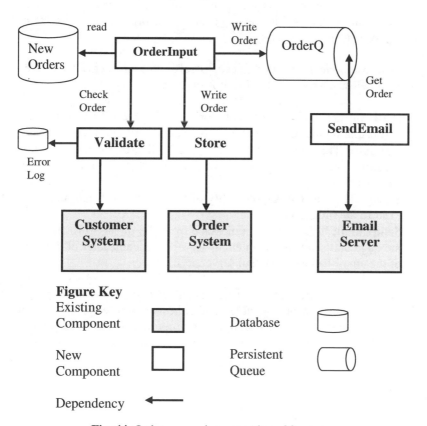

Fig. 44. Order processing example architecture

Let's explore a simple example to illustrate some of these issues. Fig. 44 is an example of a structural view of an order processing application, defined using a simple informal notation. New orders are received (from where is irrelevant) and loaded into a database. Each order must be validated against an existing customer details system to check the customer information and that valid payment options exist. Once validated, the order data is simply stored in the order processing database, and an email is generated to the customer to inform them that their order is being processed.

The general architecture framework is based on straightforward messaging. The customer order details are read from the database, validated, and if valid, they are stored in the order application and written to a queue. Information about each valid order is removed from the queue, formatted as an email and sent to the customer using the mail server. Hence, using a message queue this architecture decouples the order processing from the email formatting and delivery.

Four components are introduced to solve this problem. These are described below, along with their responsibilities:

- **OrderInput:** This is responsible for accessing the new orders database, encapsulating the order processing logic, and writing to the queue.
- **Validate:** This encapsulates the responsibility of interacting with the customer system to carry out validation, and writing to the error logs if an order is invalid.
- **Store:** This has the responsibility of interacting with the order system to store the order data.
- **SendEmail:** This removes a message from the queue, formats an email message and sends it via an email server. It encapsulates all knowledge of the email format and email server access.

So, each component has clear dependencies and a small set of responsibilities, creating a loosely coupled and cohesive architecture. We'll return to this example and further analyze its properties in the next section, in which the validation of an architecture design is discussed.

5.3   Validation

During the architecture process, the aim of the validation phase is to increase the confidence of the design team that the architecture is fit for purpose. The validation has to be achieved within the project constraints of time and budget, as the detailed design and implementation cannot generally fully commence until the architecture is agreed. The trick is to be as rigorous and efficient as possible.

Validating an architecture design poses some tough challenges. Whether it's the architecture for a new application, or an evolution of an existing system, the proposed design is, well, just that – a design. It can't be executed or tested to see that it fulfills its requirements. It will also likely consist of new components that have to be built, and black box off-the-shelf components such as middleware and specialized libraries and existing applications. All these parts have to be integrated and made to work together.

So, what can sensibly be done? There are two main techniques that have proved useful. The first essentially involves manual testing of the architecture using test scenarios. The second involves the construction of a prototype that creates a simple archetype of the desired application, so that its ability to satisfy requirements can be assessed in more detail through prototype testing. The aim of both is to identify potential flaws and weaknesses in the design so that they can be improved before implementation commences. These approaches should be used to explicitly identify potential risk areas for tracking and monitoring during the subsequent build activities.

5.3.1 Using Scenarios

Scenarios are a technique developed at the SEI to tease out issues concerning an architecture through manual evaluation and testing. Scenarios are related to architectural concerns such as quality attributes, and they aim to highlight the consequences of the architectural decisions that are encapsulated in the design.

The SEI ATAM work describes scenarios and their generation in great detail. In essence though, scenarios are relatively simple artifacts. They involve defining some kind of stimulus that will have an impact on the architecture. The scenario then involves working out how the architecture responds to this stimulus. If the response is desirable, then a scenario is deemed to be satisfied by the architecture. If the response is undesirable, or hard to quantify, then a flaw or at least an area of risk in the architecture may have been uncovered.

Scenarios can be conceived to address any quality requirement of interest in a given application. Some general hypothetical examples are shown in Table 9. These scenarios highlight the implications of the architecture design decisions in the context of the stimulus and the effects it elicits. For example, the "availability" scenario shows that messages can be lost if a server fails before messages have been delivered. The implication here is that messages are not being persisted to disk, most likely for performance reasons. The loss of messages in some application contexts may be acceptable. If it is not, this scenario highlights a problem, which may force the design to adopt persistent messaging to avoid message loss.

Table 9. Scenario examples

Quality Attribute	Stimulus	Response
Availability	The network connection to the message consumers fails.	Messages are stored on the MOM server until the connection is restored. Messages will only be lost if the server fails before the connection comes back up.
Modifiability	A new set of data analysis components must be made available in the application.	The application needs to be rebuilt with the new libraries, and the all configuration files must be updated on every desktop to make the new components visible in the GUI toolbox.
Security	No requests are received on a user session for ten minutes.	The system treats this session as potentially insecure and invalidates the security credentials associated with the session. The user must logon again to connect to the application.
Modifiability	The supplier of the transformation engine goes out of business.	A new transformation engine must be purchased. The abstract service layer that wraps the transformation engine component must be re-implemented to support the new engine. Client components are unaffected as they only use the abstract service layer.
Scalability	The concurrent user request load doubles during the 3 week enrollment period.	The application server is scaled out on a two machine cluster to handle the increased request load.

Let's look at some more specific examples for the order processing example introduced in the previous section. The design in Fig. 44 needs to be validated, and the scenarios in Table 10 probe more deeply into the architecture, looking to expose flaws or areas of risk.

Table 10. Scenarios for the order processing example

Quality Attribute	Stimulus	Response
Modifiability	The *Customer System* packaged application is updated to an Oracle database.	The *Validate* component must be rewritten to interface to the Oracle system.
Availability	The email server fails.	Messages build up in the *OrderQ* until the email server restarts. Messages are then sent by the *SendEmail* component to remove the backlog. Order processing is not affected.
Reliability	The *Customer* or *Order* systems are unavailable.	If either fails, order processing halts and alerts are sent to system administrators so that the problem can be fixed.

The first two scenarios seem to elicit positive responses from the design. The *Validate* component bounds the changes needed to accommodate a new customer database, and hence it insulates other components from change. And should the email server be unavailable, then the implication is that emails are merely delayed until the email server returns.

The failure of the *Customer* or *Order* applications is more revealing however. The communications with these two systems is synchronous, so if either is not available, order processing must halt until the applications are restored. This may be less than desirable.

Note the design does not discriminate between the interactions with the two applications. It's pretty obvious, however, that the interaction with the *Customer System* requires a response saying whether the order data is valid. If it is not, it is written to an error log and the order processing ceases for that order. The *Order System* though simply stores the order data for subsequent processing. There's no need for the *Store* component to require an immediate response.

So, the reliability scenario has highlighted an area where the architecture could be improved. An order can't be processed until it has been successfully validated, so a response from the *Customer System* is necessary. If it is unavailable, processing can't continue.

But the *Order System* is a different matter. Asynchronous communications is better in this case. *Store* could just write to a persistent queue, and order processing can continue. Another component could then be introduced to read the order from the queue and add the details to the *Order*

System. This solution is more resilient to failure, as the *Order System* can be unavailable but order processing can continue.

5.3.2 Prototyping

Scenarios are a really useful technique for validating a proposed architecture. But some scenarios aren't so simple to answer based only on a design description. Consider a performance scenario for the order processing system:

"On Friday afternoon, orders must be processed before close-of-business to ensure delivery by Monday. Five thousand orders arrive through various channels (Web/Call centre/business partners) five minutes before close-of-business."

The question here then is simply, can the five thousand orders be processed in five minutes? This is a tough question to answer when some of the components of the solution don't yet exist.

The only way to address such questions with some degree of confidence is to build a prototype. Prototypes are minimal, restricted or cut-down versions of the desired application, created specifically to test some high risk or poorly understood aspects of the design. Prototypes are typically used for two purposes:

1. **Proof-of-concept:** Can the architecture as designed be built in a way that can satisfy the requirements?
2. **Proof-of-technology:** Does the technology (middleware, integrated applications, libraries, etc) selected to implement the application behave as expected?

In both cases, prototypes can provide concrete evidence about concerns that are otherwise difficult, if not impossible to validate in any other way.

To answer our performance scenario above, what kind of prototype might we build? The general answer is one that incorporates all the performance sensitive operations in the design, and that executes on a platform as similar as possible (ideally identical) to the one the application will be deployed on.

For example, the architect might know that the queue and email systems are easily capable of supporting five thousand messages in five minutes, as these solutions are used in another similar application. There would therefore be no need to build this as part of the prototype. However, the throughput of interactions between the *Customer* and *Order* applications using their APIs are an unknown, and hence these two must be tested to see if they can process five thousand messages in five minutes. The simplest way to do this is:

- Write a test program that calls the *Customer System* validation APIs five thousand times, and time how long this takes.
- Write a test program that calls the *Order System* store APIs five thousand times, and time how long this takes.

Once the prototypes have been created and tested, the response of the architecture to the stimulus in the scenario can be answered with a high degree of confidence.

Prototypes should be used judiciously to help reduce the risks inherent in a design. They are the only way that concerns related to performance, scalability, ease of integration and capabilities of off-the-shelf components can be addressed with any degree of certainty.

Despite their usefulness, a word of caution on prototyping is necessary. Prototyping efforts should be carefully scoped and managed. Ideally a prototype should be developed in a day or two, a week or two at most. Most proof-of-technology and proof-of-concept prototypes get thrown away after they've served their purpose. They are a means to an end, so don't let them acquire a life of their own and become an end in themselves.

5.4 Summary and Further Reading

Designing an application architecture is an inherently creative activity. However, by following a simple process that explicitly captures architecturally significant requirements, exploits known architecture patterns and systematically validates the design, some of the mystique of design can be exposed.

The three step process described in this chapter is inherently iterative. The initial design is validated against requirements and scenarios, and the outcome of the validation can cause the requirements or the design to be revisited. The iteration continues until all the stakeholders are happy with the architecture, which then becomes the blueprint from which detailed design commences.

The process is also scalable. For small projects, the architect may be working mostly directly with the customer, or there may in fact be no tangible customer (often the case in new, innovative product development). The architect is also likely to be a major part of the small development team that will build the project. In such projects, the process can be followed informally, producing minimal documentation. For large projects, the process can be followed more formally, involving the requirements and design teams, gathering inputs from the various stakeholders involved, and producing extensive documentation.

Of course, other architecture processes exist, and probably the most widely used is the Rational Unified Process (RUP). A good reference to RUP is:

P. Kruchten. The Rational Unified Process: An Introduction (2nd Edition). Addison-Wesley, 2000

The most comprehensive source of information on methods and techniques for architecture evaluation is:

P. Clements, R. Kazman, M. Klein. Evaluating Software Architectures: Methods and Case Studies. Addison-Wesley, 2002

This describes the ATAM process, and provides excellent examples illustrating the approach. Its focus is evaluating large, complex systems, but many of the techniques are appropriate for smaller scale applications.

A group of luminaries in the software architecture area got together in 1999 and produced a report known as the Software Architecture Review and Assessment (SARA) Report. This is a comprehensive source of experience-based guidance that can be employed to carry out architecture reviews. The best way to find this report is to google for it, as at the time of writing, its location seems to be transient!

6 Documenting a Software Architecture

6.1 Introduction

Architecture documentation is often a thorny issue in IT projects. It's common for there to be little or no documentation covering the architecture in many projects. Sometimes, if there is some, it's out-of-date, inappropriate and basically not very useful.

At the other extreme there are projects that have masses of architecture related information captured in various documents and design tools. Sometimes this is invaluable, but at times it's out-of-date, inappropriate and not very useful!

Clearly then, experience tells us that documenting architectures is not a simple job. But there are many good reasons why we want to document our architectures, for example:

- Others can understand and evaluate the design. This includes any of the application stakeholders, but most commonly other members of the design and development team.
- We can understand the design when we return to it after a period of time.
- Others in the project team and development organization can learn from the architecture by digesting the thinking behind the design.
- We can do analysis on the design, perhaps to assess its likely performance, or to generate standard metrics like coupling and cohesion.

Documenting architectures is problematic though, because:

- There's no universally accepted architecture documentation standard.
- An architecture can be complex, and documenting it in a comprehensible manner is time consuming and non-trivial.
- An architecture has many possible views. Documenting all the potentially useful ones is time consuming and expensive.

- An architecture design often evolves as the system is incrementally developed and more insights into the problem domain are gained. Keeping the architecture documents current is often an overlooked activity, especially with time and schedule pressures in a project.

I'm pretty certain the predominant tools used for architecture documentation are Microsoft Word, Visio and PowerPoint, along with their non-Microsoft equivalents. And the most widely used design notation is informal "block and arrow" diagrams, just like we've used in this book so far, in fact. Both these facts are a bit of an indictment on the state of architecture documentation practices at present. We should be able to do better.

This chapter examines some of the most useful architecture views to document, and shows how the latest incarnation of the *Unified Modeling Language*, UML v2.0, can help with generating these views. Using these techniques and supporting tools, it's not overly difficult or expensive to generate useful and valuable documentation.

6.2   What to Document

Probably the most crucial element of the "what to document" equation is the complexity of the architecture being designed. A two-tier client server application with complex business logic may actually be quite simple architecturally. It might require no more than an overall "marketeture" diagram describing the main components, and a perhaps a structural view of the major components (maybe it uses a model-view-controller architecture) and a description of the database schema, no doubt generated automatically by database tools. This level of documentation is quick to produce and routine to describe.

Another factor to consider is the likely longevity of the application. Will the system serve a long-term business function, or is it being built to handle a one-off need for integration, or is it just a stop-gap until a full ERP package is installed? Projects with little prospect of a long life probably don't need a lot of documentation. Still, never let this be an excuse to hack together some code and throw good design practices to the wind. Sometimes these stop-gap systems have a habit of living for a lot longer than initially anticipated, and someone (maybe even you) might pay for these hacks one day.

The next factor to consider is the needs of the various project stakeholders. The architecture documentation serves an important communications role between the various members of the project team, including architects, designers, developers, testers, project management, customers, partner organizations, and so on. In a small team, interpersonal communication is often good, so that the documentation can be minimal, and maybe even maintained on a whiteboard or two. In larger teams, and especially when groups are not co-located in the same offices or building, the architecture documentation becomes of vital importance for describing design elements such as:

- Component interfaces;
- Subsystems constraints;
- Test scenarios;
- third party component purchasing decisions;
- Team structure and schedule dependencies;
- External services to be offered by the application.

So, there's no simple answer here. Documentation takes time to develop, and costs money. It's therefore important to think carefully about what documentation is going to be most useful within the project context, and produce and maintain this as key reference documents for the project.

6.3 UML 2.0

There's also the issue of how to document an architecture. So far in this book we've used simple box-and-arrow diagrams, with an appropriate diagram key to give a clear meaning to the notation used. This has been done deliberately, as in my experience, informal diagrammatical notations are the most common vehicle used to document IT application architectures.

There are of course many ways to describe the various architecture views that might be useful in a project. Fortunately for all of us, there's an excellent book that describes many of these from Paul Clements et al. (see Further Reading), so no attempt here will be made to replicate that. But there's been one significant development since that book was published, and that's the emergence of UML 2.0.

For all its greatly debated strengths and weaknesses, the UML has become the predominant software description language used across the whole range of software development domains. It has wide and now quality and low-cost tool support, and hence is easily accessible and useable for software architects, designers, developers, students – everyone in fact.

UML 2.0 is a major upgrade of the modeling language. It adds several new features and, significantly, it formalizes many aspects of the language.

This formalization helps in two ways. For designers, it eliminates ambiguity from the models, helping to increase comprehensibility. Second, it supports the goal of model-driven development, in which UML models are used for code generation. There's also a lot of debate about the usefulness of model-driven development, and this topic is specifically covered in a later chapter, so we won't delve into it now.

The UML 2.0 modeling notations cover both structural and behavioral aspects of software systems. The structure diagrams define the static architecture of a model, and specifically are:

- **Class diagrams:** Show the classes in the system and their relationships.
- **Component diagrams:** Describe the relationship between components with well-defined interfaces. Components typically comprise multiple classes.
- **Package diagrams:** Divide the model into groups of elements and describe the dependencies between them at a high level.
- **Deployment diagrams:** Show how components and other software artifacts like processes are distributed to physical hardware.
- **Object diagrams:** Depict how objects are related and used at run-time. These are often called instance diagrams.
- **Composite Structure diagrams:** Show the internal structure of classes or components in terms of their composed objects and their relationships.

Behavior diagrams show the interactions and state changes that occur as elements in the model execute:

- **Activity diagrams:** Similar to flow charts, and used for defining program logic and business processes.
- **Communication diagrams:** Called collaboration diagrams in UML 1.x, they depict the sequence of calls between objects at run-time.
- **Sequence diagrams:** Often called swim-lane diagrams after their vertical timelines, they show the sequence of messages exchanged between objects.
- **State Machine diagrams:** Describe the internals of an object, showing its states and events, and conditions that cause state transitions.
- **Interaction Overview diagrams:** These are similar to activity diagrams, but can include other UML interaction diagrams as well as activities. They are intended to show control flow across a number of simpler scenarios.

- **Timing diagrams:** These essentially combine sequence and state diagrams to describe an object's various states over time and the messages that alter the object's state.
- **Use Case diagrams:** These capture interactions between the system and its environment, including users and other systems.

Clearly then, UML 2.0 is a large technical area in itself, and some pointers to good sources of information are provided at the end of this chapter. In the following sections though, we'll describe some of the most useful UML 2.0 models for representing software architectures.

6.4   Architecture Views

Let's return to the order processing example introduced in the previous chapter. Fig. 44 shows an informal description of the architecture using a box and arrow notation. In Fig. 45, a UML component diagram is used to represent an equivalent structural view of the order processing system architecture. Note though, based on the evaluation in the previous chapter, a queue has been added to communicate between the *OrderProcessing* and *OrderSystem* components.

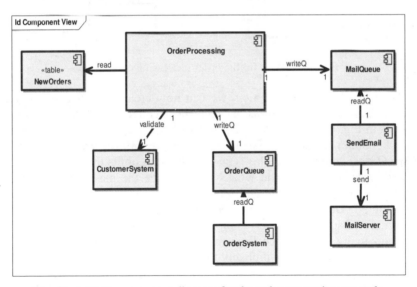

Fig. 45. A UML component diagram for the order processing example

Only two of the components in the architecture require substantial new code to be created. The internal structure of the most complex of these, *OrderProcessing*, is shown in the class diagram in Fig. 46. It includes a class essentially to encapsulate each interaction with an existing system. No doubt other classes will be introduced into the design as it is implemented, for example one to represent a new order, but these are not shown in the class diagram so that they do not clutter it with unnecessary detail. These are design details not necessary in an architecture description.

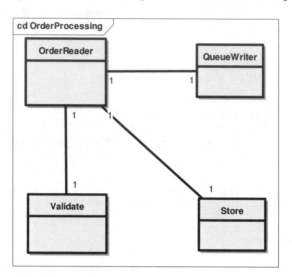

Fig. 46. Classes for the order processing component

With this level of description, we can now create a sequence diagram showing the main interactions between the architectural elements. This is shown in Fig. 47, which uses the standard UML stereotypes for representing *Boundary* (*CustomerSystem, OrderQueue, MailQueue*) and *Entity* (*NewOrder*) components. This sequence diagram omits the behavior when a new order is invalid, and what happens once the messages have been placed on the *OrderQueue* and *MailQueue*. Again, this keeps the model uncluttered. Descriptions of this additional functionality could either be described in subsequent (very simple) sequence diagrams, or just in text accompanying the sequence diagram.

Sequence diagrams are probably the most useful technique in the UML for modeling the behavior of the components in an architecture. One of their strengths actually lies in their inherent weakness in describing complex processing and logic. Although it is possible to represent loops and selection in sequence diagrams, they quickly become hard to understand and unwieldy to create. This encourages designers to keep them relatively simple, and focus on describing the major interactions between architecturally significant elements in the design.

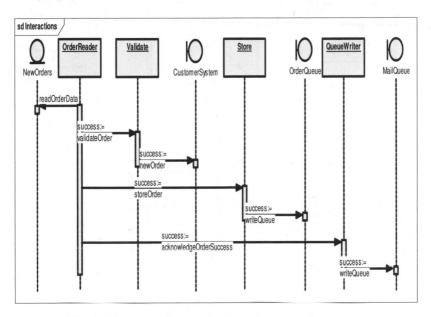

Fig. 47. Sequence diagram for the order processing system

Quite often in this style of business integration project, it's possible to create a UML deployment diagram showing where the various components will execute. This is because many of the components in the design already exist, and the architect must show how the new components interact with these in the deployment environment. An example of a UML deployment diagram for this example is given in Fig. 48. It allocates components to servers and shows the dependencies between the components. It's often useful to label the dependencies with a name that indicates the protocol that is used to communicate between the components. For example, the *OrderProcessing* executable component requires JDBC[28] to access the *NewOrders* table in the *OrdersDB* database.

---

[28] Java Database Connectivity

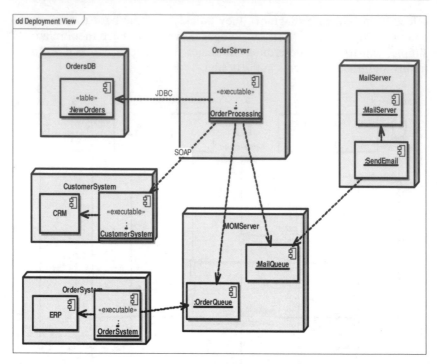

Fig. 48. UML Deployment diagram for the order processing system

6.5   More on Component Diagrams

Component diagrams are very useful for sketching out the structure of an application architecture. They clearly depict the major parts of the system, and can show which off-the-shelf technologies will be used as well as the new components that need to be built. UML 2.0 has also introduced improved notations for representing component interfaces. An interface is a collection of methods that a component supports. In addition to the UML 1.x "lollipop" notation for representing an interface supported by a component (a "provided" interface), the 'socket' notation can be used to specify that a component needs a particular interface to be supported by its environment (a "required" interface). These are illustrated in Fig. 49. Interface definition is particularly important in an architecture, as it allows independent teams of developers to design and build their components in isolation, ensuring that they support the contracts defined by their interfaces.

By connecting provided and required interfaces, components can be "plugged" or "wired" together, as shown in Fig. 49. The provided interfaces are named, and capture the dependencies between components. Interface names should correspond to those used by off-the-shelf applications in use, or existing home-grown component interfaces.

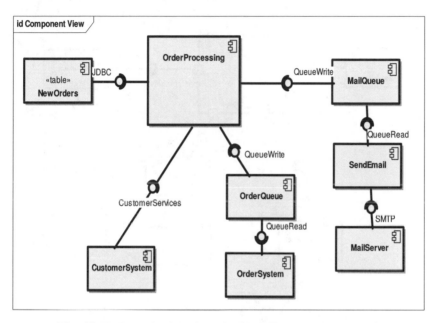

Fig. 49. Representing interfaces in the order processing example

UML 2.0 makes it possible to refine interface definitions even further, and depict how they are supported within the context of a component. This is done by associating interfaces with 'ports'. Ports define a unique, optionally named interaction point between a component and its external environment. They are represented by small squares on the edge of the component, and have one or more provides or requires interfaces associated with them.

The order processing system architecture using ports for the *OrderProcessing* and *CustomerSystem* components is depicted in Fig. 50. All the ports in this design are unidirectional, but there is nothing stopping them from being bidirectional in terms of supporting one or more provides or requires interfaces. UML 2.0 composite diagrams enable us to show the internal structure of a design element such as a component. As shown in Fig.

51, we can explicitly depict which objects comprise the component implementation, and how they are related to each other and to the ports the component supports. The internal objects are represented by UML 2.0 "parts". Parts are defined in UML 2.0 as run-time instances of classes that are owned by the containing class or component. Parts are linked by connectors and describe configurations of instances that are created within an instance of the containing component/class.

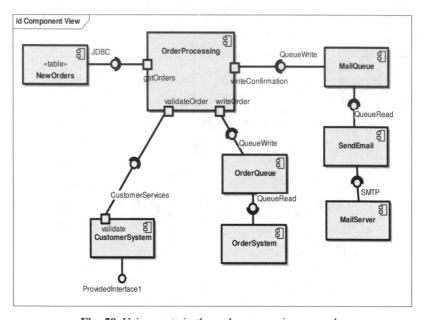

Fig. 50. Using ports in the order processing example

Composite diagrams are useful for describing the design of complex or important components in a design. For example, a layered architecture might describe each layer as a component that supports various ports/interfaces. Internally, a layer description can contain other components and parts that show how each port is supported. Components can also contain other components, so hierarchical architectures can be easily described. We'll see some of these design techniques in the case study in the next section.

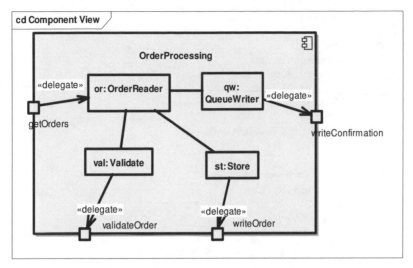

Fig. 51. Internal design of the *OrderProcessing* component

6.6   Architecture Documentation Template

It's always useful for an organization to have a document template avail
able for capturing project specific documentation. Templates reduce the
start-up time for projects by providing ready-made document structures for
project members to use.

Once the use of the templates becomes institutionalized, the familiarity
gained with the document structure aids in the efficient capture of project
design details. Templates also help with the training of new staff as they
tell developers what issues the organization requires them to consider and
think about in the production of their system.

Fig. 52 shows the headings structure for a documentation template that
can be used for capturing an architecture design. To deploy this template in
an organization, it should be accompanied by explanatory text and illustra-
tions of what information is expected in each section. However, instead of
doing that here, this template structure will be used to show the solution to
the ICDE case study problem in the next chapter.

Architecture Documentation Template
Project Name: XXX
1   Project Context
2   Architecture Requirements
    2.1   Overview of Key Objectives
    2.2   Architecture Use Cases
    2.3   Stakeholder Architectural Requirements
    2.4   Constraints
    2.5   Non-functional Requirements
    2.6   Risks
3   Solution
    3.1   Relevant Architectural Patterns
    3.2   Architecture Overview
    3.3   Structural Views
    3.4   Behavioral Views
    3.5   Implementation Issues
4   Architecture Analysis
    4.1   Scenario analysis
    4.2   Risks

Fig. 52. Architecture documentation outline

6.7   Summary and Further Reading

Generating architecture documentation is nearly always a good idea. The trick is to spend just enough effort to produce only documentation that will be useful for the project's various stakeholders. This takes some upfront planning and thinking. Once a documentation plan is established, team members should commit to keeping the documentation reasonably current, accurate and accessible.

I'm a bit of a supporter of using UML-based notations and tools for producing architecture documentation. The UML, especially with version 2.0, makes it pretty straightforward to document various structural and behavioral views of a design. Tools make creating the design quick and easy, and also make it possible to capture much of the design rationale, the design constraints, and other text based documentation within the tool repository. Once it's in the repository, generating design documentation becomes a simple task of selecting the correct menu item and opening up a browser or walking to the printer. Such automatic documentation production is a trick that is guaranteed to impress non-technical stakeholders, and even sometimes the odd technical one!

In addition, it's possible to utilize UML 2.0 flexibly in a project. It can be used to sketch out an abstract architecture representation, purely for communication and documentation purposes. It can also be used to closely model the components and objects that will be realized in the actual implementation. This "closeness" can be reduced further in the extreme case to "exactness", in which elements in the model are used to generate executable code. If you're doing this, then you're doing so-called model-driven development (MDD).

There's all manner of debates raging about the worth and value of using the UML informally versus the precise usage required by MDD. Back in Chapter 1, the role of a software architecture as an abstract representation of the system was discussed. Abstraction is a powerful aid to understanding, and if our architecture representation is abstract, then it argues for a more informal usage of the UML in our design. On the other hand, if our UML models are a precise representation of our implementation, then they are hardly much of an abstraction. But such detailed models make code generation possible, and bridge the semantic gap between models and implementation. I personally think there's a place for both, it just depends what you're building and why. Like many architecture decisions, there's no right or wrong answer, as solutions need to be evaluated in the context of their problem definition. Now there's a classic consultant's answer.

For in-depth discussions on architecture documentation approaches, the *Views & Beyond* book from the SEI is the current font of knowledge:

P. Clements, F. Bachmann, L. Bass, D. Garlan, J. Ivers, R. Little, R. Nord, J. Stafford. *Documenting Software Architectures: Views and Beyond*. Addison-Wesley, 2002

Good UML 2.0 books are starting to emerge. The one I find useful is:

S. W. Ambler. *The Object Primer 3rd Edition: Agile Model Driven Development with UML 2*. Cambridge University Press, 2004

This book also gives an excellent introduction into agile development methods, and how the UML can be used in lightweight and effective ways.

There's an IEEE standard, IEEE 1471-2000, for architecture documentation, which is well worth a read if you're looking at defining architecture documentation standards for your organization. This can be found at:

http://standards.ieee.org/reading/ieee/std_public/description/se/1471-2000_desc.html

7 Case Study Design

7.1 Overview

In this chapter, a design for the ICDE case study described in Chap. 2 is given. First, a little more technical background to the project is given, so that the design details are more easily digested. Then the design description is presented, and is structured using the architecture documentation template introduced in the previous chapter. The only section that won't be included in the document is the first, the "Project Context", as this is basically described in Chap. 2. So, without further ado, let's dive into the design documentation.

7.2 ICDE Technical Issues

Chapter 2 gave a broad, requirements level description of the ICDE v1.0 application and the goals for building the next version. Of course, this description is necessary in order to understand architectural requirements, but in reality, it's only the starting point for the technical discussions that result in an actual design. The following sections describe some of the technical issues, whose solutions are reflected in the resulting design description in section 7.3.

7.2.1 Large Data

The ICDE database stores information about the actions of each user when using their workstation and applications. This means events such as opening and closing applications, typing in data, moving the mouse, accessing the Internet, and so on all cause data to be written to the database. Although the database is periodically purged (e.g. every day/week) to archive old data and control size, some database tables can quickly grow to a size of several million rows.

This is not a problem for the database to handle, but it does create an interesting design issue for the ICDE API. With the two-tier ICDE v1.0 application, the data analysis tool can issue naïve database queries (the classic *SELECT * from VERYBIGTABLE* case) that can return very large data sets. These are inevitably slow to execute and can bring down the analysis tool if the data set returned is very large.

While inconvenient, according to the "you asked for it, you got it!" principle, this isn't a serious issue for users in a single user system as in ICDE v1.0. They only do harm to themselves, and presumably after bringing down the application a few times, will learn better.

However, in order to lower deployment costs and management complexity, moving to a ICDE system shared amongst multiple users is a potentially attractive option because:

- It reduces database license costs, as only one is needed per deployment, not per user.
- It reduces the specification of the PC that users need to run the ICDE application, as it doesn't need to run the database, just the ICDE client software. Simply, this saves money for a deployment.
- It reduces support costs, as there's only one shared ICDE server application to manage and monitor.

If the database is to be shared by multiple users, it would still be possible to use a two-tier or three-tier application architecture. The two-tier option would likely provide better performance for small deployments, and be easier to build as less components would be needed (basically, no middle tier). The three-tier option would likely scale better as deployments approach a 100-150 users, as the database connections can be pooled and additional processing resources deployed in the middle tier.

Regardless, when a shared infrastructure is used, the behavior of each client impacts others. In this case, issues to consider are:

- Database performance
- For the three-tier option, resource usage in the middle tier

Memory usage in the middle tier is an important issue to consider, especially as clients (users and third party tools) might request result sets with many thousands of rows. While the middle tier server could be configured with a large memory heap, if several clients request sizeable result sets simultaneously, this could easily consume all the servers memory resources, causing thrashing and poor performance. In some cases this will cause requests to fail due to lack of memory and timeouts, and will likely bring down the server in extreme cases.

For third party tools written to the ICDE API, this is not at all desirable. If potentially huge result sets can be returned from an API request, it means it is possible to create applications using the API that can fail unpredictably. The failure circumstances would depend on the size of the result set and the concurrent load on the server exerted by other clients. One API call might bring down the server, and cause all applications connected to the server to fail too. This is not likely to make the development or support teams happy as the architecture would not be providing a reliable application platform.

7.2.2 Notification

There are two scenarios when event notification is needed.

1. A third party tool may want to be informed when the user carries out a specific action, for example, accesses a new site on the Internet.
2. The third party tools can share useful data that they store in the ICDE database with other tools. Therefore they need a mechanism to notify any interested parties about the data they have just written into the ICDE system.

Both of these cases, but especially the first, require the notification of the event to be dispatched rapidly, basically as the event occurs. With a two-tier architecture, instant notification is not so natural and easy to achieve. Database mechanisms exist that can be exploited such as triggers, but these have disadvantages potentially in terms of scalability, and also flexibility. A database trigger is a block of statements that are executed when there is an alteration (INSERT, UPDATE, DELETE) to a table in the database. Trigger mechanisms tend to exploit database vendor specific features, which would inhibit portability.

Flexibility is the key issue here. The ICDE development team cannot know what events or data the third party tools wish to share a priori (simply, the tools don't exist yet). Consequently, some mechanism that allows the developers themselves to create and advertise events types "on demand" is needed. Ideally, this should be supported by the ICDE platform without requiring intervention from an ICDE programmer or administrator.

7.2.3   Data Abstraction

The ICDE database structure evolved considerably from v1.0 to v2.0. The reasons were to incorporate new data items, and to optimize the internal organization for performance reasons. Hence it is important that the internal database organization is not exposed to API developers. If it were, every time the schema changed, their code would break. This would be a happy situation for precisely no one.

7.2.4   Platform and Distribution Issues

Third party tool suppliers want to be able to write applications on non-Windows platforms such as Linux. Some tools will want to run some processes on the same workstation as the user (on Windows), others will want to run their tools remotely and communicate with the user through ubiquitous mechanisms like email and instant messaging. Again, the key here is that the ICDE solution should make both options as painless as possible.

7.2.5   API Issues

The ICDE API allows programmatic access to the ICDE data store. The data store captures detailed, time-stamped information about classes of events of user actions, including:

- Keyboard events
- Internet browser access events
- Application (e.g. word processor, email, browser) open and close events
- Cut and paste events
- File open and close events

Hence the API must provide a set of interfaces for querying the event data stored in the database. For example, if a third party tool wants to know the applications a user has opened since they last logged on (their latest ICDE "session"), in pseudo code the API call sequence might look something like:

```
Session sID = getSessionID(userID, CURRENT_SESSION);
ApplicationData[] apps = getApplicationEvent(sID,
    APP_OPEN_EVENT, NULL); //NULL = all applications
```

The `apps` array can now be walked through and, for example, the web pages opened by the user in their browser during the session can be accessed[29] and analyzed using more API calls.

The ICDE API should also allow applications to store data in the data store for sharing with other tools or perhaps the user. An API for this purpose, in pseudo-code, looks like:

```
ok = write( myData, myClassifier, PUBLISH, myTopic);
```

This stores the data in a pre-designated database table, along with a classifier that can be used to search for and retrieve the data. The API also causes information about this event to be published on topic `myTopic`.

In general, to encourage third party developers, the ICDE API has to be useful in terms of providing the developers with the facilities they need to write tools. It should therefore:

- Be easy to learn and flexibly compose sequences of API queries to retrieve useful data.
- Be easy to debug.
- Support location transparency. Third party tools should not have to be written to a particular distributed configuration that relies on certain components being at known, fixed locations.
- Be resilient as possible to ICDE platform changes. This means that applications do not break when changes to the ICDE API or data store occur.

7.2.6 Discussion

Taken together, the above issues weave a reasonably complex web of requirements and issues. The event notification requirements point strongly to a flexible publish-subscribe architecture to tie together collaborating tools. The need to support multiple platforms and transparent distributed configurations points to a Java solution with the various components communicating over protocols like RMI and JMS. The large data and data store abstraction requirements suggest some layer is needed to translate API calls into the necessary SQL requests, and then manage the safe and reliable return of the (potentially large) result set to the client.

---

[29] The ICDE data store keeps copies of all accessed web pages so that even dynamically changing web pages (e.g. www.bbc.co.uk) can be viewed as they appeared at the time of access.

The chosen solution selected a three-tier architecture along with a publish-subscribe infrastructure for event notification. The details of this solution, along with detailed justifications follow in the next section, which documents the architecture using the template from Chap. 6.

7.3   ICDE Architecture Requirements

This section describes the set of requirements driving the design of the ICDE application architecture.

7.3.1   Overview of Key Objectives

The first objective of the ICDE v2.0 architecture is to provide an infrastructure to support a programming interface for third party client tools to access the ICDE data store. This must offer:

- Flexibility in terms of platform and application deployment/configuration needs for third party tools.
- A framework to allow the tools to "plug" into the ICDE environment and obtain immediate feedback on ICDE user activities, and provide information to analysts and potentially other tools in the environment.
- Provide convenient and simple read/write access to the ICDE data store.

The second objective is to evolve the ICDE architecture so that it can scale to support deployments of 100-150 users. This should be achieved in a way that offers a low cost per workstation deployment.

The approach taken must be consistent with the stakeholder's needs, and the constraints and non-functional requirements detailed in the following sections.

7.3.2   Architecture Use Cases

Two basic use cases regarding the API usage have been identified from discussions with a small number of potential third party tool vendors. These are briefly outlined below:

- **ICDE data access:** Queries from the third party tools focus on the activities of a single ICDE user. A query sequence starts by getting information about the user's current work assignment, which is basically the project (i.e. analyze Pfizer Inc financials) they are working on. Query navigation then drills down to retrieve detailed data about the user's activity. The events retrieved are searched in the time sequence they occur, and the application logic looks for specific data items (e.g. window titles, keyboard valucs, document names, URLs) in the retrieved records. These values are used to either initialize activity in the third party analysis tool, or create an informational output that appears on the user's screen.

- **Data Storage:** Third party tools need to be able to store information in the ICDE data store, so that they can share data about their activities. A notification mechanism is needed for tools to communicate about the availability of new data. The data from each tool is diverse in structure and content. It must therefore contain associated discoverable meta-data if it is to be useful to other tools in the environment.

7.3.3 Stakeholder Architectural Requirements

The requirements from the perspectives of the three major project stakeholders are covered in the following sections.

7.3.3.1 Third Party Tool Producers

- **Ease of data access:** The ICDE data store comprises a moderately complex software component. The relational database has approximately fifty tables, with some complex interrelationships. In the ICDE v1.0 environment, this makes the SQL queries to retrieve data non-trivial to write and test. Also, as the functional requirements evolve with each release, changes to the database schema are inevitable, and these might break existing queries. For these reasons, a mechanism to make it easy for third party tools to retrieve useful data is needed, as well as an approach to insulate thc tools from database changes. Third party tools should not have to understand the database schema and write complex queries.
- **Heterogeneous platform support:** Several of the third party tools are developing technologies on platforms other than Windows. The ICDE v1.0 software is tightly coupled to Windows. Also, the relational database used is available only on the Windows platform. Hence, the ICDE v2.0 must adopt strategies to make it possible for software not executing on Windows to access ICDE data and plug into the ICDE environment.
- **Instantaneous event notification:** The third party tools being developed aim to provide timely feedback to the analysts (ICDE users) on their activities. A direct implication of this is that these tools need access to the events recorded by the ICDE system as they occur. Hence,

some mechanism is needed to distribute ICDE user-generated events as they are captured in the *Data Store*.

7.3.3.2   ICDE API Programmers
From the perspective of the ICDE API programmer, the API should:

1. Be easy and intuitive to learn.
2. Be easy to comprehend and modify code that uses the API.
3. Provide a convenient, concise programming model for implementing common use cases that traverse and access the ICDE data.
4. Provide an API for writing tool specific data and metadata to the ICDE data store. This will enable multiple tools to exchange information through the ICDE platform.
5. Provide the capability to traverse ICDE data in unusual or unanticipated navigation paths. The design team cannot predict exactly how the data in the data store will be used, so the API must be flexible and not inhibit "creative" uses by tool developers.
6. Provide "good" performance, ideally returning result sets in a small (1-5) number of seconds on a typical hardware deployment. This will enable tool developers to create products with predictable, fast response times.
7. Be flexible in terms of deployment options and component distribution. This will make it cost-effective to establish ICDE installations for small workgroups, or large departments.
8. Be accessible through a Java API.

7.3.3.3   ICDE Development Team
From the ICDE development team's perspective, the architecture must:

1. Completely abstract the database structure and server implementation mechanism, insulating third party tools from the details of, and changes to, the ICDE data store structure.
2. Support ease of server modification with minimal impact on the existing ICDE client code that uses the API.
3. Support concurrent access from multiple threads or ICDE applications running in different processes and/or on different machines.
4. Be easy to document and clearly convey usage to API programmers.
5. Provide scalable performance. As the concurrent request load increases on an ICDE deployment, it should be possible to scale the system with no changes to the API implementation. Scalability would be achieved by adding new hardware resources to either scale up or scale out the deployment.

6. Significantly reduce or ideally remove the capability for third party tools to cause server failures, consequently reducing support effort. This means the API should ensure that bad parameter values in API calls are trapped, and that no API call can acquire all the resources (memory, CPU) of the ICDE server, thus locking out other tools.
7. Not be unduly expensive to test. The test team should be able to create a comprehensive test suite that can automate the testing of the ICDE API.

7.3.4 Constraints

1. The ICDE v2.0 database schema must be used.
2. The ICDE v2.0 environment must run on Windows platforms.

7.3.5 Non-functional Requirements

- **Performance:** The ICDE v2.0 environment should provide sub five second response times to API queries that retrieve up to 1000 rows of data, as measured on a "typical" hardware deployment platform.
- **Reliability:** The ICDE v2.0 architecture should be resilient to failures induced by third party tools. This means that client calls to the API cannot cause the ICDE server to fail due to passing bad input values or resource locking or exhaustion. This will result in less fault reports and easier and cheaper application support. Where architectural trade-offs must be made, mechanisms that provide reliability are favored over those that provide better performance.
- **Simplicity:** As concrete API requirements are vague (because few third party tools exist), simplicity in design, based on a flexible[30] foundation architecture, is favored over complexity. This is because simple designs are cheaper to build, more reliable, and easier to evolve to meet concrete requirements as they emerge. It also ensures that, as the ICDE development team is unlikely to possess perfect foresight, highly flexible[31] and complex, but perhaps unnecessary functionality is not built until concrete use cases justify the efforts. A large range of features supported comes at the cost of complexity, and complexity inhibits design agility and evolvability.

---

[30] Flexible in terms of easy to evolve, extend and enhance, and not including mechanisms that preclude easily adopting a different architectural strategy.
[31] Flexible in terms of the range of sophisticated features offered in the API for retrieving GB data.

7.3.6 Risks

The major risk associated with the the design is as follows:

Risk	Mitigation Strategy
Concrete requirements are not readily available, as only a few third party tool vendors are sufficiently knowledgeable about ICDE to provide useful inputs.	Keep initial API design simple and easily extensible. When further concrete use cases are identified, extend the API where needed with features to accommodate new requirements.

7.4   ICDE Solution

The following sections outline the design of the ICDE architecture.

7.4.1   Relevant Architectural Patterns

The following architecture patterns are used in the design:

- **Three-tier:** Third party tools are clients, communicating with the API implementation in the middle tier, which queries the ICDE v2.0 data store.
- **Publish-subscribe:** The middle tier contains a publish-subscribe capability.
- **Layered:** Both the client and middle tier employ layers internally to structure the design.

7.4.2   Architecture Overview

The ICDE v2.0 architecture overview is depicted in Fig. 53. ICDE clients use the *ICDE API Client* component to make calls to the *ICDE API Services* component. This is hosted by a J2EE application server, and translates API calls into JDBC calls on the data store.

The existing *Data Collection* client in ICDE v1.0 is refactored to remove all functionality with data store dependencies. All data store access operations are relocated into a set of J2EE hosted components which offer data collection services to clients.

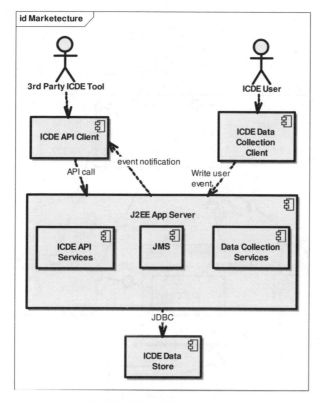

Fig. 53. ICDE API architecture

Event notification is achieved using a publish-subscribe infrastructure based on the Java Messaging Service (JMS).

Using J2EE as an application infrastructure, ICDE can be deployed so that one data store can support:

- Multiple users interacting with the data collection components.
- Multiple third party tools interacting with the API components.

7.4.3 Structural Views

A component diagram for the API design is shown in Fig. 54.

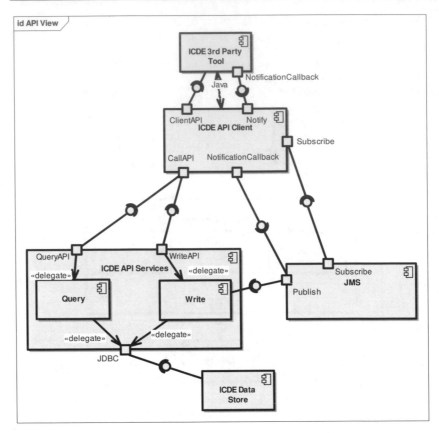

Fig. 54. Component diagram for ICDE API architecture

This shows the interfaces and dependencies of each component, namely:

- **ICDE Third Party Tool**: This uses the *ICDE API Client* component interface. The API interface supports the services needed for the third party tool to query the data store, write new data to the data store, and to subscribe to events that are published by the JMS. It must provide a callback interface that the *ICDE API Client* uses to deliver published events.
- **ICDE API Client:** This implements the client portion of the API. It takes requests from third party tools, and translates these to EJB calls to the API server components that either read or write data from/to the data store. It also packages the results from the EJB and returns these to the third party tool. This component encapsulates all knowledge of the use

of J2EE, insulating the third party tools from the additional complexity (locating, exceptions, large data sets) of interacting with an application server. Also, when a third party tool requests an event subscription, the *ICDE API Client* issues the subscription request to the JMS. It therefore becomes the JMS client that receives published events, and it passes these on using a callback supported by the third party tools.

- **ICDE API Services:** The API services component comprises stateless session EJBs for accessing the *ICDE Data Store* using JDBC. The *Write* component also takes a topic parameter value from the client request and publishes data about the event on the named topic using the JMS.
- **ICDE Data Store:** This is the ICDE v2.0 database.
- **JMS:** This is a standard J2EE Java Messaging Service, and supports a range of topics used for event notification using the JMS publish-subscribe interfaces.

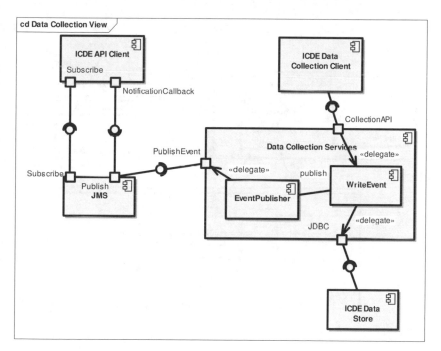

Fig. 55. Data collection components

A component diagram for the data collection functionality is depicted in Fig. 55. The responsibilities of the components are:

- **ICDE Data Collection Client**: This is part of the ICDE client application environment. It receives event data from the client application, and calls the necessary method in the *CollectionAPI* to store that event. It encapsulates all knowledge of interacting with the J2EE application server in the ICDE client application.
- **Data Collection Services:** This comprises stateless session EJBs that write the event data passed to them as parameters to the *ICDE Data Store*. Some event types also cause an event notification to be passed to the *EventPublisher*.
- **EventPublisher:** This publishes event data on the JMS using a set of pre-configured topics for events that should be published (not all user generated events are published, e.g. moving the mouse). These events are delivered to any *ICDE API Client* components that have subscribed to the event type.

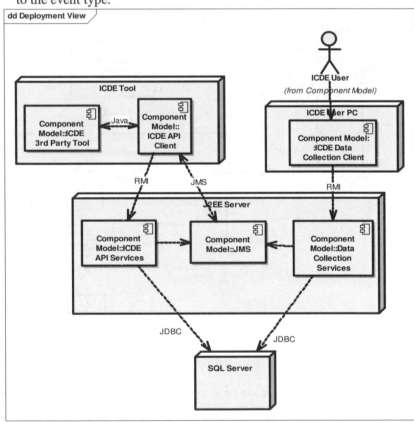

Fig. 56. ICDE deployment diagram

A deployment diagram for the ICDE architecture is shown in Fig. 56. It shows how the various components are allocated to nodes. Only a single ICDE user and a single third party tool are shown, but the J2EE server can support multiple clients of either type. Issues to note are:

- Although the third party tools are shown executing on a different node to the ICDE user workstation, this is not necessarily the case. Tools, or specific components of tools, may be deployed on the user workstation. This is a tool-dependent configuration decision.
- There is one *ICDE API Client* component for every third party tool instance. This component is built as a JAR file that is included in the tool build.

7.4.4 Behavioral Views

A sequence diagram for a query event API call is shown in Fig. 57. The API provides an explicit "Initialize" call which tools must invoke. This causes the *ICDE API Client* to establish references to the EJB stateless session beans using the J2EE directory service (JNDI).

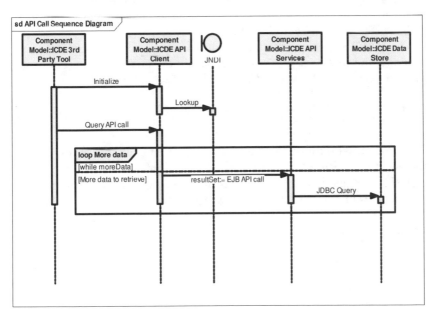

Fig. 57. Query API call sequence diagram

Once the API layer is initialized, the third party tool calls one of the available query APIs to retrieve event data (perhaps a list of keys pressed while using the word processor application on a particular file). This request is passed on to an EJB instance that implements the query, and it issues the JDBC call to get the events that satisfy the query.

All the ICDE APIs that return collections of events may potentially retrieve large result sets from the database. This creates the potential for resource exhaustion in the J2EE server, especially if multiple queries return large event collections simultaneously.

To alleviate this potential performance and reliability problem, the design employs:

- Stateless session beans that release the resources used by a query at the end of every call
- A variation of the page-by-page iterator pattern[32] to limit the amount of data each call to the session bean retrieves

The *ICDE API Client* passes the parameter values necessary for constructing the JDBC query, along with a *start index* and *page size* value. The page size value tells the session bean the maximum number of objects[33] to return from a single query invocation, and for the initial query call, the start index is set to NULL.

The JDBC call issued by the session bean exploits SQL features to return only the first *page size* rows that satisfy the query criteria. For example in SQL Server, the TOP operator can be used as follows:

```
SELECT TOP (PAGESIZE) * FROM KEYBOARDEVENTS WHERE (EVENTID
> 0 AND USER = "IAN" AND APP_ID = "FIREFOX")
```

The result set retrieved by the query is returned from the session bean to the client. If the result set has *page size* elements, the *ICDE API Client* calls the EJB query method again, using the key of the last element of the returned result set as the *start index* parameter. This causes the session bean to re-issue the same JDBC call, except with the modified *start index* value used. This retrieves the next *page size* rows (maximum) that satisfy the query.

The *ICDE API Client* continues to loop until all the rows that satisfy the request are retrieved. It then returns the aggregated event collection to its

---

[32] http://java.sun.com/developer/technicalArticles/J2EE/J2EEpatterns/

[33] The 'page size' value can be tuned for each type of event to attempt to maximize server and network performance. A typical value is 1000.

caller (the third party tool). Hence this scheme hides the complexity of retrieving potentially large result sets from the ICDE application programmer.

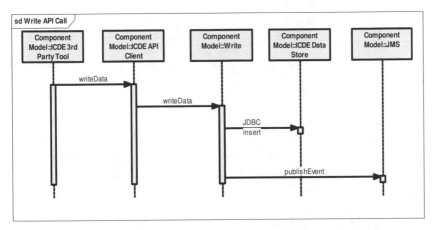

Fig. 58. Sequence diagram for the write API

A sequence diagram depicting the behavior of a *write* API call is shown in Fig. 58. The write API call contains parameter values that allow the *ICDE API Client* to specify whether an event should be published after a successful write, and if so, on which topic the event should be published.

A sequence diagram for storing an ICDE user-generated event is shown in Fig. 59. An event type may require multiple JDBC INSERT statements to be executed to store the event data; hence the container transaction services should be used. After the event data is successfully stored in the database, if it is a publishable event type, the event data is published using the JMS. The JMS publish operation is outside the transaction boundary to avoid the overheads of a two-phase commit.[34]

---

[34] There's a performance trade-off here. As the JMS publish operation is outside the transaction boundary, there can be failures that result in data being inserted into the data store, but with no associated JMS message being sent. In the ICDE context, this is undesirable, but will not cause serious problems for client applications. Given the likely frequency of such failures happening (i.e. not very often), this is a trade-off that is sensible for this application.

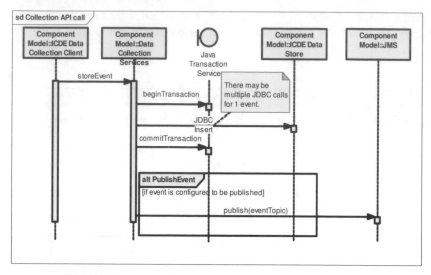

Fig. 59. Sequence diagram for storing user generated events

7.4.5 Implementation Issues

The Java 2 Enterprise Edition platform has been selected to implement the ICDE v2.0 system. Java is platform neutral, satisfying the requirement for platform heterogeneity. There are also quality open source versions available for low-cost deployment, as well as high performance commercial versions for larger mission-critical sites. In addition, J2EE has inherent support for distributed component-based systems, publish-subscribe event notification and database access.

Additional implementation issues to consider are:

- **Threading:** The *ICDE API Client* component should be thread-safe. This will enable tool developers to safely spawn multiple application threads and issue concurrent API calls.
- **Security:** ICDE tools authenticate with a user name and password. The API supports a *login* function, which validates the user/password combination against the credentials in the ICDE data store, and allows access to a specified set of ICDE user data. This is the same mechanism used in v1.0.
- **EJBs:** The *Data Collection Services* session beans issue direct JDBC calls to access the database. This is because the JDBC calls already exist

in the two-tier ICDE v1.0, and hence using these directly in the EJBs makes the refactoring exercise less costly.

7.5 Architecture Analysis

The following sections provide an analysis of the ICDE architecture in terms of scenarios and risks.

7.5.1 Scenario Analysis

The following scenarios are considered:

- **Modify ICDE Data Store organization:** Changes to the database organization will necessitate code changes in the EJB server-side components. Structural changes that do not add new data attributes are contained totally within these components and do not propagate to the ICDE API. Modifications that add new data items will require interface changes in server-side components, and this will be reflected in the API. Interface versioning and method deprecation can be used to control how these interface changes affect client components.
- **Move the ICDE architecture to another J2EE supplier:** As long as the ICDE application is coded to the J2EE standards, and doesn't use any vendors extension classes, industry experience shows that J2EE applications are portable from one application server to another with small amounts of effort (e.g. less than a week). Difficulties are usually encountered in the areas of product configuration and application-server specific deployment descriptor options.
- **Scale a deployment to 150 users:** This will require careful capacity planning[35] based on the specification of the available hardware and networks. The J2EE server tier can be replicated and clustered easily due to the use of stateless session beans. It is likely that a powerful database server will be needed for 150 users. It should also be feasible to partition the ICDE data store across two physical databases.

---

[35] Capacity planning involves figuring out how much hardware and software is needed to support a specific ICDE installation, based on the number of concurrent users, network speeds and available hardware.

7.5.2 Risks

The following risks should be addressed as the ICDE project progresses.

Risk	Mitigation Strategy
Capacity planning for a large site will be complex and costly.	We will carry out performance and load testing once the basic application server environment is in place. This will provide concrete performance figures that can guide capacity planning for ICDE sites.
The API will not meet emerging third party tool supplier needs.	The API will be released as soon as an initial version is complete for tool vendors to gain experience with. This will allow us to obtain early feedback and adapt/extend the design if/when needed.

7.6 ˙ Summary

This chapter has described and documented some of the design decisions taken in the ICDE application. The aim has been to convey the thinking and analysis that is necessary to design such an architecture, and demonstrate the level of design documentation that should suffice in many projects.

Note that some of the finer details of the design are necessarily glossed over due to the space constraints of this forum. But the ICDE example is representative of a medium complexity application, and hence provides an excellent exemplar of the work of a software architect.

8 Looking Forward

The world of software technology is a fast moving and ever changing place. As our software engineering knowledge, methods and tools improve, so does our ability to tackle and solve more and more complex problems. This means we create "bigger and better" applications, while still stressing the limits of our ever-improving software engineering skills. Not surprisingly, many in the industry feel like they are standing still. They don't seem to be benefiting from the promised quality and productivity gains of improved development approaches. I suspect that's destined to be life for all of us in the software industry for at least the foreseeable future.

8.1 The Challenges of Complexity

It's worth dwelling for a moment to consider what might be some of the major challenges for IT system builders in the next few years. It's probably pretty uncontroversial to state the inevitability that business applications will continue to become more and more complex. Complexity is a multi-dimensional attribute though. Which aspects of complexity exactly are most likely to influence the way we design and build the next generation of IT applications?

From a business perspective, it seems highly likely that the following will be drivers for much of what the IT profession does in the next decade:

- Enterprises will insist their IT infrastructure supports increasingly complex business processes that increase their organizational efficiency and reduce their cost of business.
- For many enterprises, the rate of change in their business environment will require their IT systems to be easily and quickly adaptable. Agility in the way an enterprise responds to their business needs will impact on their bottom line.
- Enterprises always want increased benefit from IT and to simultaneously reduce their IT costs. Too many enterprises have seen massive

waste on unsuccessful IT systems. As a consequence, they now need seriously convincing of the necessity to heavily invest in IT, and will insist that their IT department continually "do more with less".

Let's discuss each of these and see what implications they may have, especially from an IT architect's perspective.

8.1.1   Business Process Complexity

In large enterprises, high value business processes inevitably span multiple, independent business applications, all operating in a highly heterogeneous IT infrastructure. In such environments, the tools and technologies for business process definition and enactment become of critical importance. In practical terms, this means business process orchestration technologies are likely to become commodity, mission critical components in many enterprises.

Today's business process orchestration tools are proven and effective, and the mature ones are increasingly able to support high requests loads and to scale. But there are some fundamental problems that currently lie outside their capabilities. Probably the key need is moving from "static" to "dynamic" processes. What does this mean exactly?

A highly attractive aim for business processes is dynamic composition. For example, an organization may have a stock purchasing business process defined for purchasing from suppliers. Unexpectedly, one supplier goes out of business, or another raises prices above the threshold the organization wants to pay. With current technologies, it's likely that the business process will have to be manually modified to communicate with a new supplier. This is costly and slow.

Ideally, a business process would be able to "automagically" reconfigure itself, following a set of business rules to connect to a new supplier and reestablish a purchasing relationship. This would all happen in a few seconds, alleviating the need for programmer involvement.

This kind of dynamic business process evolution isn't too hard as long as the environment is highly constrained. If there is a fixed, known set of potential partners, each with known (ideally the same) interfaces, then business processes can be constructed to modify their behavior when certain conditions occur (like a partner interface disappears). However, once these constraints are removed, the whole problem becomes exponentially more difficult.

To start with, if potential business partners are not known in advance, the business process has to find a suitable new partner. This requires some form of directory or registry, which can flexibly searched based on a number of properties. That's not too hard, and a search might yield one or more possibilities for the business process to connect to. Assuming more than one, how does the process decide which? How does it know which potential partner will provide the process with the levels of service needed in terms of reliability and security? There has to be some mechanism for describing provided service levels and establishing trust dynamically for all this to work.

Once a trusted partner has been selected based on the service levels they advertise, it's next necessary to figure out exactly how to communicate with the partner. There's no guarantee that every possible partner has the same interface and accepts and understands the same set of messages. It's therefore necessary for the requesting business process to ensure that it sends requests in the correct format.

The killer problem here though is that an interface will typically only describe the format of the requests it receives and sends, and not the semantics of the data in the request. This means a message that tells you the price of an item may or may not be in US dollars. If it's in Euros, and you're expecting US dollars, then depending on exchange rates, you might be in for a shock or a pleasant surprise.

In their general forms, these problems of discovery, trust and data semantics are pretty much unsolved. Efforts are underway to tackle the discovery and trust problems with Web services technologies, and the semantic problems with a collection of technologies known as the Semantic Web. These are described in chapters 12 and 13 respectively.

8.1.2 Agility

Agility is a measure of how quickly an enterprise can adapt its existing applications to support new business needs. If a business can get a new business service on-line before its competitors, it can start making money while the competition struggles to catch up.

From a technical perspective, agility is very closely related to modifiability. If an enterprise's architecture is loosely-coupled and application and technology dependencies are abstracted behind sensible interfaces, implementing new business processes might not be too onerous.

One genuine barrier to agility is heterogeneity. An architecture might be beautifully designed, but if for example it suddenly becomes necessary to get a new .NET application talking to existing J2EE application using a JMS, then life can get painfully messy. In reality, the sheer number of incompatible technology combinations in an enterprise is usually not something that is pleasurable to think about.

Finally however, a solution is on the horizon. Of course, heterogeneity is never going to go away. But it doesn't have to if we can hide this diversity behind a standards-based integration architecture. XML Web services have emerged in the last five years as a set of technologies which are supported by every major vendor. They define a standard protocol and mechanisms for plugging applications together, both within and across enterprises. Chapter 12 describes the features of the Web services technology stack. While some of the elements of the standards are still evolving at the time of writing this, it's a better than even bet that Web services are going to be in the IT world for the long haul.

Web services bring increased agility through standards-based integration. But integration is not the only impediment to increasing an enterprise's ability to modify and deliver new applications. Improved development technologies that make change less difficult and costly can also greatly increase an enterprise's agility. Two emerging approaches in this vein are aspect technologies and Model-Driven Architectures (MDA).

Aspect technologies structure an application as a collection of independent but related "aspects" of a solution, and provide tools to merge these aspects at build or run-time. As aspects can be created, understood and modified independently, they enhance development agility.

MDA, or model-driven development as it's increasing known, promotes application development using abstract UML-based models of a solution. Executable code is generated from these models using MDA tools. MDA raises the abstraction level of the development process, in theory making changes easier to effect in the models rather than in detailed code. MDA code generation tools also hide detailed platform-specific knowledge from the application. If the underlying platform (e.g. MOM technology) changes, a code generator for the new platform is simply acquired. The application can then be automatically regenerated from the model to use the new platform. Now there's agility for you! That's the theory, anyway.

Aspects and MDA are described in Chap. 10 and Chap. 11 respectively.

8.1.3   Reduced Costs

The heady days of the late 1990s "dot.com" boom and massive IT spends have gone, likely for a very long time. Now businesses rightly demand to know what business benefit their IT investments will bring, and what return-on-investment they can expect. As an architect, writing business cases for investments and acquisitions is a skill you'll need to acquire, if you haven't already of course.

In terms of reducing what we spend, while still achieving our business goals, the place to start is to begin by working smarter. As a whole, the IT industry has struggled to deliver on the promises of increased efficiency and lower costs from new development technology adoption. Object and component technologies were meant to make it easy for us to design and deliver reusable components that could be used in many applications. Build something once, and use it for essentially no cost, many times over. That's a deal no one can possibly refuse, and one which is simple for management to understand.

The truth is that the IT industry has pretty much failed to deliver on the reuse promise. Successful reuse tends to take place with large scale, infrastructural components like middleware and databases. Similarly, Enterprise Resource Planning (ERP) systems like SAP and their like have managed to deliver generalized, customizable business processes to a wide spectrum of organizations. None of these have been without their difficulties of course. But think of how much of somebody else's code (i.e. investment) you're using when you deploy an Oracle database or a J2EE application server. It's significant indeed.

But on a smaller scale, reusable components have pretty much failed to materialize. The reason for this is simple and well explained by much research in the software engineering community. The argument goes like this.

Essentially, it costs money to build software components so they can be used in a context which they were not originally designed for. You have to add more features to cater for more general use. You need to test all these features extensively. You need to document the features and create examples of how to use the component. Studies indicate that it costs between three and ten times as much to produce quality reusable components.

Of course, all this investment may be worthwhile if the components are used over and over again. But what if they're not? Well, basically you've just invested a lot of time and effort in generalizing a component for no purpose. That's not smart.

Fortunately, some very smart architects thought about this problem a few years back. They realized that successful reuse didn't just happen "by magic", but it could be achieved if a product strategy was understood and planned out. Hence the term "product line architecture" was coined. These are explained in Chap 9. They represent a set of proven practices that can be adopted and tailored within an enterprise to leverage investments in software architectures and components. They represent the state-of-the art in working smart right now.

8.2   What Next?

The remaining chapters in this book each cover an emerging area of practice or technology that is likely to have a profound effect on the future life
of a software architect. These are:

- Software Product Lines
- Aspect-Oriented Programming
- Model-Driven Architectures (MDA)
- Service-Oriented Architectures and Web Services
- The Semantic Web
- Agent technologies

Some of these, like software product lines, have proven their utility in
certain application domains like telecommunications and defense, while
others are still in their relative infancy. All are likely to contribute in some
manner to the way we design and build IT systems in ten years from now.

Each of the chapters that follow describes the fundamentals of each approach, addresses the state-of-the-art, and speculates about future potential
and adoption. They also describe how the techniques or technologies can
be applied to the ICDE case study to provide enhanced features and functionality.

Hopefully these chapters will arm you with sufficient knowledge to at
least seem intelligent and informed when a client or someone in your project catches you by surprise and suggests adopting one of these approaches. In such circumstances, a little knowledge can go a long way.

9 Software Product Lines

Mark Staples

9.1 Product Lines for ICDE

The ICDE system is a platform for capturing and disseminating information that can be used in different application domains. However, like any generically applicable horizontal technology, its broad appeal is both a strength and weakness. The weakness stems from the fact that a user organization will need to tailor the technology to suit its application domain (e.g. finance), and make it easy for their users to learn and exploit. This takes time and money, and is hence a disincentive to adoption.

Recognizing this, the product development team decided to produce a tailored version of the ICDE platform for their three major application domains, namely financial analysis, intelligence analysis and government policy research. Each of the three would be marketed as different products, and contain specific components that make the base ICDE platform more user-friendly in the targeted application domain.

To achieve this, the team brainstormed several strategies that they could employ to minimize the design and development effort of the three different products. The basic idea they settled on was to use the base ICDE platform unchanged in each of the three products. They would then create additional domain-specific components on top of the base platform, and build the resulting products by compiling the base platform with the domain-specific components. This basic architecture is depicted in Fig. 60.

What the team had done was to take the first steps to creating a product line architecture for their ICDE technology. Product lines are a way of structuring and managing the on-going development of a collection of related products in a highly efficient and cost-effective manner. Product lines achieve significant cost and effort reductions through large scale reuse of software product assets such as architectures, components, test cases and documentation.

The ICDE product development team already benefits from software reuse in a few different ways. They reuse some generic libraries (like JDBC drivers to handle database access), and sometimes even reuse entire off the shelf applications (like the relational database in the ICDE data store). Market forces are driving the introduction of the three tailored versions of the ICDE product. But if the team developed each of these separately, it could triple their development or maintenance workload. Hence their plan is to reuse core components for the fundamental ICDE functionality and to create custom components for the functionality specific to each of the three product's markets. This is a kind of software product line development, and it should significantly reduce their development and maintenance costs.

The remainder of this chapter overviews product line development and architectures, and describes a range of reuse and variation mechanisms that can be adopted for product line development.

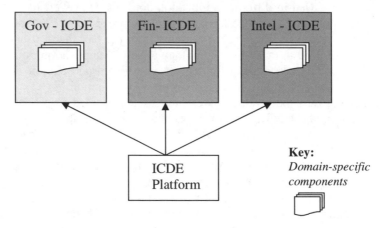

Fig. 60. Developing domain-specific products for the ICDE platform

9.2   Software Product Lines

Widespread software reuse is a "holy grail" for software engineering. It promises a harmonious world where developers can quickly assemble high-quality solutions from a suite of pre-existing software components. The quest for effective software reuse has in the past stereotypically focused on "reuse in the small", exploiting techniques to reuse individual functions, or libraries of functions for data-types and domain-independent technologies. Collection class and mathematical function libraries are good examples. Such approaches are proven to be beneficial, but they have not realized the full promise of software reuse.

Reusing software is easy if you know it already does exactly what you want. But software that does 'almost' what you want is usually completely useless. To realize the full benefits of software reuse, we need to practice effective "software variation" as well. Modern approaches to software reuse, such as Software Product Line (SPL) development, support software variation "in the large", with an architectural basis and a domain-specific focus. Software Product Line development has proved to be an effective way to benefit from software reuse and variation. It has allowed many organizations to reduce development costs, reduce development duration, and increase product quality.

In SPL development, a collection of related products is developed by combining reused core assets with product-specific custom assets that vary the functionality provided by the core assets. A simple conceptual example of a product line is shown in Fig. 61. In the picture, two different calculator products are developed, with both using the same core asset internal boards. The different functionalities of the two calculator products are made available by each of their custom assets, including the two different kinds of buttons that provide the individualized interface to the generic, reused functionality.

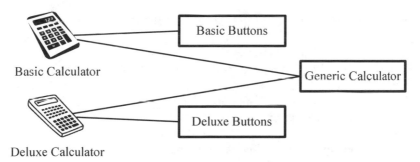

Fig. 61. A schematic view of a simple product line

From this simple perspective, SPL development is just like more traditional hardware-based product line development, except that in SPL development, the products are of course software![36]

---

[36] Product lines are also widely used in the embedded systems domain, where products are a software/hardware combination.

For any product in a SPL, almost everything is implemented by reused core assets. These core assets implement base functionality which is uniform across products in the SPL, as well as providing support for variable features which can be selected by individual products. Core asset variation points provide an interface to select from among this variable functionality. Product-specific custom assets instantiate the core assets' variation points, and may also implement entire product-specific features.

Software variation has a number of roles in SPL development. The most obvious role is to support functional differences in the features of the SPL. Software variation can also be used to support non-functional differences (such as performance, scalability, or security) in features of the SPL. Another less recognized role for software variation is to help resolve change control conflicts on core assets.

SPL development is not simply a matter of architecture, design, and programming. SPL development impacts existing processes across the software development lifecycle, and requires new dimensions of process capability for the management of reused assets, products, and the overarching SPL itself. The Software Engineering Institute has published Product Line Practice guidelines (see Further Reading at the end of the chapter) for these processes and activities that support SPL development. We will refer to these practice areas later within this chapter.

9.3   Benefiting from SPL Development

When an organization develops a set of products that share many commonalities, a SPL becomes a good approach. Typically an organization's SPL addresses a broad market area, and each product in the SPL targets a specific market segment. Some organizations also use an SPL to develop and maintain variants of a standard product for each of their individual customers.

The scope of a product line is the range of possible variation supported by the core assets in a SPL. The actual products in a SPL will normally be within the SPL scope, but custom assets provide the possibility for developing functionality beyond the normal scope of the SPL. To maximize the benefit from SPL development, the SPL scope should closely match both the markets of interest to the company (to allow new products within those markets to be developed quickly and efficiently), and also the full range of functionality required by the actual products developed by the company. These three different categories of product (the company's markets of interest, the SPL scope, and the actual products developed by the company) are depicted in a Venn diagram in Fig. 62.

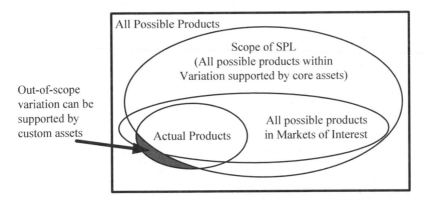

Fig. 62. The scope of an SPL

The most obvious benefit from SPL development is increased productivity. The costs of developing and maintaining core assets are not borne by each product separately, but are instead spread across all products in the SPL. Organizations can capture these economies of scale to benefit from the development of large numbers of products. The SPL approach scales well with growth, as the marginal cost of adding a new product should be small.

However, SPL development also has other significant benefits. When the core assets in an SPL are well established, the time required to create a new product in the SPL is much smaller than with traditional development. Instead of having to wait for the redevelopment of functionality in the core assets, customers need only wait for the development of functionality that is unique to their needs.

Organizations can also experience product quality benefits from SPL development. In traditional product development, a defect might be repeated across many products, but in SPL development, a defect in a core asset only needs to be fixed once. Moreover, although the defect might be initially found in the use of only one product, every product in the SPL will benefit from the defect fix. These factors allow more rapid improvements to product quality in SPL development.

There are additional second-order benefits to SPL development. For example, SPL development provides organizations with a clear path enabling them to turn customized project work for specific customers into product line features reused throughout the SPL. When organizations have processes in place to managed reused assets, the development of customer-specific project work can initially be managed in a custom asset. If the features prove to have wider significance, the custom asset can be moved into the reused core asset base.

Another related benefit is that the management of core and custom assets provides a clear and simple view of the range of products maintained by the organization. This view enables organizations to more easily:

- upgrade products to use a new core version;
- see what assets are core for the business;
- see how products differ from each other;
- consider options for future functionality for the SPL.

9.3.1   Product Lines for ICDE

The three planned ICDE products all operate in a similar way and the differences for each of the products are fairly well understood. The Government product will have a user interface that supports policy and governance checklists, the Financial product will support continually-updated displays of live market information, and the Intelligence product will integrate views of data from various sources of classified data.

The variation required in the product line can be defined largely in terms of the data collection components. The GUI options and the access to domain specific data sources will have to be supported by variation points in the collection components. This means the *Data Collection* client component will need variation points in order to support access to application domain-specific data sources. This will require custom components to handle the specific details of each of the new government/financial/intelligence data sources. The *Data Store* component should not need to support any variation for the three different products. It should be able to be reused as a simple core asset.

9.4   Product Line Architecture

SPL development is usually described as making use of a Product Line Architecture (PLA). A PLA is a reuse-oriented architecture for the core assets in the SPL. The reuse and variation goals of a PLA are to:

- systematically support a pre-planned scope of variant functionality

- allow products within the SPL to easily choose options from among that variant functionality.

A PLA achieves these goals using a variety of technical mechanisms for reuse and variation that are described in the following sections.

Jan Bosch[37] has identified three levels of PLA maturity:

1. Under-specified architecture (ad-hoc variation)
2. Specified architecture
3. Enforced architecture (all required variation supported by planned architectural variation points)

Increasing levels of architectural maturity provide more benefits from systematic variation by making product development faster and cheaper. However, increasingly mature PLAs provide fewer opportunities for ad-hoc variation, which can reduce opportunities for reuse. Nonetheless, increasing levels of reuse can be achieved if there is better systematic variation, that is, better adaptation of the PLA to the scope and application domain of the SPL.

A PLA is not always necessary for successful SPL development. The least mature of Bosch's maturity levels is "under-specified architecture", and experiences have been reported of the adoption of SPL development with an extremely under-specified PLA. Although products in an SPL will always have some sort of architecture, it docs not necessarily have to be a PLA, namely one designed to support goals of reuse and variation. Some non-architectural mechanisms to achieve reuse and variation are discussed in the following sections.

9.4.1 Reuse Mechanisms

To reuse software, developers must:

1. find and understand the software,
2. make the software available for use by incorporating it into their development context, and
3. use the software by invoking it.

---

[37] J. Bosch, *Maturity and Evolution in Software Product Lines*. In Proceedings of the Second International Software Product Line Conference (San Diego, CA, U.S.A., August 19-22 2002). Springer LNCS Vol. 2379, 2002, pp. 257-271.

Let's look at each of these steps in turn.

9.4.1.1   Find and Understand Software

Software engineers use API documentation and reference manuals to support the simple reuse of software libraries. For SPL development, the Product Line Practice guidelines from the SEI (see Further Reading) describe the *Product Parts Pattern* which addresses the discovery and understanding of core asset software for SPL development. This pattern relies on the documentation of procedures to use and instantiate core assets in the construction of products.

9.4.1.2   Bring Software into the Development Context

After finding the software, a developer has to make it available to be used. There are many ways to bring software into a development context, which can be categorized according to their "binding time". This is the time at which the names of reused software assets are bound to a specific implementation. The main binding times and some example mechanisms are:

- Programming time – by version control of source code
- Build time – by version control of static libraries
- Link time – by operating system or virtual machine support for dynamic libraries
- Run time – by middleware or application-specific mechanisms for configuration or dynamic plug-ins, and by programming language mechanisms for reflection

Earlier binding times (such as programming or build time) make it easier to use ad-hoc variation. Later binding times (such as link or run time) delay commitment to specific variants, and so make it easier to benefit from the options provided by systematic variation. Increasingly mature PLAs for SPL development tend to use later binding time mechanisms. This enables them to maximize the benefits from an SPL scope that is well understood and has a good fit with the company's markets of interest.

9.4.1.3   Invoke Software

To invoke software, programming languages provide procedure/function/method call mechanisms. For distributed systems, interoperation standards such as CORBA and SOAP provide remote invocation mechanisms that are tied into programming language mechanisms, to allow developers to invoke software systems running on other machines. These invocation mechanisms are the same for SPL development as for traditional software development.

9.4.2 SCM for Reuse

For organizations that are adopting SPL development, the most common binding times for reuse are programming time and build time. This makes software configuration management (SCM) a critical supporting process area for SPL development. SCM includes version control and change control for software assets.

SCM for SPL development is more complicated than in normal product development partly because configuration identification (CI) is more complicated. CI is the SCM activity of specifying the names, attributes, and relationships between configurations (a versioned collection of versioned objects). In normal product development, a product's configuration usually has a simple structure (e.g. a single versioned binary or versioned file system directory hierarchy). However in SPL development, each core asset, custom asset, and product is a configuration that must be identified and the relationships between these configurations must be specified and managed. Basically, SCM gets much more architectural for SPL development.

One approach to SCM for SPL development is depicted in Fig. 63. In this approach, core assets and products each have their own line of development (LOD). Each product version includes its own custom assets, as well as versions of core assets. The version control system ensures that reused core assets are read-only for a product, and that they not modified solely within the context of a specific product's LOD. However, a product's LOD can take a later version of a core asset which has been produced on its own LOD.

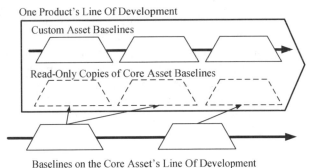

Fig. 63. A SCM branching pattern for SPL development

This view of SPL development provides a quantitative basis for seeing why SPL development can prove so effective. The LOD for each product contains source code for customer-specific assets and also (read-only) source code for core assets. So each LOD contains essentially the same source code as it would were PLD not being used. However the total volume of branched code has been reduced, because the size of core assets is not multiplied across every product. Core assets are not branched for each product, and so low level design, coding and unit test costs within core assets can be shared across many products.

In the ICDE example there are three products, and let's assume that the core components have 140,000 LOC (Lines of Code) and each product's custom part have 10,000 LOC. In normal product development, each product would be maintained on a separate LOD, giving a total of:

*(140,000 + 10,000) * 3 = 450,000 branched LOC.*

In SPL development, the core is on its own LOD, and each product has a LOD only for changing their custom assets, giving a total of:

*140,000 + (10,000 * 3) = 170,000 branched LOC.*

That's only 38% of the original total. The improvement gets better when developing more products, or when the size of the custom assets compared to core assets is proportionately smaller.

9.4.3 Variation Mechanisms

In an SPL, core assets support variable functionality by providing variation points. A SPL typically has a PLA that gives an architectural basis for variation. A PLA uses specific architectural variation mechanisms to implement variable functionality. However an SPL can also use non-architectural variation mechanisms to vary software functionality.

In addition to architectural-level variation mechanisms, there are design-level and source-level variation mechanisms. These different types of variation are not incompatible. For example, it is possible to use file-level variation at the same time as architectural variation. This section describes some of the variation mechanisms at these different levels of abstraction. This classification is similar to the taxonomy of variability realization techniques in terms of software entities that has been proposed by Svahnberg et al.[38]

---

[38] M. Svahnberg, J. van Gurp, J. Bosch, *A Taxonomy of Variability Realization Techniques*, Technical paper, Blekinge Institute of Technology, Sweden, 2002.

9.4.3.1   Architecture-Level Variation Points

Architectural variation mechanisms are high-level design strategies intended to let systems support a range of functionality. These strategies are only very loosely related to the facilities of any specific programming language. Examples of these include frameworks, and plug-in architectures. Even the formal recognition of a space of configuration options or parameters for selecting between variant functionality can be considered to be an architectural variation mechanism.

9.4.3.2   Design-Level Variation

The boundary between architecture and design is not always a clear one. Here we will say that design-level mechanisms are those supported directly by programming language facilities, and that architecture-level mechanisms must be created by programming. Programming language mechanisms can be used to represent variation. These mechanisms include component interfaces that can allow various functionally different implementations, and inheritance and overriding that similarly allow objects to have variant functionality that satisfies base classes.

9.4.3.3   File-Level Variation

Development environments and programming languages provide ways to implement variation at the level of source code files. Some programming languages provide conditional compilation or macro mechanisms that can implement functional variation. In any event, build scripts can perform logical or physical file variation that can be used to represent functional variation.

9.4.3.4   Variation by Software Configuration Management

The main role of SCM for SPL development is to support asset reuse, by identifying and managing the versions of (and changes to) products and their constituent component assets. New product versions do not have to use the most recent version of a core asset. SCM systems can allow a product to use whatever core asset version meets the needs of the product's stakeholders. The version history and version branching space within an SCM tool can be used to represent variation.

In a version control tool, a branched LOD of a core asset can be created to contain variant functionality. Branching reused core assets in order to introduce ongoing variation is a sort of technical decay that reduces the benefits of SPL development. In the extreme case where every product has its own branch of core assets, an organization will have voided SPL development completely and will be back doing ordinary product development. Nonetheless, in some circumstances a temporary branch is the most pragmatic way to introduce variation into a component in the face of a looming delivery deadline.

9.4.4   Product Line Architecture for ICDE

Early on the in the development of the ICDE product the development team had put considerable effort into the product architecture. This means that they're in the fortunate position of already having many architectural variation mechanisms in place, making the adoption of SPL development easier. For example, the *Data Source* adapter mechanism provides all the required variability for the three new products. These existing variation mechanisms form the heart of the product line architecture for the ICDE product line.

The team need to define some new variation mechanisms too. To support the real-time display of market information for the Financial product, the existing GUI components need new functionality. The GUI is currently too rigid, so the team plans to extend the GUI framework to let them add new types of "plug-in" panels connected to data sources. When this framework is extended, it'll be much easier to implement the real-time display panel, connect it to the market data source, and include it in the GUI for the Financial product build.

However, although the ICDE team thought the *Data Store* would be the same for all three products, it turns out that separating the classified data for the Security product is a non-trivial problem, with requirements quite different to the other two products. The team has to come up with some special-purpose *Data Store* code just for that product. The easiest way to make these special changes is in a separate copy of the code, so in their version control tool they create a branch of the *Data Store* component just for the Security product. Having to maintain two different implementations of the *Data Store* might hurt a little, but it's the best the team can do under a tight deadline. Once the product ships they'll have time to design a better architectural variation mechanism for the next release, and move all the products onto that new *Data Store* component.

9.5   Adopting Software Product Line Development

Like many radical business changes, the adoption of SPL development in an organization is often driven in response to a crisis (what Schmid and

Verlage[39] diplomatically called a "reengineering-driven" situation). This may be an urgent demand to quickly develop many new products, or to reduce development costs, or to scale new feature development in the face of a growing maintenance burden. This section points out some paths and processes relevant to the adoption of SPL development.

9.5.1 Starting Points for Adopting SPL Development

There are two different starting points in the adoption of SPL development:

1. **Green Fields:** where no products initially exist;
2. **Ploughed Fields:**, where a collection of related legacy products have already been developed without reuse in mind.

Each situation has special considerations, as described below.

9.5.1.1 Green Fields Adoption of SPL Development

For Green Fields adoption of SPL development, the SEI's *What to Build* pattern is particularly relevant. This pattern describes how a number of interacting practice areas can result in the generation of an SPL Scope (to know what SPL will be built) and a business case (to know why building the SPL is a good investment for the organization). The SEI's *Scoping* and *Building a Business Case* practice areas that are directly responsible for these outputs are supported by the *Understanding Relevant Domains*, *Market Analysis*, and *Technology Forecasting* practice areas.

An organization has to decide on their markets of interest, their medium-to-long term SPL scope, and their short-to-medium term product production plans. In terms of the Venn diagram depicted in Fig. **62**, the organization must plan and evaluate the various investment options of having the PLA of the core asset base support a large-enough SPL scope. This makes it possible to trade off the potential for return from the products that can be generated within that scope for the markets of interest to the organization.

Investing in a PLA at the beginning of an SPL will provide a better long-term return assuming that the products in the SPL are successful in the market. However, the cost and technical difficulty of creating such a PLA *ex nihlio* can pose a barrier to the adoption of SPL development, es-

[39] K. Schmid, M. Verlage, *The Economic Impact of Product Line Adoption and Evolution*. In IEEE Software, July/August 2002, pp. 50-57.

pecially if the organization is not already expert within the application do-main being targeted by the SPL.

9.5.1.2   Ploughed Fields Adoption of SPL Development

When a set of products exists and is being transitioned to an SPL, an or-ganization will, as for Green Fields adoption, need to decide on the SPL scope and markets of interest for the SPL. However, organizations in this position will generally already have a good understanding about these. The scope of the SPL will largely be driven by the functionality of existing products and future product plans. The other significant considerations for Ploughed Fields adoption are potential barriers related to change control, and defining the core assets and PLA.

Change control issues can pose a barrier to the adoption of SPL devel-opment for an organization's legacy products. The stakeholders of existing products will already have established expectations about how their prod-uct releases change. As discussed in the SCM section, every product in the SPL has stakeholders that influence changes made to core assets, and these core asset changes in the SPL will ultimately affect every product in the SPL, including other stakeholders. This change in the nature of product re-leases must be understood and accepted by the products' stakeholders.

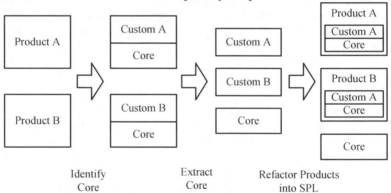

Identify Core   Extract Core   Refactor Products into SPL

Fig. 64. Mining core assets from a collection of existing products

When initially defining an SPL for an existing set of independent prod-ucts, the organization must decide what is core for every product, and what is custom or specific to any individual product. Instead of throwing away the existing assets for the organization's products and starting from a blank slate, it is possible to use an extractive approach to mine core assets from existing products. The SEI describes a product line practice area *Mining Existing Assets* addressing this activity. In many ways, the extraction of core assets is like a giant refactoring exercise, as depicted in Fig. 64. Starting from an initial collection of products, the goal of the exercise is to finish with identical products, except now all built using a common core asset.

When defining the core assets, the organization can also define a PLA to cater for variation that is identified among the products. Svahnberg et al. have presented a set of minimally necessary steps to introduce variability into a SPL. These are:

- identification of variability
- constraining variability
- implementing variability
- managing the variability

In order to reduce change control conflicts, it may be easier to introduce SPL development early in the cycle leading to the release of a major new version of a product. Product stakeholders are prepared for major changes when receiving a major new version. Although moving to SPL development need not in principle result in any functional difference to a product, there will at least be change control policy modifications, which customers may find easier to accept in the context of a major new product version.

An organization adopting SPL development can also reduce business and technical risks by incrementally rolling out the SPL within the organization. Adoption can be incremental either by progressively increasing the size of the core assets, by progressively adding more products to use the core assets, or a combination of both.

9.6 Product Line Adoption Practice Areas

The adoption of SPL development has impact outside the technical development context. Regardless of the starting point for SPL adoption (Green or Ploughed Fields) and regardless of the specific product and technical process changes that are to be made, many organizational management issues must be dealt with to successfully transition to SPL development. The SEI product line practice guidelines describe the *Cold Start Pattern* that groups together practice areas that can help an organization effectively prepare for the launch of its first SPL. The structure of the pattern is shown in Fig. 65.

Although the details of these practice areas are beyond the scope of this chapter, the pattern as a whole highlights the fact that SPL development must have broad business support from within the adopting organization and from its customers.

Fig. 65. The structure of product line practice areas in SEI's *Cold Start* pattern (after Clements and Northrup 2002, p383)

9.6.1   Product Line Adoption for ICDE

The ICDE team was driven to SPL development by the daunting prospect of developing three new products at once. They are creating three new products for three specific markets, but are using their existing product as a starting point. Their adoption of SPL development is thus a Ploughed Field scenario. They have to mine reusable components from their existing code base.

Luckily their existing customers aren't going to be too concerned initially about the move to a PLA, because the move is part of the development of a major new version of the product. The customers will be happy to upgrade because of the new features they'll also be getting.

9.7   Ongoing Software Product Line Development

SPL development must be effective not just for the initial development of new products, but also for their ongoing maintenance and enhancement. Although SPL development can have many benefits, it is more complicated than normal product development. Enhanced processes are necessary to make ongoing SPL development effective. This section gives an overview of a few of these SPL development processes. We pay particular attention to "change control" and "architectural evolution" for SPL development, but also summarize other SEI Product Line Practice areas for ongoing SPL development.

9.7.1 Change Control

Software change control is related to software configuration management, and is concerned with planning, coordinating, tracking, and managing the impact of change to software artifacts (e.g. source code). Change control is harder when you do software reuse, and this affects SPL development.

In any kind of product development, every product has a collection of stakeholders that is concerned with how their product changes to accommodate their needs for new functionality. In addition, stakeholders are concerned about non-functional characteristics (such as release schedule, product reliability) related to the release of their products. Risk-averse stakeholders (such as those using safety-critical software or those in the banking industry) are often motivated to ensure that their products do not change at all! Such stakeholders sometimes prefer to be confident in their understanding of the product (bugs and all) rather than use new, perhaps better versions.

9.7.1.1 Change Control is Harder for SPL Development

Change control is harder when you do software reuse, including software reuse for SPL development. For ordinary product development, each product is developed separately, and so each product's stakeholders are kept separate too. However, in SPL development each product depends on reused core assets, and so these products' stakeholders also vicariously depend on these reused core assets. If one product's customer has a change request that involves a change to a core asset, then implementing that will force that change on every other customer who uses the new version of that core asset. The many, often conflicting, needs of the products' stakeholders will need to be simultaneously satisfied by the reused core assets.

9.7.1.2 Long, Medium, and Short Term Change Control

There are a range of strategies to help address the problems of change control for SPL development, but there is no silver bullet to solve them. Good discipline and a combination of long, medium, and short term change management are required.

An important long term way to reduce change control conflicts is to develop higher quality core assets. Change control is easier if changes are not required, and higher quality core assets can reduce the need for change. Serendipitously, one benefit of SPL development is that the quality of core assets will tend to increase over time, because many different products will exercise the core assets in slightly different patterns of use, which will tend to expose more defects for correction.

An SPL Road Map is a medium-to-long term approach to manage change. A SPL Road Map is a formal plan for changes to core assets, which can be useful in managing the expectations and plans of the products' stakeholders. This can help to avoid differing expectations among stakeholders about product release schedules and functionality. An SPL Road Map is the place where proactive architectural changes are scheduled, to add variation points to core assets. This helps to minimize the problems associated with changing PLA core asset variation points.

Many organizations use CCBs (Change Control Boards) to make decisions about the implementation of change requests in individual products. A product's CCB contains representatives from the development team and the product's stakeholders. In SPL development, products can still have CCBs, but the SPL as a whole requires a Core CCB. A Core CCB makes decisions about the implementation of change requests affecting core assets. The Core CCB is the forum for short-to-medium term negotiation between the product stakeholders to decide on the disposition of change requests that have not been previously agreed to within the SPL Road Map.

If a short term or emergency core asset change is required and is not approved by the Core CCB, it may be possible to "fake" a core change by instead changing a product's custom assets. File-level variation mechanisms are particularly well suited to this. Fake core changes are work-arounds that can add to the longer-term maintenance cost and decrease the economies of reuse. To avoid an accumulation of these inefficiencies, when a fake core change is implemented, it is best to also have the Core CCB agree to schedule a "real" medium-term core asset change in the SPL Road Map, and when this is implemented, undo the fake change in the custom assets.

9.7.1.3   Change Tracking

The increased complexity of SCM configuration identification for SPL development noted earlier also has an impact on the complexity of change tracking. In SPL development, core assets, custom assets, and products are all separately managed as CIs. Changes can be made to any of these CIs. Some changes observable at the product level are seen by product stakeholders conceptually as single changes (e.g. fixing a product defect), but within the SPL they are implemented as changes to both core and custom assets. Change tracking only at the asset level may create seemingly spurious changes at the product level, while change tracking only at the product level will cause confusion about the nature and scope of the changes with an individual asset.

To address these change tracking problems a change tracking system for SPL development needs to be able to track changes at both the asset level, and also in an aggregated way at the product level. One way to do this is to separately track change requests (at the product level) and their related changes (at the asset level).

9.7.2 Architectural Evolution for SPL Development

In SPL development there is constant evolution of both individual product custom assets and the reused core assets. The PLA is the architectural basis for the variation supported by core assets. A change to a core assets' interface is a change to the PLA, and can force changes in all products that use the new version of these core assets. How then should the new or enhanced core features be added to a SPL? That is, how should changes be made to the PLA?

There are three ways to time the introduction of variation points into core assets:

- **Proactive:** Plan ahead for future features, and implement them in core assets before any product needs them.
- **Reactive:** Wait until a new feature is actually required by a product, and then implement it in core assets at that time.
- **Retroactive:** Wait until a new feature is actually required by a product, and then implement it in a custom asset at that time. When enough products implement the feature in their custom assets, add it to the core assets. New products can use the new core assets' feature, and the older products can drop their custom asset implementation in favor of the core assets' implementation.

It is possible to use a mix of these approaches, for different enhancements. For example, enhancements on a long-term SPL Road Map could be added in a proactive way, by planning architectural changes to support the future increased scope of the SPL. Limited but generally useful enhancements to core assets could be added in a reactive way, by modifying the PLA as required by those enhancements. Enhancements needed by one product that are more speculative or are less well defined could be added retroactively.

Each of these strategies has different costs, benefits, and risks. The choice of strategy for a particular feature will be driven by consideration of these tradeoffs in the organization's business context. Table 11 summarizes some of the differences between the three approaches:

Table 11. Comparing strategies for architecture evolution

	Proactive	Reactive	Retroactive
No long-term investment	No	Yes	Yes
Reduces risk of core asset change conflict	Yes	No	Yes
Reduces lead time to add feature to first product	Yes	No	No
Reduces risk of core feature not required in a number of products	No (0 products)	No (1 product)	Yes

9.7.3   Product Line Development Practice Areas

The SEI product line practice guidelines provide the *Factory* pattern that links together other patterns and their constituent practice areas relevant to the ongoing development and maintenance of a SPL. The *In Motion* pattern groups together organizational management practice areas. Other relevant SEI patterns are the *Monitor*, *Process*, and *Curriculum* patterns that describe ongoing aspects of SPL development.

For technical practice areas, the SEI's *Each Asset* pattern describes practice areas that are relevant to the development of core assets. The *Product Parts* pattern ties together the core assets with the product development. The *Product Builder* pattern describes practice areas relevant to the development of any specific product. The *Assembly Line* pattern describes how products are output from the SPL.

9.7.4   Product Lines with ICDE

Doing SPL development wasn't just an architectural issue for the ICDE team. Each of the products had a customer steering group that was involved in defining requirements for the new products, and defined enhancement requests that they wanted to track through to the delivery of the products. But the ICDE team didn't want the Financial product customer steering group to see all the details of the Security product steering group, and vice-versa. The problem was that some enhancement requests were the same (or similar), and the team didn't want to get confused about duplicate requests when they started coding.

So, the ICDE team set up different customer-facing request systems for each of the products. These linked to an internal change request system which could track changes to each of the main reused sub-systems and also the product-specific custom components.

Eventually the first product was released. Instead of releasing all three products at once, the team shipped the simplest product first, namely the Government product. The Government customers quickly raised a few post-release defect reports, but the ICDE development team was able to respond quickly too. The good news was that one of the defects that was fixed was in the core *Data Collection* component, so when the other two products were released later, their customers wouldn't see that problem. The ICDE team was beginning to see some quality benefits from SPL development.

The bad news came after the other products were released. The Security and Financial customers were happy to have the new version, though the Financial customers did raise a defect report on the *Data Analysis* component. It would have been easy to fix in the core component, but by that time the Government customers had gone into production. They hadn't seen that problem in the *Data Analysis* area, and in fact the bug was related to the framework extensions required to support the Financial product real-time display panel.

However, if the *Data Analysis* component changed in any way at all, the Government customers would have to follow their policy and re-run all of the related acceptance tests, which would cost them time and money. So they really didn't want to see any changes, and put pressure on the ICDE sales team to try to stop the change.

The ICDE development team really wanted to change the core version, but how could they satisfy everyone? They thought about faking the core changes in custom assets just for the Financial product, but in the end they decided to keep the Government product on the old version of the *Data Analysis* component, and implemented the fix in the core. The ICDE development team also created a Core CCB involving representative members from each of the three customer steering groups. This meant that in future the negotiations could be managed inside the Core CCB, instead of via the ICDE sales team.

A bright spot on the horizon was that the Security customers were starting to talk about their need to see real-time visualization of news reports. The ICDE development team could implement that just by reusing the real-time display panel developed for the Financial product. The company had already accounted for the costs of developing that feature, so being able to sell it again to other customers would mean all the new revenue would go straight to the bottom line.

9.8   Conclusions

SPL development has already given many organizations orders of magnitude improvements to productivity and time to market, and significant improvements in product quality. If we think about SPL development simply from a SCM perspective, we can see that (proportionately large) core assets are not branched for each product, and so the total number of branched lines of code is vastly reduced for the whole SPL.

What does the future hold for SPL development? Because of its massive potential, SPL development is likely to become even more widely known, better understood, and increasingly used. However, SPL development will also have impacts on software architecture practices, as architectural mechanisms for reuse in the large become better and more widely understood.

Improved architectural practices combined with a deeper understanding of specific application domains can also support increasingly declarative variation mechanisms. This could transform software reuse to be more like the mythical vision of software construction using software building blocks. Simple reuse relies heavily on procedural variation, writing ad-hoc code to achieve the particular functionality that is required. Increasing architectural sophistication and domain knowledge can support configurable variation, realized by systematic variation supported by core assets interfaces.

Choosing a variant for such a system requires choosing values from a list of configuration options. When an application domain is very well understood, then a domain-specific language becomes a viable way of declaratively specifying product variation. Sentences in this language can specify system variants, and can be dynamically interpreted by the core assets.

Other architectural and design approaches such as aspect-oriented programming and model-driven development also have promise as variation or mass-customization mechanisms that may be able to support SPL development. These two topics are described in the next two chapters.

SPL development is just one approach to benefit from software reuse. In SPL development, variation of reused assets is usually performed with the use of custom assets that are created at development time. Other approaches for benefiting from software reuse are based on variation incorporating assets at later binding times. For example, configurable product bases have no (or almost no) custom assets and all variation occurs at build time or load time. Continuing to the extreme, dynamically configurable product bases have no custom assets and all variation occurs dynamically at run time.

As the time of system variation extends out of the development context, so does the need to extend the control and management of variation. For systems that can vary at installation time, load time, or run time, the need to control and manage system variation does not end when the system is released from development. Software configuration management supports control and management of variation during development. However, for installation, load or run time, existing package management and application management frameworks have very weak facilities for version and variation control. In future, the boundaries between configuration management, package management, and application management will become blurred. A unified framework is therefore required to control and manage variation across the entire product lifecycle.

9.9 Further Reading

The Software Engineering Institute has been a leader in defining and reporting the use of software product lines. An excellent source of information is the following book by two of the pioneers of the field:

P. Clements, L. Northrop. *Software Product Lines: Practices and Patterns.* Addison Wesley, 2001.

The SEI's web site also contains much valuable information and links to other product line related sources:

http://www.sei.cmu.edu/productlines/index.html

Another excellent reference is:

K. Pohl, G. Böckle, F. J. van der Linden. Software Product Line Engineering: Foundations, Principles and Techniques. Springer-Verlag 2005

Software configuration management is a key part of software product lines. A good book on this topic is:

S.P. Berczuk, B. Appleton. Software Configuration Management Patterns: Effective Teamwork, Practical Integration. Addison-Wesley, 2002.

A case study describing how to exploit file-based variation to create a software product line is:

M. Staples, D. Hill. *Experiences Adopting Software Product Line Development without a Product Line Architecture*. Proceedings of the 11th Asia-Pacific Software Engineering Conference (APSEC 2004), Busan, S. Korea, 30 Nov-3 Dec 2004, IEEE, pp. 176-183.

A slightly different perspective on product lines is the Software Factories work by Jack Greenfield et al. This book is definitely worth a read.

J. Greenfield, K. Short, S. Cook, S. Kent, J. Crupi, Software Factories: Assembling Applications with Patterns, Models, Frameworks, and Tools, Wiley 2004

10 Aspect Oriented Architectures

Yan Liu

10.1 Aspects for ICDE Development

The ICDE 2.0 environment needs to meet certain performance requirements for API data retrievals. To try and guarantee this performance level,
the actual behavior of an ICDE implementation needs to be monitored.
Performance monitoring allows remedial actions to be taken by the development team if the required performance level is not met.

However, ICDE v2.0 is a large, multithreaded and distributed system,
comprising both off-the-shelf and custom written components. Such systems are notoriously difficult to monitor and isolate the root cause of performance problems, especially when running in production.

The time-honored strategy for monitoring application performance and
pinpointing components causing performance bottlenecks is to instrument
the application code with calls to log timing and resource usage. However
this approach leads to duplicate code being inserted in various places in the
source. As always, duplicate code is error prone and makes it more difficult to maintain the application as the ICDE application evolves.

The ICDE team was aware of the engineering problems of inserting performance monitoring code throughout the ICDE code base. Therefore they
sought a solution that could separate the performance monitoring code
from the application implementation in a modular, more maintainable way.
Even better would be if it were possible to inject the performance monitoring code into the application without the need to recompile the source
code.

So, the ICDE team started to look in to aspect-based approaches and
technologies to address their performance monitoring problem. Aspect-
oriented programming (AOP) structures code in modules known as aspects. Aspects are then merged at either compile time or run time to form a
complete application.

The remainder of this chapter provides an overview of AOP, its essential elements and tool support. It also discusses the influence of aspect-based approaches on architecture and design. Finally, the chapter describes how the ICDE system could leverage aspect-based techniques to monitor application performance in a highly flexible, modular and maintainable way.

10.1.1 Introduction to Aspect-Oriented Programming

Aspect-oriented programming (AOP) is an approach to software design invented at Xerox PARC in the 1990s[40]. The goal of AOP is to let designers and developers better separate the "crosscutting concerns" that a software system must address. Crosscutting concerns are elements of a system's behavior that cannot be easily localized to specific components in an application's architecture. Common crosscutting concerns are error handling, security checks, event logging and transaction handling. Each component in the application must typically include specific code for each crosscutting concern, making the component code more complex and harder to change.

To address crosscutting concerns, AOP provides mechanisms for systematic identification, separation, representation and composition. Crosscutting concerns are encapsulated in separate modules, called "aspects", so that localization can be achieved.

AOP has a number of potential benefits. First, being able to identify and explicitly represent crosscutting concerns helps architects consider crosscutting behavior in terms of aspects at an early stage of the project lifecycle. Second it allows developers to easily reuse the code for an aspect in many components, and thus reduces the effort of utilizing (often this means copying) the code. Third, AOP promotes better modularity and encapsulation as component code is succinct and uncluttered.

Structuring applications with aspects and directly implementing the design using aspect-oriented programming languages has the potential for improving the quality of software systems. Aspects may make it possible for large and complex software systems to be factored and recomposed into simpler and higher quality offerings. To see how this works, let's look at this approach in more details.

---

[40] Kiczales, G., Lamping, J., Mendhekar, A., Maeda, C., Videira Lopes, C., Loingtier, J.-M., and Irwin, J, *Aspect-Oriented Programming*, Proceedings European Conference on Object-Oriented Programming, Vol. 1241. Springer-Verlag, (1997) 220-242.

10.1.2 Crosscutting Concerns

Separation of concerns is a fundamental principle of software engineering. This principle helps manage the complexity of software development by identifying, encapsulating and manipulating those parts of the software relevant to a particular concern. A "concern" is a specific requirement or consideration that must be addressed in order to satisfy the overall system goal.

Any application is composed of multiple functional and non-functional concerns. Functional concerns are relevant to the actual use of the application, whereas non-functional concerns pertain to the overall quality attributes of the system, such as the performance, transactions and security. Even applications that are designed in a highly modular fashion suffer from tangling of functional and non-functional aspects. For example, caching logic to improve database performance might be embedded in the business logic of many different components, thus mixing or tangling functional and performance concerns. Other examples of crosscutting concerns include performance monitoring, transaction control, service authorization, error handling, logging and debugging. The handling of these concerns spans across multiple application modules, replicating code and making the application more complex.

10.1.3 Managing Concerns with Aspects

Using conventional design techniques, a crosscutting concern can be modularized using an interface to encapsulate the implementation of the concern from its invoking client components. Although the interface reduces the coupling between the clients and the implementation of the concern, the clients still need to embed code to call the interface methods from within its business logic.

With aspect-oriented design and programming, each crosscutting concern is implemented separately in a component known as an aspect. In Fig. 66, the difference between implementing a logging concern using conventional programming and AOP is demonstrated. The aspect defines execution points in client components that require the implementation of the crosscutting concern. For each execution point, the aspect then defines the behavior necessary to implement the aspect behavior, such as calling a logging API.

Importantly, the client modules no longer contain any code to invoke the aspect implementation. This leads to client components that are unpolluted by calls to implement one or more concerns.

Once defined, the use of an aspect is specified in composition rules. These composition rules are input to a programming utility known as a "weaver". A weaver transforms the application code, composing the aspect with its invoking clients. Aspect-oriented programming languages such as AspectJ provide weaving tools, and hence AOP languages and tools are necessary to effectively implement aspect-oriented designs.

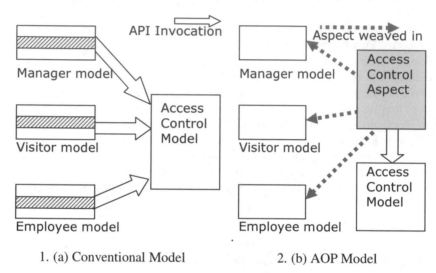

1. (a) Conventional Model   2. (b) AOP Model

Fig. 66. Implementation of a logging concern

10.1.4 AOP Syntax and Programming Model

"Crosscutting" is an AOP technique to enable identification of concerns and structuring them into modules in a way that they can be invoked at different points throughout an application. There are two varieties of crosscutting, static and dynamic. Dynamic crosscutting modifies the execution behavior of an object by weaving in new behavior at specific points of interest. Static crosscutting alters the static structure of a component by injecting additional methods and/or attributes at compile time.

The basic language constructs and syntax used to define crosscutting in AOP are as follows:

• A "join point" is an identifiable point of execution in an application, such as a call to a method or an assignment to a variable. Join points are important, as they are where aspect behaviours are woven in to the application.

- A "pointcut" identifies a join point in the program at which a crosscutting concern needs to be applied. For example, the following defines a pointcut when the *setValue* method of the *Stock* class is called:

```
pointcut log(String msg):args(msg)
execution(void Stock.setValue(float))
```

- An "advice" is a piece of code implementing the logic of a crosscutting concern. It is executed when a specified pointcut is reached.
- An "introduction" is a crosscutting instruction that can make static changes to the application components. An introduction may, for example, add a method to a class in the application.
- An aspect in AOP is equivalent to a class in object-oriented programming. It encapsulates pointcuts and associated advice and introductions.

In Fig. 67 the relationship between these AOP terms is illustrated.

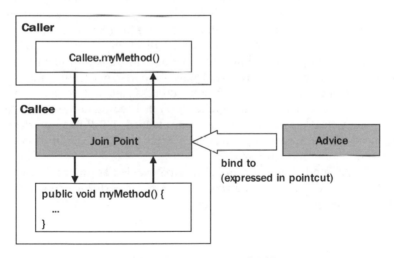

Fig. 67 The anatomy of AOP

10.1.5 Weaving

Realizing an aspect-oriented design requires programming language support to implement individual aspects. The language also defines the rules for weaving an aspect's implementation with the rest of the application code. Weaving can follow a number of strategies, namely:

1. a special source code pre-processor executed during compilation;
2. a post-processor that patches binary files;
3. an AOP-aware compiler that generates woven binary files;
4. load-time weaving (LTW); for example, in the case of Java, weaving the relevant advice by loading each advice class into the JVM.
5. run-time weaving (RTW); intercepting each join point at runtime and executing all relevant advices. This is also refered to as "hotswapping" after the class is loaded.

Most AOP languages support compile-time weaving (CTW) using one of the first three options. In the case of Java, the way it typically works is that the compiler generates standard Java binary class files, which any standard JVM can execute. Then the *.class* files are modified based on the aspects that have been defined. CTW isn't always the best choice though, and sometimes it's simply not feasible (e.g. with Java Server Pages).

LTW offers a better solution with greater flexibility. In the case of Java, LTW requires the JVM classloader to be able to transform or instrument classes at runtime. The JDK[41] v5.0 now supports this feature through a simple standard mechanism. LTW must process Java bytecode at runtime and create data structures (this can be slow) that represent the bytecode of a particular class. Once all the classes are loaded, LTW has no effect on the speed of the application execution. AspectJ[42], JBoss AOP[43] and AspectWerkz[44] now support LWT.

RTW is a good choice if aspects must be enabled at runtime. However, like LTW, RTW can have drawbacks in terms of performance at runtime while the aspects are being weaved in.

---

[41] Java Development Kit
[42] http://eclipse.org/aspectj/
[43] http://www.jboss.org/products/aop
[44] http://aspectwerkz.codehaus.org/

10.1.6 Example of a Cache Aspect

In this section we'll use a simple example to illustrate the AOP programming model[45]. This simple application calculates the square of a given integer. In order to improve performance, if a particular input value has been encountered before, its square value is retrieved from a cache. The cache is a crosscutting concern, not an essential part of computing the square of an integer.

```java
//Source code of Application.java
package Caching;

public class Application {
  public static void main(String[] args) {
    System.out.println("The square of 45 is " + calculateSquare(45));
    System.out.println("The square of 64 is " + calculateSquare(64));
    System.out.println("The square of 45 is " + calculateSquare(45));
    System.out.println("The square of 64 is " + calculateSquare(64));
  }
  private static int calculateSquare(int number) {
    try {
      Thread.sleep(6000);
    }
    catch (InterruptedException ie) {}
    return number * number;
  }
}
```

```java
//Source code of Cache.aj
package Caching;
import java.util.Hashtable;

public aspect Cache {
  private Hashtable valueCache;
  pointcut calculate(int i) : args(i)
      && (execution(int Application.calculateSquare(int)));
  int around(int i) : calculate(i) {
    System.out.println("Cache aspect is invoked for parameter "+i);
    if (valueCache.containsKey(new Integer(i))) {
      return ((Integer) valueCache.get(new Integer(i))).intValue();
    }
    int square = proceed(i);
    valueCache.put(new Integer(i), new Integer(square));
    return square;
  }
  public Cache() {
    valueCache = new Hashtable();
  }
}
```

Fig. 68. A cache aspect implemented using AspectJ

---

[45] Chapman, M., Hawkins, H. *Aspect-oriented Java applications with Eclipse and AJDT*, IBM developerWorks,
http://www-128.ibm.com/developerworks/library/j-ajdt/

The example is implemented using AspectJ and shown in Fig. 68. The cache is implemented as an aspect in *Cache.aj* and separated from the core application implementation, *Application.java*. The method *calculateSquare* is a join point and it is identified by the pointcut *calculate* in the *Cache* aspect, as in the following:

```
pointcut calculate(int i):args(i)
    && (execution(int Application.calculateSqure(int)));
```

The implementation of the cache function, retrieving a value from a *java.util.Hashtable*, is provided inside the *around* advice. Note that this advice is only applied to the class *Application*. The cache aspect is weaved into the application code at compile time using an AspectJ compiler.

The following output from executing the program demonstrates the advice is invoked at the join point.

```
Cache aspect is invoked for parameter 45
The square of 45 is 2025
Cache aspect is invoked for parameter 64
The square of 64 is 4096
Cache aspect is invoked for parameter 45
The square of 45 is 2025
Cache aspect is invoked for parameter 64
The square of 64 is 4096
```

10.2 Aspect-Oriented Architectures

An aspect relating to a system's quality attributes heavily influences the application architecture, and many such aspects are basically impossible to localize. For example, to guarantee the performance of a loosely coupled application, consideration must be paid to the behavior of individual components and their interactions with one another. Therefore, concerns such as performance tend to crosscut the system's architecture at the design level, and they can not be simply captured in a single module.

AOP provides a solution for developing systems by separating crosscutting concerns into modules and loosely coupling these concerns to functional requirements. In addition, design disciplines like aspect-oriented design (AOD) and aspect-oriented software development (AOSD) have been proposed to extend the concepts of AOP to earlier stages in the software lifecycle. With AOD and AOSD, the separation of concerns is addressed at two different levels.

First at the design level, there must be a clear identification and definition of the structure of components, aspects, joint points and their relationship. Aspect design and modeling are the primary design activities at this level. Individual concerns tend to be related to multiple architectural artifacts.

For example, a concern for performance may be associated with a set of use cases in the architecture requirements, a number of components in the design and some algorithms for efficiently implementing specific logical components. The requirements for each aspect need to be extracted from the original problem statement, and the architecture needs to incorporate those aspects and identify their relationship with other components. It is also important to identify potential conflicts that arise when aspects and components are combined at this level. To be effective, this approach requires both design methodologies and tool support for modeling aspects.

Second, at the implementation level, these architectural aspects need to be mapped to an aspect implementation and weaved into the implementation of other components. This requires not only the expressiveness of an AOP language that can provide semantics to implement join points, but also a weaving tool that can interpret the weaving rules and combine the implementations of aspects.

10.2.1 Architectural Aspects and Middleware

As explained in Chap. 4, component-based middleware technologies such as J2EE and .NET provide services that support, for example, distributed transaction processing, security, directory services, integration services, database connection pooling, and so on. The various issues handled by these services are also the primary non-functional concerns targeted by AOSD. In this case, both component technology and AOP address the same issue of separation of concerns.

Not surprisingly then, middleware is one of the most important domains for applying AOP. Research on aspect mining[46] shows that 50% of the classes in three CORBA ORB implementations are responsible for coordination with a particular aspect. AOP has been used in such cases to effectively refactor a CORBA ORB and modularize its functionality.

Following on from such endeavors, attempts have been made to introduce AOP to encapsulate middleware services in order to build highly configurable middleware architectures. Distribution, persistence and transac-

---

[46] Zhang, C., Jacobsen, H. *Refactoring middleware with aspects*. In IEEE Transactions on Parallel and Distributed Systems, IEEE Computer Society, (2003), 14(11):1058 – 1073

tion aspects for software components using AspectJ have been successfully implemented, and AspectJ2EE extends AspectJ to implement the EJB model and several J2EE services. In the open source product world, JBoss AOP provides a comprehensive aspect library for developing Java-based application using AOP techniques.

The major problem in applying AOP to build middleware frameworks is that middleware services are not generally orthogonal. Attaching a service (aspect) to a component without understanding its interaction with other services is not sensible, as the effects of the services can interact with each other.

For example, aspects are commonly used for weaving transactional behavior with application code. Database transactions can be committed using either one phase or two phase (for distributed transactions) commit protocols. For any individual transaction, only one protocol is executed, and hence only one aspect, and definitely not both, should be weaved for any join point. In general, handling interacting aspects is a difficult problem. Either a compile-time error or a run-time exception should be raised if the two interacting aspects share a join point.

10.3 State-of-the-Art

Recent research and development efforts have been dedicated to various aspect-oriented technologies and practices. These include AOP language specification, tool support for aspect modeling and code generation, and integration with emerging technologies such as metadata based programming. Let's discuss each of these.

10.3.1 Aspect Oriented Modeling in UML

Several approaches exist to support aspect modeling for AOD and AOSD. Most of these approaches extend UML by defining a new UML profile for AOSD. This enables UML extensions with aspect concepts to be integrated into existing CASE tools that support standard UML.

An advantage of aspect oriented modeling is the potential to generate code for aspects from design models. In aspect oriented modeling and code generation, aspect code and non-aspect code is generated separately. Using Model Driven Architecture (MDA) approaches, tools use a transformation definition to transform a platform independent model (PIM) into one or more platform specific models (PSMs), from which the automated generation of aspect code and weaving can take place. MDA technologies are explained in detail in the next chapter.

10.3.2 AOP Tools

The fundamental model of AOP is the join point model. All AOP tools employ this model to provide a means of identifying where crosscutting concerns are applied. However, different tools implement the specifics of the aspect model in their own way, and introduce new semantics and mechanisms for weaving aspects.

For example, in JBoss AOP, advices are implemented through "interceptors" using Java reflection, and pointcuts are defined in an XML file that describes the place to weave in an advice dynamically at run time. In AspectJ, both advices and pointcuts are defined in an aspect class and weaved statically.

This diversity in AOP tools is problematic for software development using aspects, because of the semantic differences of different AOP models and the different ways an aspect is weaved with other classes. It is not possible to simply redevelop an existing aspect in order for it to be weaved with other aspects developed with another AOP model.

In order to address this problem, AspectWerkz has proposed an open architecture model for an "aspect container" for Java-based AOP tools. The basic idea is to provide a weaver and a container that can weave, deploy and run any aspect no matter how it is implemented and defined. It is the aspect container's responsibility to resolve the semantic differences between the different aspect models. Such a container can allow aspects developed by different AOP models and tools to coexist in one single runtime environment. Currently, AspectWerkz has implemented an extension model for aspects that implements the AOP Alliance interfaces, Spring AOP and AspectJ.

10.3.3 Annotations and AOP

The join point model can utilize the properties of program elements such as method signatures to capture join points. However it cannot capture join points needed to implement certain crosscutting concerns, such as transaction and role-based security, as there is no information in an element's name or signature to suggest the need for transactional or authorization related behaviors. Adding metadata to AOP systems is therefore necessary to provide a solution for such cases.

In the programming language context, metadata known as "annotations", capture additional information attached to program elements such as methods, fields, classes, and packages. The J2SE v5.0 and the C#/VB .NET languages provide language standards to attach annotations to program elements. A good example of applying annotations is declaring transactions in the J2EE and .NET frameworks. For example, the following annotation declares the transaction attribute of the method *update()* in EJB 3.0:

```
@TransactionAttribute
      (TransactionAttributeType.REQUIRED)
  public void update (double newvalue)
      throws Exception
```

Annotations are widely supported by AOP tools, such as JBoss AOP and AspectWerkz. Using AspectWerkz, aspects can be utilized to implement EJB 3.0 annotations. For example, a pointcut must be defined to match any method in a class that is annotated with the javax.transaction.TransactionAttribute annotation. Such a pointcut can be expressed as

```
execution(@javax.ejb.TransactionAttribute * *.*(..))
```

An advice that encapsulates the transaction management according to the annotated transaction attribute can be implemented as follows:

```
                            The aspect instance is per JVM

@Aspect("perJVM")
public abstract
        class TransactionAttributeAspect {

@Expression("execution(@javax.ejb.TransactionAttribute *
*.*(..))")
    Pointcut transactedMethods;

                            The pointcut that picks out all
                            transacted methods
```

10.4 Performance Monitoring of ICDE with AspectWerkz

When running in production, it is desirable to be able to inject performance monitoring code into ICDE components without recompiling the complete application. Using aspects, this can be achieved using LTW. Hence the

ICDE team starts to design an aspect-based architecture using Aspect-Werkz as shown in Fig. 69.

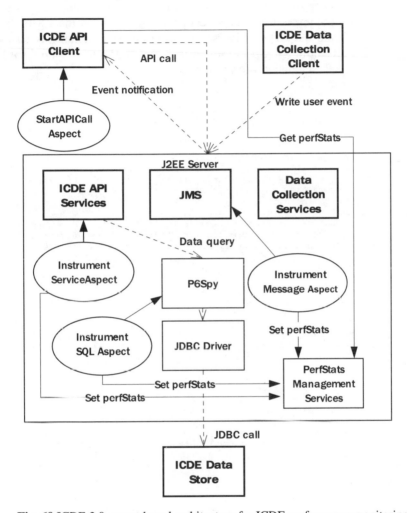

Fig. 69 ICDE 2.0 aspect-based architecture for ICDE performance monitoring

In this architecture, the performance instrumentation for different ICDE components is encapsulated in a dedicated aspect that can be injected into the ICDE application. This is necessary because the metrics that must be recorded are different in nature. For example, the performance monitoring of a JMS server measures both the message processing rate and the message size, while the instrumentation of SQL statements measures response time.

In order to instrument the database query response time, an open source component, P6Spy[47], is used. This acts as a layer between the J2EE connection pool and the JDBC drivers, capturing the SQL statements issued by J2EE application. An aspect must also be applied to this component to retrieve the SQL statement information.

```
public class InstrumentSQLAspect
{
    public Object logJdbcQueries(final JoinPoint joinPoint)
            throws Throwable
    {
        //access Runtime Type Information
        MethodRtti rtti = (MethodRtti)joinPoint.getRtti();
        String query = (String) rtti.getParameterValues()[0];
        Long startTime = System.currentTimeMillis();
        //execute the method
        final Object result = joinPoint.proceed();
        Long endTime = System.currentTimeMillis();
        // log the timing information for this SQL statement execution
        perfStatsManager.log(query,"Statement",endTime-startTime);
        return result;
    }

    public Object logValuesInPreparedStatement(final JoinPoint
    joinPoint) throws Throwable
    {
        MethodRtti rtti = (MethodRtti)joinPoint.getRtti();
        Integer index = (Integer)rtti.getParameterValues()[0];
        Object value = rtti.getParamterValues()[1];
        String query = "index="+ index.intValue()+ " value="
                         + value.toString();
        Long startTime = System.currentTimeMillis();
        //execute the method
        Final Object result = joinPoint.proceed();
        Long endTime = System.currentTimeMillis();
        //log the timing information for this PreparedStatement
        //execution
        perfStatsManager.log(query,"PreparedStatement",endTime-
        startTime);
        return result;
    }
};
```

Fig. 70 SQL statement instrumentation aspect implementation

Once all the performance data is captured, there are a variety of options to make it available for subsequent processing. It can be simply written to log file periodically or loaded into a database. A more flexible and effi-

---

[47] http://www.p6spy.com/

cient solution to provide direct access to live system performance data is to use a standard protocol such as Java Management eXtension (JMX)[48] that existing J2EE management tools can display and track.

To illustrate the design, implementation and deployment of Aspect-Werkz aspects, we'll describe in detail the `InstrumentSQLAspect`. To measure SQL statement response times, we need to locate all method calls where a `java.sql.Statement` is created and inject timing code immediately before and after the SQL query is executed. We also have to trace all method calls where a value is set in a `java.sql.PreparedStatement` instance. The resulting code snippet for the `InstrumentSQLAspect` is illustrated in Fig. 70.

The next step is to compile the aspects as a normal Java class with the AspectWerkz libraries. The weaving rules for binding the advice to the pointcut is specified in the *aop.xml* file as shown in Fig. 71.[49]

LTW for AspectWerkz is achieved by loading the AspectWerkz library for the JDK v5. The ICDE application can then be booted normally and the aspect code will be weaved in at load-time

In summary, using AOP techniques, instrumentation code can be separated and isolated into aspects. The execution of the aspects can be weaved into the system at runtime without the need to recompile the whole system.

```xml
<aspectwerkz>
   <system id="ICDE">
      <package name="com.icde.perf.aop">
         <aspect class="InstrumentSQLAspect"
               deployment-model="perThread">
            <pointcut name="Statement" expression=
               "execution(* java.sql.Connection+.prepare*(..))" />
            <pointcut name="PreparedStatement" expression=
               "execution(void java.sql.PreparedStatement+.set*(..))" />
            <advice name="logJdbcQueries(final JoinPoint joinPoint)"
               type="around" bind-to="Statement" />
            <advice name="logValuesInPreparedStatement(final JoinPoint
               joinPoint)" type="around" bind-to="PreparedStatement" />
         </aspect>
      </package>
   </system>
</aspectwerkz>
```

Fig. 71. `InstrumentSQLAspect` XML definition file

---

[48] http://java.sun.com/products/JavaManagement/

[49] Note that as J2EE containers are multi-threaded, and individual requests are handled by threads held in a thread pool, the aspect is deployed in *perThread* mode.

10.5 Conclusions

AOP was originally introduced as a programming mechanism to encapsulate crosscutting concerns. Its success has seen aspect-oriented techniques become used in various application domains, such as middleware frameworks. It has also spawned modeling and design techniques which influence the architecture of a software system built using aspect-oriented techniques.

AOP brings both opportunities and challenges for the software architect. In limited domains, AOP has demonstrated a great deal of promise in reducing software complexity through providing a clear separation and modularization of concerns. Potentially fruitful areas for the future include further integrating AOP and middleware to increase the flexibility of configuring middleware platforms. Even in this example though, challenging problems remain, namely coordinating multiple aspects to deal with conflicts, as crosscutting concerns are not completely orthogonal.

Aspect oriented design and implementation requires the support of efficient AOP tools. With such tools, on-going research and development is still attempting to provide better solutions in several areas, namely:

- **Maintenance**: Designing quality aspect-oriented systems means paying attention to defining robust pointcuts and sensibly using aspect inheritance. Pointcuts that capture more join points than expected or miss some desired join points can lead to brittle implementations as the system evolves. Consequently an efficient debugging tool is needed to detect the faulty join point and the pointcut implementation.
- **Performance:** Using AOP introduces extra performance overheads in applications, both during the weaving process and potentially at runtime. The overhead of AOP needs to be minimized to provide good build and runtime performance.
- **Integration:** The reusability of aspects hasn't been explored sufficiently, so that designers could utilize libraries of aspects instead of developing each aspect from scratch. As each AOP tool only provides aspect implementations specific to its own AOP model, an aspect implemented by one AOP model can not be easily weaved into a system with aspects using a different AOP model. This is potentially a serious hurdle to the adoption of aspect-orientation in a wide range of software applications.

In summary, aspect-oriented techniques are still developing and maturing. Only limited use-cases exists in which AOP-based mechanisms have proven useful. These include security, logging, monitoring, transactions and caching. Whether aspect-orientation will become a major design and development paradigm is very much open to debate. However it seems inevitable based on current adoption that aspect-oriented techniques will gradually be infused into the software engineering mainstream.

10.6 Futhur Reading

A good comparison of four leading Java AOP tools, namely AspectJ, AspectWerkz, JBoss AOP and Spring AOP, in terms of their language mechanisms and development environments is:

M. Kersten, *AOP Tools Comparison*. IBM developerWorks,
http://www-128.ibm.com/developerworks/library/j-aopwork1/

A source of wide-ranging information on aspects is maintained at the AOSD wiki at http://aosd.net/wiki/index.php?title=Main_Page

The home page for *Aspectwerkz* is http://aspectwerkz.codehaus.org/

A good practical guide to AspectJ is:

R. Laddad, AspectJ in Action: Practical Aspect-Oriented Programming. Manning 2003

11 Model-Driven Architecture

Liming Zhu

11.1 Model-Driven Development for ICDE

One problem lurking at the back of the ICDE development team's mind is related to capacity planning for new ICDE installations. When an ICDE installation supports multiple users, the request load will become high, and the hardware that the platform runs on needs to be powerful enough to support this request load. If the hardware becomes saturated, it will not be able to process all user generated events, and important data may be lost. The situation is exacerbated by the following issues:

- Different application domains and different individual installations within each domain will use ICDE in different ways, and hence generate different request loads per user.
- Different installations will deploy ICDE on different hardware platforms, each capable of supporting a different number of users.
- The ICDE platform will be ported to different J2EE application servers, and each of these has different performance characteristics.

All of these issues relate to the software engineering activity of capacity planning. Capacity planning is concerned with how large, in terms of hardware and software resources, an installation must be to support its expected request load. Mathematical modeling techniques can sometimes be used to predict a platform's capacity for standardized components and networks[50]. But more typically, benchmark tests are executed on a prototype or complete application to test and measure how the combined hardware/software deployment performs.

---

[50] For example, Microsoft's Capacity Manager and its support for Exchange deployments.

The only realistic way the ICDE team could anticipate to carry out capacity planning was to execute a test load on specific deployment platforms. For each installation, the team would need to:

- Install ICDE on the target hardware platform, or one that is as close as
  possible in specification to the expected deployment platform.
- Develop sample test requests generated by software *robots* to generate a
  load on the platform, and measure how it responds. The test requests
  should reflect the expected usage profile of the users operating on that
  ICDE installation.

So, for each installation, a set of tests must be developed, each of which
will execute a series of requests on the ICDE platform and measure the response time and throughput. This is shown in Fig. 72.

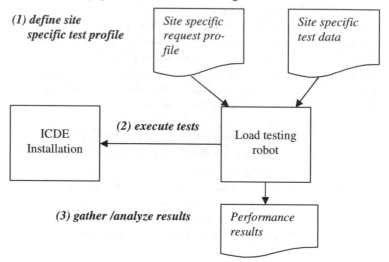

Fig. 72. Capacity planning for ICDE installations

Not surprisingly, the ICDE team were extremely interested in making
this whole capacity planning exercise as efficient and painless as possible.
This would mean minimizing the amount of site-specific development. So
for example, instead of writing a test robot specific for every installation,
they would like to define the test load and test data externally to the code,
and somehow input this into the robot to interpret. They would also like
the performance results from test runs to be produced and collated automatically as graphs for easy analysis.

To achieve this, the team decided to exploit model-driven architecture methods and supporting development technologies. Model-driven approaches encourage the components of a software system to be described in UML models. These models are then input into code generators that automatically produce executable code corresponding to the model. The team hoped they could develop a single model of an ICDE test robot. Then, by simply changing parameters in the model, they could generate an installation-specific load test at the press of a button.

This chapter describes the essential elements of model-driven architecture approaches. It then shows how the ICDE team could use model-driven techniques to automate the development, deployment and results gathering of an ICDE installation for efficient capacity planning purposes.

11.2 What is MDA

One recurring theme in the evolution of software engineering is the ongoing use of more abstract formal languages for modelling solutions. In much mainstream software development, abstract descriptions, for example in Java or C#, are transformed by tools into executable forms. Developing solutions in abstract notations increases productivity and reduces errors because the translation from abstract to executable forms is automated by translation tools like compilers.

Of course, few people believe the nirvana of abstract programming languages is Java, C# or any of their modern contemporaries. In fact, the history of programming languages research is strewn with many proposals for new development languages, some general-purpose, some restricted to narrow application domains. A small minority ever see the light of day in "developerland". This doesn't stop the search from continuing however.

Model-driven architecture (MDA) is a recent technology that leads the pack in terms of more abstract specification and development tools (and use of new acronyms) aimed at the IT market. MDA is defined by the OMG[51] as "*an approach to IT system specification that separates the specification of functionality from the specification of the implementation*".

As the name suggests, an "application model" is the driving force behind MDA. A model in MDA is a formal specification of the function, structure and/or behaviour of an application or system. In the MDA approach, an IT system is first analysed and specified as a "Computation Independent Model" (CIM), also known as a domain model. The CIM fo-

---

[51] Object Management Group: www.omg.org

cuses on the environment and requirements of the system. The computational and implementation details of the system are hidden at this level of description, or are yet to be determined.

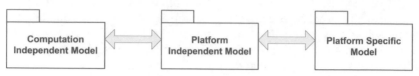

Fig. 73. Model transformation in MDA

As Fig. 73 shows, the CIM is transformed into a "Platform Independent Model" (PIM) which contains computational information for the application, but no information specific to the underlying platform technology that will be used to eventually implement the PIM. Finally, a PIM is transformed into a "Platform Specific Model" (PSM), which includes detailed descriptions and elements specific to the targeted implementation platform.

A "'platform" in MDA is defined as any set of subsystems and technologies that provide a coherent set of functionalities through interfaces and specified usage patterns. An MDA platform is therefore a very broad concept. Platforms often refer to technology specific sets of subsystems which are defined by a standard, such as CORBA or J2EE. Platforms can also refer to a vendor specific platform which is an implementation of a standard, like BEA's WebLogic J2EE platform, or a proprietary technology like the Microsoft .NET platform.

MDA is supported by a series of OMG standards, including the UML, MOF (Meta-Object Facility), XMI (XML Metadata Interchange), and CWM (Common Warehouse Metamodel). MDA also includes guidelines and evolving supporting standards on model transformation and pervasive services. The standards in MDA collectively define how a system can be developed following a model driven approach and using MDA compatible tools. Each MDA standard has its unique role in the overall MDA picture.

In MDA, models need to be specified by a modelling language. This can range from generic modelling languages applicable to multiple domains (e.g. UML) to a domain specific modelling language. The MOF provides facilities to specify any modelling language using MOF's metamodeling facilities, as depicted in Fig. 74.

The MOF also provides mechanisms to determine how any model defined in a modelling language can be serialized into XML documents or be represented by programmable interfaces. Any existing modelling language can be made MDA compatible by creating a MOF representation of the language. There are many debates on MOF's expressiveness and complexity for specifying some languages. The OMG has recognized these limitations and is actively working to address them in future versions.

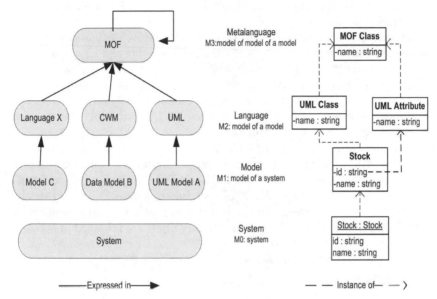

Fig. 74. The role of MOF in MDA

The UML and CWM are two relatively generic MOF-defined modelling languages and are included in the MDA standards package. UML focuses on object modelling and CWM focuses on data modelling.

The XMI standard in MDA is a mapping which can be used to define how an XML schema and related XML serialization facilities can be derived from a modelling language metamodel specified using the MOF. For example, the OMG has applied XMI to the UML metamodel to come up with an XML schema for representing UML models. Consequently, the XML schema for UML models can be used by UML modelling tool vendors to interchange UML models.

So, from business domain models, to analysis models, to design models and finally code models, MDA principles cover every phase of the software development process, artefacts and tooling. In the next sections, we will discuss the overall benefits of MDA and give some examples.

11.3 Why MDA?

Models play the central role in MDA. But why exactly do we need models? Here's the answer.

Models provide abstractions of a system that allow various stakeholders to reason about the system from different viewpoints and abstraction levels. Models can be used in many ways, for example, to predict the qualities (e.g. performance) of a system, validate designs against requirements, and to communicate system characteristics to business analysts, architects and software engineers. And importantly in the MDA world, they can be used as the blueprint for system implementation.

The three primary goals of MDA are portability, interoperability and reusability, achieved through architectural separation of concerns. Critical design issues concerning the CIM, PIM and PSM are very different in nature and can evolve independently of each other. Multiple CIMs, PIMs and PSMs can exist for one application, reflecting different refinement levels and viewpoints. Let's see how these primary goals are achieved in MDA.

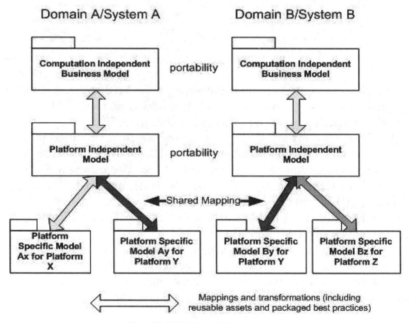

Fig. 75. MDA model mappings

11.3.1 Portability

Portability is achieved by model separation and transformation. High level models do not contain low level platform and technical details. As Fig. 75 illustrates, when the underlying platforms change or evolve, the upper level models can be transformed to a new platform directly, without any remodelling.

Portability is also achieved by making models moveable across different tool environments. The MOF and XMI standards allow a UML model to be serialized into XML documents that can be imported into a new tool for different modelling and analysis purposes.

11.3.2 Interoperability

There is rarely an application which does not communicate with other applications. Enterprise level applications particularly need to communicate across internal and external organizational boundaries in a heterogenous and distributed manner. Most of the time, you have limited control over the other systems you need to interoperate with.

Using MDA, interoperability is achieved through horizontal model mapping and interaction (see Fig. 76). Early versions of MDA guidelines refer to integration as the single biggest goal for MDA, which aims to improve interoperability in two ways:

- The interoperability problem can be seen as a problem of horizontal model mapping and interaction. For simplification, let's suppose we have two sets of CIM/PIM/PSM for the two systems, as shown in Fig. 76. The interaction between higher level CIMs and PSMs can be first modelled and analysed. These cross model mappings and interactions then can be mapped to detailed communication protocols or shared databases supported by the underlying models. Since explicit vertical transformations exist between models in each system, the elements involved in the high level mapping can be easily traced or even automatically translated into lower level elements.
- The same problem can also be seen as a problem of refining a single high level model into multiple models operating across two or more platforms. Different parts of the higher level models are refined into models specific to different platforms. Associations in the original models are refined into communication channels or shared databases between platform specific models.

With unified metamodeling facilities and explicit model transformation tools, these two approaches become feasible in practice.

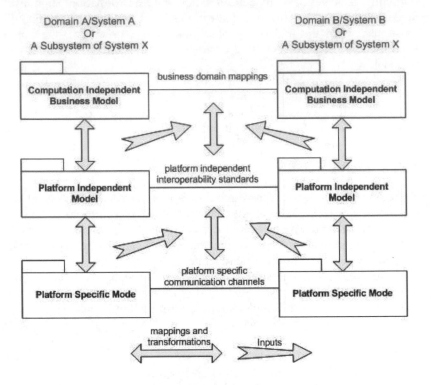

Fig. 76. Horizontal model mapping for interoperability

11.3.3 Reusability

Reusability is the key to improving productivity and quality. MDA encourages reuse of models and best practices in designing applications, especially in creating families of applications as in software product lines (see Chap. 9). MDA supports software product line approaches with increasing levels of automation. For example, the PIM is intended for reuse by mapping to different PSMs that a product line supports, and an MDA platform is designed for reuse as a target for multiple applications in a product line.

11.4 State-of-Art Practices and Tools

Although it is possible to practice parts of the MDA without tool support, this is only recommended for the brave and dedicated. A large portion of the standards is aimed at tooling and tool interoperation. Some standards are meant to be mainly machine readable, and not for general human consumption.

Since MDA standards, especially the guidelines, are intentionally suggestive and non-prescriptive, there has been a plethora of tools claming to support MDA, all with very different features and capabilities. Some loosely defined parts of MDA have caused problems in terms of tool interoperability and development artefact reusability. However, the correct balance between prescriptive and non-prescriptive standards is hard to determine *a priori* and requires real world inputs from industry users.

We'll now discuss some promising tool examples from the J2EE/Java platform community because of its relatively wide adoption of MDA. The .NET platform is also moving towards model driven approaches through its own Domain Specific Language (DSL) standard. This is not compatible with MDA although third party vendors have successfully developed MDA tools for .NET Platform.

Although the tools discussed in the following have their roots in J2EE/Java technologies, all here have the capability to support other platforms. The architecture and infrastructure services of these tools all allow extensions and "cartridges" to be built to support other platforms. Some of them simply have out of the box support for J2EE related technologies.

11.4.1 AndroMDA

AndroMDA is an open source MDA framework. It has a plug-in architecture in which platforms and supporting components can be swapped in and out at any time. It heavily exploits existing open source projects for both platform specific purposes (e.g. XDoclet for EJB) and general infrastructure services (Apache Velocity for transformation templating).

In AndroMDA, developers can extend the existing modelling language through facilities known as "metafacades". The extension is reflected as a UML profile in modelling libraries and templates in transformation tools. AndroMDA's current focus is to generate as much code as possible from a marked PIM using UML tagged values, without having an explicit PSM file (it exists only in memory). Hence it does not provide opportunities for PSM inspection and bi-directional manipulation between PSM and PIM.

The reason for this is mainly because of the trade off between the complexity of bi-directional PIM/PSM traceability and the benefits of maintaining explicit PSMs for different platforms. At the UML stereotype level, this approach usually works well because only general platform independent semantics are involved, but for code generation, markings through tagged values usually includes platform dependent information which pollutes PIMs to a certain degree.

11.4.2 ArcStyler

Arcstyler is one of the leading commercial tools in the MDA market. It supports the J2EE, and .NET platforms out of the box. In additional to UML profiles, ArcStyler uses its own MDA "marks" as a way to introduce platform dependent information in PIMs without polluting the model with platform level details. Like AndroMDA, ArcStyler supports extensible cartridges for code generation. The cartridges themselves can also be developed within the ArcStyler environment following MDA principles. The tool also supports model to model transformation through external explicit transformation rule files.

11.4.3 Eclipse Modelling Framework (EMF)

The inseparable link between MDA models and the code created through code generation requires consistent management of models and code in a single IDE. EMF is the sophisticated metamodeling and modelling framework behind the Eclipse IDE. Although EMF was only released publicly as an Eclipse sub-project in 2003, it has a long heritage as a model driven metadata management engine in IBM's Visual Age IDE.

EMF is largely MDA compatible with only minor deviations from some of the standards. For example, the base of EMF's metamodelling language is known as Ecore, which is close but not identical to the Essential MOF (EMOF) in MOF 2.0. EMF can usually load an EMOF constructed metamodel, and mappings and transformations have been developed between EMOF and Ecore.

EMF comes with standard mechanisms for building metamodels and persisting them as programmable interfaces, code and XML (see Fig. 77). A model editor framework and code generation framework are also provided. However, EMF does not include any popular platform support out of the box, and it didn't initially impress the MDA community as a full fledged ready-to-use MDA tool for platform-based distributed systems.

However, EMF's tight integration with the Eclipse IDE and the capability of leveraging the Eclipse architecture and common infrastructures supports the integration of disparate metadata across multiple tools cooperating in a common Eclipse-based ecosystem. This raises the level of tool interoperability while being largely compatible with MDA practices.

This is also an example that demonstrates that model driven principles and standards go beyond the modelling of the system, and include modelling of all aspects of system construction. With little fanfare, IBM has migrated many of its development tools to Eclipse and manages their metadata via EMF. Third party vendors are also actively developing EMF based tools.

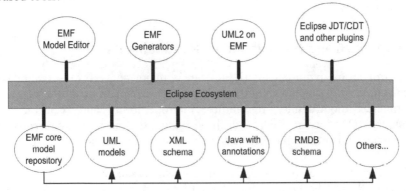

Fig. 77. The Eclipse Modeling Framework

Due to the ongoing standardization of model transformation and the significant production gains from code generation, most existing tools focus on code generation from models. The support for model to model transformation is usually lacking. This results in primitive support for bi-directional CIM-PIM-PSM transformation. Overall though, the MDA market is maturing with both industry strength commercial and open source tools emerging.

11.5 MDA and Software Architecture

Most of models in MDA are essentially representations of a software architecture. In a broad sense, domain models and system models are abstractions and different viewpoints of software architecture models. Generated code models possess the characteristics of the architecture models along with implementation details. The code can in fact be used in reverse engineering tools to reconstruct the application architecture.

A software architecture can be described in an architecture description language (ADL). There have been many ADLs developed in recent years, each with their expressiveness focused on different aspects of software systems and application domains. Many useful ADL features have recently been either absorbed into revisions of the UML, or specified as lightweight (through UML profiles) or heavyweight (MOF) UML extensions. Hence, the UML is used in MDA as an ADL.

Some exotic formalisms and dynamic characteristics of certain ADLs still can not be fully expressed using UML. But the growing MDA/UML expertise pool in industry along with high quality architecture and UML modelling tools outweighs the downside of some modelling limitations in most domains.

11.5.1 MDA and Non-Functional Requirements

Non-functional requirements (NFRs) are a major concern of software architecture. NFRs include requirements related to quality attributes like performance, modifiability, reusability, interoperability and security. Although MDA does not address each individual quality attribute directly, it promotes and helps achieving these quality attributes because:

- A certain degree of interoperability, reusability and portability is built into all models through the inherent separation of concerns. We have explained how these benefits are achieved in previous sections.
- The MOF and UML profile mechanisms allow UML to be extended for modelling requirements and design elements specifically targeting NFRs. UML profiles for expressing NFRs exist, such as the OMG's profile for performance, scheduling and time .
- Along with NFR modelling extensions for requirements and design, explicit model mapping rules encourage addressing quality attributes during model transformation.

11.5.2 Model Transformation and Software Architecture

A large part of software architecture R&D concerns how to design and validate software architectures that fulfil their requirements and are implemented faithfully to the design. One major obstacle in architecture design is the difficulty of designing an architecture that clearly captures how the various aspects of the design satisfy the requirements. For this reason, it can be difficult to systematically validate whether the architecture models fulfil the requirements, as traceability between requirements and design elements is not formalized. This does not help to increase confidence that the architecture is fit for purpose.

In MDA, all modelling languages are well defined by syntax and semantics in a metamodel. The process of transforming from one model (e.g. requirements) to another model (e.g. design) is a systematic process, following explicitly defined transformation rules. This explicitness and potential automation could greatly improve the quality and efficiency of validating an architecture model.

However, at the time of writing, the transformation process is still suggestive from the general MDA guidelines. A model "Query, View and Transformation" (QVT) standard is under development and many proposals have been submitted for public review, with some of these implemented in tool environments. With the adoption of this standard in the near future, it is possible that much of the tacit knowledge, best practices and design patterns used in architecture design and evaluation will be formally codified as various forms of bi-directional transformation rules. These will create rich forms of traceability in architecture models. In fact, transformations based on patterns and best practices have already been implemented in some tools in addition to normal platform specific mappings between PIMs and PSMs.

11.5.3 SOA and MDA

A strong industry direction currently is service-oriented architectures (SOA). In SOA, enterprise solutions are viewed as federations of services which communicate using intra-service communication protocols. While the communication protocols have been undergoing standardization and evolved to support both heterogenous platform communications (e.g. XML based SOAP) and pervasive services (WS-* standards), these standards do not address questions of semantic mappings and interactions between the multiple SOA based systems.

Both MDA and SOA try to solve the same interoperability problem but from a totally different perspective and level of abstraction. One is from the general semantic modelling perspective; the other is from the communication protocols and architecture style perspective. Following MDA, it is possible to consistently map high level semantic interactions and mappings between the two systems into lower level model elements and communication channels with necessary supporting services.

MDA can also increase productivity when the functions of a system need to be exposed as Web services, one of the most common requirements in SOAs. If the existing system is already modeled following MDA rules, exposing its services is just a matter of applying transformation rules for the Web services platform. For example, in AndroMDA, the "webservice" cartridge provides WSDL and WSDD file generation using a simple UML profile. To expose the same business logic as Web services, users only need to change the business process PIM (the ultimate goal is to have no change) and use the "webservice" cartridge.

In summary, SOA bridges heterogenous systems through communication protocols, pervasive services and an associated service-oriented architecture style. MDA can take care of the seamless high level semantic integration between systems and transforming the system models into lower level SOA based facilities. This synergy between MDA and SOA might mean that the next generation service oriented computing world with a highly federated and flexible architecture is not too far away.

SOA and Web Services are described in the next chapter.

11.5.4 Analytical Models are Models too

The importance of using analytical models to examine characteristics of a system is often ignored, even in the official MDA guidelines. However, the benefits of having analytical models that are also compatible with MDA are potentially huge.

According to the MDA definition, a model is defined as a description of a system in a well-defined language. This definition can be applied to a wide range of models. For example, in performance engineering, we can choose to view a system as a queue-based model which has servers and queues. In modifiability analysis, we can choose to view a system as a dependency graph model which has nodes to represent conceptual or implementation elements and edges to represent dependency relationships among them.

Currently, these models are usually expressed in their own modelling languages. In order to build an analytical model for an existing UML model, either we have to do the modelling manually or a low level transformation must be carried out based on the UML model represented in XML. This is shown in Fig. 78, and has several limitations:

- The transformation relies solely on primitive XML transformation facilities such as XSLT. Debugging and maintenance is difficult with no clear semantic mapping between the two models.
- Without a clear semantic mapping and round trip engineering facilities, it is very hard to place the results gained from the analytical model back into the original UML model context.

- The original design model will likely be further refined and eventually implemented in code. The analytical model is essentially also a derived model from the same design model. But as the analytical model is not compatible with the MDA standard, it is even harder to cross-reference the analytical model with all the other derived models for validation, calibration and other purposes.

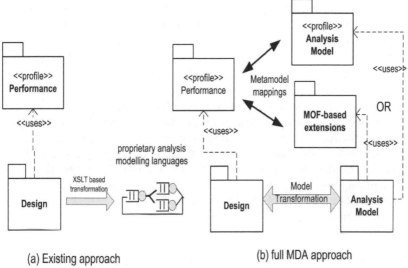

(a) Existing approach   (b) full MDA approach

Fig. 78. MDA model transformation for model analysis

11.6 MDA for ICDE Capacity Planning

In order to conduct capacity planning for ICDE installations, the ICDE team needed a test suite that could be quickly tailored to define a site-specific test load. It should then be simple and quick to execute the test suite on the intended deployment environment, and gather the performance statistics such as throughput and response time.

After a close look at their performance testing requirements, the ICDE team found that their needs for rapid development across different J2EE platforms were amenable to applying MDA principles, leveraging its support for portability, interoperability and reusability. The reasons are as follows:

- For different J2EE application servers, only the platform related plumbing code and deployment details differ. Using MDA, a generic application model could be used, and platform specific code and plumbing generated from the model. This leverages the portability inherent in MDA.
- The generation of repetitive plumbing code and deployment configuration is supported for many J2EE application servers code by a number of open source MDA projects. These code generation cartridges are usually maintained by a large active user community, and are of high quality. Thus the ability to reuse these cartridges in MDA tools was very attractive.
- The ICDE team has extensive experience in performance and load testing. By refactoring their existing libraries into a reusable framework, much of this can be easily reused across J2EE platforms. However, each site-specific test will require custom code to be created to capture client requirements. Using MDA, these site-specific features can be represented using UML stereotypes and tagged values, as a combination of modelling details and configuration information. From this design description, the MDA code generation cartridge can produce the site-specific features and hook these in with the team's reusable framework components.

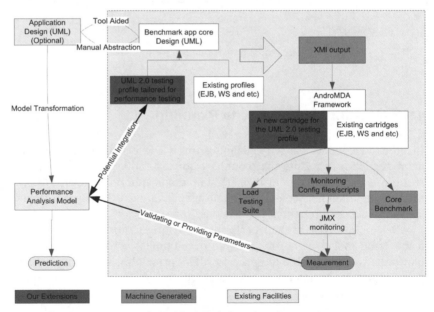

Fig. 79. Overview of ICDE's MDA-based performance test generator

So, the ICDE team designed a UML profile and a tool to automate the generation of complete ICDE performance test suites from a design description. The input is a UML-based set of design diagrams for the benchmark application, along with a load testing client modeled in a performance tailored version of the UML 2.0 Testing Profile.[52] The output is a deployable complete benchmark suite including monitoring/profiling/reporting utilities. Executing the generated benchmark application produces performance data in analysis friendly formats, along with automatically generated performance graphs. The tool is built on top of an open source extensible framework – AndroMDA. The overall structure of the benchmark generation and related process workflow is presented in the boxed area in Fig. 79.

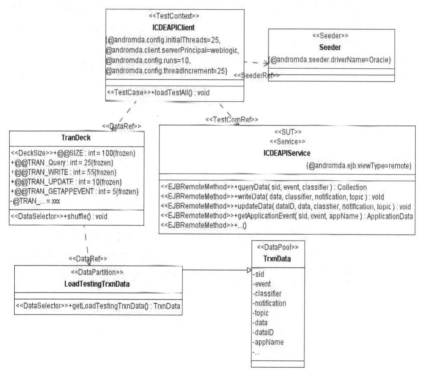

Fig. 80. ICDE performance test model

A snippet of the model is represented in Fig. 80. The load testing entry point is the *ICDEAPIService*. It is the front end component of the system

---

under test, which is marked with the <<SUT>> stereotype. *ICDEAPIClient* is the <<TestContext>> which consists of a number of test cases. Only the default *loadTestAll()* test case is included with its default generated implementation.

All the test data to be used for calling ICDE APIs is modeled in the *TrxnData* class. The *TranDeck* class contains values that configure the transaction mix for a test using tagged values, shown in Fig. 80. For example, calls to the ICDE API *queryData* represents 25% of all transactions and *writeData* represents 55% for the test defined in this model. This data is used to randomly generate the test data which simulates the real work load of the ICDE installation under test.

In Fig. 81, example test outputs are depicted for the response time distribution for two different application servers under a workload of 150 concurrent clients.

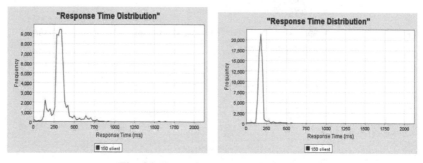

Fig. 81. Example response time results

The amount of time saved using MDA can be considerable. Community-maintained technology cartridges automatically generate repetitive and error prone plumbing code, and the best practices inherited through using the cartridges improve the quality of the performance testing software. Above all, MDA principles raise the abstraction level of the test suite development, making it easy and cheap to modify and extend.

For more information on this work, please refer to the MDABench reference at the end of the chapter.

11.7 Summary and Further Reading

MDA, as the industry wide standardization of model driven software development, is proving successful and is continuing to evolve. MDA impacts on software architecture practices, as it requires the architecture team to create formal models of their application using rigorously defined modeling languages and supporting tools. This essentially represents raising the level of abstraction for architecture models. The software industry has been raising abstraction levels in software development (e.g. from machine code to assembly language to 3GLs to object-oriented languages and now to models) for the best part of five decades. MDA is the latest step in this direction, and if it achieves it goals the industry could attain new levels of development productivity only dreamt of today.

Still, MDA draws criticism from many sides concerning its limitations, some of which are arguably intrinsic and hard to improve without a major revision. Microsoft has chosen not to comply with MDA standards and follow its own path, defining and using its own DSL as the modelling language in its Visual Studio IDE. While this may splinter the development community and create incompatible models and tools, both the OMG's and Microsoft's promotion of general model-driven development principles is likely to have positive outcomes for the software community in the years to come.

The best reference for all MDA-related information is the OMG's web site:

OMG, *MDA Guide Version 1.0.1.* 2003. http://www.omg.org/mda/

Two good books on MDA from prominent authors are:

S. J. Mellor, S. Kendall, A. Uhl, D. Weise. *MDA Distilled.* Addison-Wesley, 2004.
A. Kleppe, J. Warmer, W. Bast. *MDA Explained: The Model Driven Architecture--Practice and Promise.* Addison-Wesley, 2003.

For some further details on the MDA-based performance and capacity planning tools, see:

L. Zhu, J. Liu, I. Gorton, N. B. Bui. *Customized Benchmark Generation Using MDA.* in Proceedings of the 5th Working IEEE /IFIP Conference on Software Architecture, Pittsburgh, November 2005.

12 Service-Oriented Architectures and Technologies

Paul Greenfield

12.1 Service-Oriented Architecture for ICDE

The initial release of the ICDE platform offered a Java based API that let third party tool vendors access the data in the ICDE data store. This was a good approach for most third parties, but it still had two important limitations:

1. The tools had to be written in Java (or use some nasty language bridging approach to call Java from another language)
2. Requests to EJB methods are not generally allowed to pass through organizational firewalls and this meant that the ICDE API was only accessible to tools running in the same administrative domain as the ICDE platform deployment. Unfortunately, this was inconvenient for a collection of powerful analytical tools that needed to run on dedicated cluster machines and remotely access an ICDE deployment over the Internet.

The development team wished to remove both of these restrictions in order to make it easier to integrate tools into ICDE deployments. Some approach was needed that would allow tools to be written in a wider range of programming languages such as C++ and C#, and these tools needed a way to securely access the ICDE API across the Internet from a remote site, as shown in Fig. 82.

Fortunately for the ICDE team, an architectural approach and supporting technologies had been evolving over the last five years which satisfied both these requirements. Web services technologies support inter-application communication over the Internet using XML documents and the SOAP protocol. Web services also support a design approach known as service-oriented architecture, in which applications communicate via exchanging SOAP messages in a loosely coupled fashion.

This chapter delves into the intricacies of Web services and service-oriented architectures. It describes why service-oriented architectures are desirable, and how the various Web services technologies make building secure, reliable service-based applications a reality.

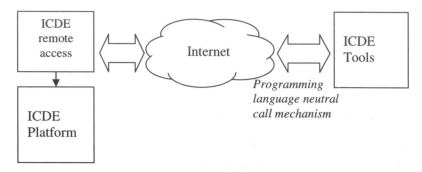

Fig. 82. Remote, language-neutral access to the ICDE platform

12.2 Background

Service-oriented architectures and Web services are the latest step in the development of application integration middleware. They attempt to fix the interoperability problems of the past and provide a foundation for future Internet-scale distributed applications. They also mark the end of the "middleware wars" with all major vendors finally agreeing on a single rich set of technology standards for application integration and distributed computing.

Application integration middleware is used for many purposes, from linking together local components to create simple desktop or Web server applications, to building global supply chains that span the Internet. Traditional technologies in this space, such as J2EE application servers and messaging, can be excellent solutions for building applications from components or integrating applications running within the same organization. However, they fall well short of what is needed to link together business processes run by independent organizations that are connected over the global Internet. Web services and service-oriented architectures are designed to meet just this need.

In many ways, service-oriented computing and Web services are nothing new. Like earlier distributed computing technologies and architectures, their main purpose is to let applications invoke functionality provided by other applications, just as J2EE middleware lets Java client applications call methods provided by J2EE components.

The real difference here is that the focus of the services-based model and its supporting technologies is on interoperability and solving the practical problems that arise because of differences in platforms and programming languages. Although it is possible to design and build "service-oriented systems" using any distributed computing or integration middleware, only Web services technologies can meet the critical requirement for seamless interoperability that is such an important part of the service-oriented vision.

This emphasis on pragmatic interoperability is a result of accepting the diverse nature of today's enterprises, and realizing that this diversity is not going to diminish in the future. Almost all organizations today support a mix of platforms, programming languages and software packages, including business-critical legacy applications. Any integration middleware proposal that assumes the wholesale rewriting of applications or the migration of already working applications to new platforms will fail at the first hurdle as the costs and risks will be too high.

The reality is that large-scale enterprise applications are increasingly being woven together from applications, packages and components that were never designed to work together and may even run on incompatible platforms. This gives rise to a critical need for interoperability, one that becomes even more important as organizations start building a new generation of wide-area integrated applications that directly incorporate functions hosted by business partners and specialist service providers.

Web services and service-oriented architectures are the computing industry's response to this need for interoperable integration technologies.

12.3 Service-Oriented Systems

The shift to service-oriented systems is being driven by the need to integrate both applications and the business systems they support. Most existing integration technologies are closed or proprietary and only support the integration of applications built on the same technology, unless organizations are willing to bear the cost of buying or writing complex, special purpose adapter code. These restrictions may just be acceptable within a single organization, although, even then, the chances of every application and every computer system being compatible are pretty slight in reality.

There has been a need for business system integration ever since there have been business systems. This integration has traditionally been handled through the exchange of paper documents such as quotes, invoices and orders. These traditional documents are still used today, but now they are almost always produced by computerized systems. The task of integrating these business systems has changed little though and is still commonly done by sending these paper documents by post or fax, and then re-keying their data once they arrive.

The cost savings and efficiencies that come from getting rid of paper and directly integrating computer-based business systems have been obvious (and attractive) for many years, but have proved difficult to attain for just about as long. EDI (Electronic Data Interchange) was one major previous attempt to realize these potential benefits. In many ways it was before its time and so proved too costly for all but the largest organizations because of the closed and private nature of EDI networks and the high cost of proprietary EDI software.

The advent of the Internet and Web services has totally changed this picture. The Internet now potentially connects every computer system in one global network, letting businesses send documents electronically to their partners and customers anywhere in the world, quickly and at low cost. Web services addresses the other part of the problem by providing a single set of application integration standards that are implemented by every major vendor and are shipped as an integral part of all server platforms. The result of these developments is that business-level integration may soon be relatively easy, inexpensive and commonplace.

Web services are really just another application integration technology, conceptually little different to CORBA, J2EE, DCOM or any of their competitors. All of these technologies are much alike: client applications can discover servers, find out what services they are offering and invoke the functions they provide. What is different about service-oriented systems and their supporting Web services technologies is that these applications and servers are now expected to potentially be controlled and run by outside organizations and accessed over the public Internet. The result of this shift in focus is a set of standards and architectural principles that emphasize interoperability by making the fewest possible assumptions about how service providers and consumers work internally and what implementation details they have in common.

Fig. 83 shows a typical next-generation retail application. Customers see a single seamless application that lets them place orders for books and music and make payments. In reality this application consists of just a small core of business logic provided by the retailer augmented by services provided by business partners, and all running on a diverse mix of platforms and middleware. Customers can access this application using the Web or they can run friendlier and smarter client applications that make calls directly into the back-end services provided by the retailer's core application. These same services can also be used to support out-sourced order fulfillment services provided to specialized retailers, letting them own and operate their own on-line shop fronts and rely on the retailer for services such as handling orders and accepting payments.

This application could be built using any of the middleware technologies discussed in previous chapters. The architect of any such system would however face difficult and complex issues ensuring interoperability and robustness. These are precisely the areas addressed by service-oriented architectures and Web services technologies.

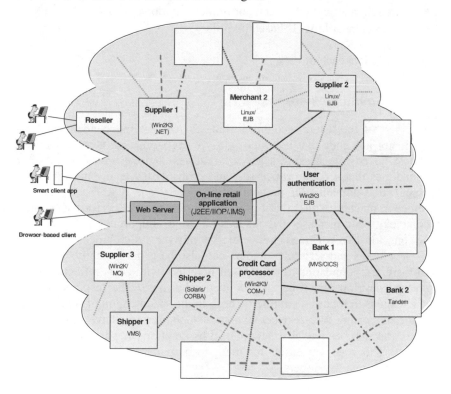

Fig. 83. Example service-based retail application

The fundamental principles underlying service-oriented architectures are not new and largely just reflect years of experience in building large-scale integrated systems that actually worked and were maintainable. Some of the principles, such as reducing the impacts of network latency by doing as much work as possible on every service call, are already common practice in high performance distributed systems. Others, such as consciously minimizing the richness of the Web services infrastructure, result from an understanding of the costs of complexity and the importance of simplicity in achieving robust interoperability.

The basic principles underlying service-oriented architectures are often expressed as four tenets:

- Boundaries are explicit.
- Services are autonomous
- Share schemas and contracts, not implementations
- Service compatibility is based on policy

Let's look at each of these.

12.3.1 Boundaries are Explicit

The first of the tenets recognizes that services are independent applications, not just code that is bound into your program that can be called at almost no cost. Accessing a service requires, at least, crossing over the boundaries that separate processes, and probably traversing networks and doing cross-domain user authentication. Every one of these boundaries (process, machine, trust) that has to be crossed reduces performance, adds complexity and increases the chances of failure. Importantly, they have to be consciously recognized and handled within the design process.

Developers and service providers can also be geographically separated, so there are boundaries to be crossed here too, with costs reflected in increased development time and reduced robustness. The response to this challenge is to focus on simplicity, both in the specification of services and in the supporting Web services standards. Good services have simple interfaces and share as few abstractions and assumptions as possible with their clients. This makes it easier for them to be understood and successfully used by remote developers.

12.3.2 Services are Autonomous

Services are autonomous independent applications, not classes or components that are tightly bound into client applications. Services are meant to be deployed onto a network, quite possibly the Internet, where they can be easily integrated into any application that finds them useful. Services need know nothing about client applications, and may accept incoming service requests from anywhere, just as long as the request messages are correctly formatted and meet specified security requirements.

Services can be deployed and managed entirely independently of other services and any possible client applications, and the owners of these services can change their definitions, implementations or requirements at any time. Version compatibility is a long-standing problem with all distributed systems and technologies, and is made worse by the open nature of services. How do you evolve a service when you have a large (possibly unknown) number of clients that depend on it?

For example, a bank running a server component that is only called by an internal teller application can know the identity and location of all client systems, so updating the service together with all of its callers is at least technically feasible. But the credit card processor who can accept authorization requests from any merchant over the Internet has no way of either knowing how to locate its clients (past, current or potential) nor of getting them to upgrade their varied calling applications to match new service definitions.

Part of the answer to this problem lies in the deliberate simplicity and extensibility of the services model. All that clients know about a service is what messages that it will accept and return, and this is the only dependency that exists between a client and a service. Owners of services can change the implementation of a service at will, just as long as currently valid messages are still accepted. They can also extend and evolve their service request and response messages, just as long as they remain backwardly compatible. Our credit card processor could totally change how their service is implemented, perhaps moving from CICS/COBOL to a C#/.NET platform, and this change will be invisible to all of their callers as long as no incompatible changes are made to the "authorize payment" message.

As services are autonomous, they are also responsible for their own security and have to protect themselves against possibly malicious callers. Systems deployed entirely on a single system or on a closed network may be able to largely ignore security or simply rely on firewalls or secure network pipes, such as SSL. However, services accessible over the open Internet have to take security much more seriously.

12.3.3 Share Schemas and Contracts, not Implementations

Years of experience has shown that building robust and reliable large-scale integrated systems is difficult. Trying to build these systems from components built using different programming models and running on different platforms is much harder still. Service-oriented technologies address this problem by deliberately aiming for simplicity as much as possible. Services aren't remote objects with inheritance, methods and complex run-time behavior, nor are they components that support events, properties and stateful method calls. Services are just applications that receive and send messages. Clients and services share nothing other than the definitions of these messages, and certainly don't share method code or complex run-time environments.

All that an application needs to know about a service is its contract: the structure (schema) of the messages it will accept and return, and whether they have to be sent in any particular order. Client applications can use such a contract to build request messages to send to a service, and services can use their schemas to validate incoming messages and make sure they are correctly formatted.

12.3.4 Service Compatibility is Based on Policy

Clients have to be completely compatible with the services they want to use. Compatibility means not simply that clients are following the specified message formats and exchange patterns, but also that they comply with other important requirements, such as whether messages should be encrypted or need to be tracked to ensure that none have been lost in transit. In the service-oriented model, these non-functional requirements are defined using policies, and not just written down as part of a service's documentation.

For example, our credit card processor may decide that all merchants submitting payment authorization requests must prove their identity using X.509-based authentication tokens. This security constraint can be represented simply as a statement in the published security policy for the authorization service.

Policies are collections of machine-readable statements that let a service define its requirements for things like security and reliability. These policies can be included as part of a service's contract, allowing it to completely specify a service's behavior and expectations, or they can be kept in separate policy stores and fetched dynamically at run-time.

Contract-based policies can be regarded as just a part of a service's documentation, but they can also be used by development tools to automatically generate compatible code for both clients and services. For example, a server-side security policy can be used to generate code that will check that required parts of an incoming message are encrypted and then decrypt this data, presenting it as plain text to the service application. All this is done without any coding effort from the developer.

The separation of policies from contracts also lets client applications dynamically adapt to meet the requirements of a particular service provider. This will become increasingly useful as services become standardized and offered by competing providers. For example, our on-line retailer may use two shippers that offer exactly the same services and use the same message schemas but have different authentication requirements. The use of dynamic policies lets our developers write a single application that supports both authentication methods and dynamically selects which one to use by fetching the target service's policy before constructing and sending any delivery requests.

12.4 Web Services

Web services are a set of integration technology standards that were designed specifically to meet the requirements arising from service-oriented architectures and systems. In many ways, Web services are really not much different to existing middleware technologies, but they do differ in their focus on simplicity and interoperability. The most important feature offered by Web services is that all major software vendors have agreed to support them. Interoperability is still not, of course, guaranteed to be painless but at least the problems encountered will be bugs and misinterpretations of common standards, not intentionally introduced incompatibilities between similar but different proprietary technologies.

All application integration technologies, including Web services and their alternatives such as COM+, J2EE and CORBA, really only provide four basic functions that let developers (and programs) do the following:

- Find suitable services (using UDDI or another directory)
- Find out about a service (using WSDL)
- Ask a service to do something (using SOAP)
- Make use of services such as security (using WS-* standards)

SOAP, WSDL and UDDI were the first Web services standards to be published but they only meet the most basic requirements for application integration. They lack support for security, transactions, reliability and many other important functions. This gap is being progressively filled by a series of standards (commonly called "WS-*") first outlined by IBM and Microsoft at a W3C workshop in 2001. The task of writing these additional standards and getting industry-wide agreement is now largely complete with production-ready implementations available for many of them. This formal standards process should be largely complete by the end of 2006, with full support from all major vendors following shortly afterwards.

Web services are XML standards. Services are defined using XML, applications request services by sending XML messages and the Web services standards make extensive use of other existing XML standards wherever possible. At the time of writing there are over thirty Web services standards and these can be organized into the categories shown in Fig. 84. This number of standards may suggest complexity rather than the desired simplicity. Overall though, the standards are as simple as possible, given that they need to support secure, robust and interoperable applications. There is also increasingly good tool and library/framework support for these standards, so developers only have to understand the capabilities offered rather than the detailed XML syntax.

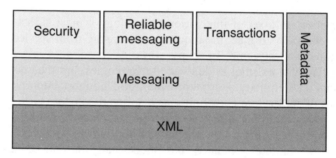

Fig. 84. Overview of Web services standards

One of the simplifying principles underlying all the Web services standards is that the various message fields and attributes used to support functions such as security and reliability are totally independent of each other. Applications only need to include just those few fields and attributes needed for their specific purposes, and can ignore all the other standards. For example, a SOAP request might identify the requestor of a service by including a username and password in the form specified in the WS-Security *UsernameToken* profile. This user/password related information is the only security-related header element included in the message. WS-Security supports other forms of user authentication, as well as encryption and digital signatures, but as these are not used by the service, they do not appear at all in the SOAP message request.

Another aim of the Web services standards is to provide good support for system architectures that make use of "intermediaries". Rather than assuming that clients always send requests directly to service providers, the intermediary model assumes that these messages can (transparently) pass along a chain of other applications on their way to their final destination. These intermediaries can do anything with the messages they receive, including routing them, logging, checking security or even adding or subtracting bits of the message's content. This model is shown in Fig. 85, where intermediaries are providing routing and auditing services.

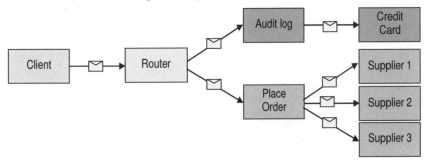

Fig. 85. Simple intermediary sequence

The Web services standards provide support for intermediary-based architectures in a number of ways. These include tagging header elements with the role of their intended recipient and supporting the "end-to-end" principle for functions such as security, so ensuring that they continue to work even if messages pass through intermediaries rather than traveling directly from client to service. For example, in the application shown in Fig. 85, the client can use mechanisms provided by WS-Security to protect sensitive information intended only for the credit card application, hiding it from the router that the message must pass through on its journey.

12.5 SOAP and Messaging

SOAP was the original Web services standard, and is still the most important and most widely used. It specifies a simple but extensible XML-based application-to-application communication protocol, roughly equivalent to DCE's RPC or Java's RMI, but much less complex and far easier to implement as a result. SOAP is simple enough for a programmer to be able to write their own implementation, making it possible to hand-write wrappers for legacy applications and technologies.

This simplicity comes from deliberately staying well away from complex problems, such as distributed garbage collection and passing objects by reference. All that the SOAP standard does is define a simple but extensible message-oriented protocol for invoking remote services, using HTTP, SMTP, UDP or other protocols as the transport layer and XML for formatting data.

SOAP messages have the simple structure shown in Fig. 86. The header holds information about the message payload, possibly including elements such as security tokens and transaction contexts. The body holds the actual message content being passed between applications. The SOAP standard does not mandate what can go in a message header, giving SOAP its extensibility as new standards, such as WS-Security, can be specified just by defining new header elements, and without requiring changes to the SOAP standard itself.

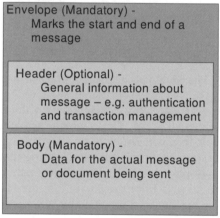

Fig. 86. SOAP message structure

SOAP originally stood for Simple Object Access Protocol but it is now officially no longer an acronym, just a word, and certainly nothing to do with accessing remote objects! SOAP really is simple though, although the use of XML can make it look anything but simple, especially when security header elements are included. SOAP clients just send XML request messages to service providers over any transport and can get XML response messages back in return. A SOAP message asking for a stock quotation is shown in Fig. 87. This corresponding to the WSDL definition is shown in Fig. 88. The request carries a username and hashed password in the header to let the service know who is making the request.

```
<?xml version-"1.0" encoding="utf-8" ?>
<soap:Envelopexmlns:soap=
    "http://www.w3.org/2003/05/soap-envelope"
xmlns:xsi="http://www.w3.org/2001/XMLSchema-instance"
xmlns:xsd="http://www.w3.org/2001/XMLSchema"
xmlns:wsa="http://schemas.xmlsoap.org/ws/2004/03/addressing"
xmlns:wsse="http://docs.oasis-open.org/wss/2004/01/oasis-
    200401-wss-wssecurity-secext-1.0.xsd"
xmlns:wsu="http://docs.oasis-open.org/wss/2004/01/oasis
    -200401-wss-wssecurity-utility-1.0.xsd">

<soap:Header>
<wsa:Action>
    http://myCompany.com/getLastTradePrice</wsa:Action>
    <wsa:MessageID>uuid:4ec3a973-a86d-4fc9-bbc4-ade31d0370dc
    </wsa:MessageID>
    <wsse:Security soap:mustUnderstand="1"
        <wsse:UsernameToken>
            <wsse:Username>NNK</wsse:Username>
            <wsse:PasswordType="http://docs.oasis-
            open.org/wss/2004/01/oasis-200401-wss-username
                -token-profile-1.0#PasswordDigest">
            weYI3nXd8LjMNVksCKFV8t3rgHh3Rw==
            </wsse:Password>
            <wsse:Nonce>WScqanjCEAC4mQoRF07sAQ==</wsse:Nonce>
            <wsu:Created>2003-07-16T01:24:32Z</wsu:Created>
        </wsse:UsernameToken>
    </wsse:Security>
</soap:Header>
<soap:Body>
    <m:GetLastTradePrice
    xmlns:m="http://myCompany.com/stockServices">
        <symbol>DIS</symbol>
    </m:GetLastTradePrice>
</soap:Body>
</soap:Envelope>
```

Fig. 87. SOAP message sample

There are a number of other standards included in the Web services Messaging category, including WS-Addressing and WS-Eventing. WS-Addressing exists because Web services really have little to do with the Web, and do not depend solely on HTTP as a transport layer. SOAP messages can be sent over any transport protocol, including TCP/IP, UDP, email (SMTP) and message queues, and WS-Addressing provides transport-neutral mechanisms to address services and identify messages. WS-Eventing provides support for the publish-subscribe model by defining the format of the subscription request messages that clients send to publishers.

Published messages that meet the provided filtering expression are sent to callers using normal SOAP messages.

12.6 UDDI, WSDL and Metadata

There is a strong theme of metadata and policy running through the Web services standards. SOAP services are normally described using WSDL (Web Services Description Language) and can be located by searching a UDDI (Universal Description, Discovery and Integration) directory. Services can describe their requirements for things like security and reliability using policy statements, defined using the WS-Policy framework and specialized policy standards such as WS-SecurityPolicy. These policies can be attached to a WSDL service definition or kept in separate policy stores and retrieved using WS-MetadataExchange.

UDDI has proven to be the least used so far of the original three Web services standards. UDDI is either the least interesting or potentially most interesting of these standards, depending on how important you think being able to dynamically discover and link to services is to your application. People are developing large complex Web services systems today without the use of global UDDI directories, using other methods of finding services such as personal contact or published lists of services on Web sites. This could all change in the future, especially when industry associations start releasing common service definitions and need to publish directories of qualified service providers.

WSDL is used to describe Web services, including their interfaces, methods and parameters. The WSDL description of a service called *StockQuoteService* that provides a single operation named *GetLastTradePrice* is depicted in Fig. 88. This operation takes one parameter *symbol* of type *string* that names the stock of interest and returns a *float* that holds the most recently traded price.

WSDL is well supported by development environments such as Visual Studio and WebSphere. These tools can generate WSDL automatically from program method and interface definitions, and they take in WSDL service definitions and make it easy for developers to write code that calls these services. One adverse side effect of this tool support is that it tends to encourage developers to think of services as remote methods, rather than moving to the preferable and richer message-based model provided by Web services.

```xml
<?xml version="1.0"?>
<definitions name="StockQuote"
    targetNamespace="http://myCompany.com/stockquote.wsdl"
    xmlns:tns="http://myCompany.com/stockquote.wsdl"
    xmlns:soap="http://schemas.xmlsoap.org/wsdl/soap/"
    xmlns:xsd="http://www.w3.org/2001/XMLSchema"
    xmlns="http://schemas.xmlsoap.org/wsdl/">

    <message name="GetLastTradePrice">
        <part name="body" type="xsd:string"/>
    </message>
    <message name="LastTradePrice">
        <part name="body" type="xsd:float "/>
    </message>

    <portType name="StockQuotePortType">
        <operation name="GetLastTradePrice">
            <input message="tns:GetLastTradePrice"/>
            <output message="tns:LastTradePrice"/>
        </operation>
    </portType>

    <binding name="StockQuoteBinding"
            type="tns:StockQuotePortType">
        <soap:binding style="document"
           transport="http://schemas.xmlsoap.org/soap/http"/>
        <operation name="GetLastTradePrice">
            <soap:operation soapAction=
                "http://myCompany.com/GetLastTradePrice"/>
            <input>
                <soap:body use="literal"/>
            </input>
            <output>
                <soap:body use="literal"/>
            </output>
        </operation>
    </binding>

<service name="StockQuoteService">
  <documentation>Stock quote service</documentation>
  <port name="StockQuotePort"
     binding="tns:StockQuoteBinding">
     <soap:address location=
        "http://myCompany.com/stockServices"/>
  </port>
</service>
</definitions>
```

Fig. 88. WSDL for the *GetLastTradePrice* service

12.7 Security, Transactions and Reliability

One of the problems faced by most middleware protocols is that they do not work well on the open Internet because of the connectivity barriers imposed by firewalls. Most organizations do not want outsiders to have access to the protocols and technologies they use internally for application integration, and so block the necessary TCP/IP ports at their perimeter firewalls.

The common technology response to this problem, and the one adopted by Web services, has been to co-opt the Web protocol, HTTP, as a transport layer because of its ability to pass through most firewalls. This use of HTTP is convenient but also creates potential security problems as HTTP traffic is no longer just innocuously fetching Web pages. Instead it may be making direct calls on internal applications.

WS-Security and its associated standards address these problems by providing strong cryptographic mechanisms to identify callers (authentication), protect content from eavesdroppers (encryption) and ensure information integrity (digital signatures). These standards are designed to be extensible, letting them be adapted easily to new security technologies and algorithms, and also supporting integration with legacy security technologies.

WS-Security supports intermediary-based application architectures by allowing multiple security header elements, each labeled with the role of their intended recipient along the processing chain, and by supporting partial encryption and partial signatures. As an illustration, in the example shown in Fig. 85, the sensitive credit card details can be hidden by encrypting them, while leaving the rest of the message unencrypted so that it can be read by the routing application.

The final set of Web services standards will also support transactions and reliable messaging. There are two types of transaction support defined in the IBM/Microsoft roadmap and these are currently supported by draft standards. WS-AtomicTransactions supports conventional distributed ACID transactions and assumes levels of trust and fast response times that make this standard suitable only for internal application integration tasks, and unusable for Internet-scale application integration purposes. WS-BusinessActivity is a framework and a set of protocol elements for coordinating the termination of loosely-coupled integrated applications. It provides some support for atomicity by invoking compensators when a distributed application finishes in failure. Its time will eventually come, but much more tool and framework development is needed before it can become generally useful in applications.

The support for reliable messaging in Web services simply ensures that all messages sent between two applications actually arrive at their destination in the order they were sent. WS-ReliableMessaging does not guarantee delivery in the case of failure, unlike queued messaging middleware using persistent queues. However, it is still a useful standard as it provides at most once, in-order message delivery over any transport layer, even unreliable ones such as UDP or SMTP.

12.8 Web Services and the Future of Middleware

Web services do not mean the end of current middleware products and technologies, although some existing technologies will be replaced for all but legacy applications, and the use of other technologies will shrink back to those applications where their strengths bring significant value.

Web services have two natural application domains:

1. Large-scale services-based applications where interoperability, security and robustness are critically important.
2. Small-scale application integration tasks within organizations where Web services are used because they are good enough, available and well understood.

Web services have no strong competitors in the first of these domains. There are some closed and proprietary offerings being used today, but these will quickly be replaced by standards-based alternatives that offer better interoperability and reduced complexity.

The second domain sees Web services competing directly with alternative protocols such as Java's RMI and CORBA's IIOP. These alternative protocols are richer, as they support remote objects rather than simple services, but Web services has the advantage of being a standard which is supported on all platforms and development environments. This makes it an acceptable lowest-common-denominator even for internal application integration. Why go with a more complex and less open integration protocol when you can easily use Web services from your current application platform and tools, and pick up the ability to do cross-platform integration at no extra cost? It's a compelling story for many organizations if they don't actually need the richer capabilities provide by these non-standard alternatives.

12.9 ICDE with Web Services

The ICDE team identified Web services as a potential remedy to their interoperability and remote access problems.

The interoperability problem stemmed from the fact that the ICDE API effectively demanded that potential third–party tool developers write their analysis applications in Java. This edict didn't help persuade non-Java developers of the benefits of building tools for the ICDE platform, particularly if they had existing non-Java analysis applications. What was needed was a remote service invocation mechanism that would work with any language. This is exactly what the Web services standards gave us.

Java supports the core Web services standards, SOAP and WSDL, so all that had to be done was change the ICDE *API Services* code to export the *QueryAPI* and *WriteAPI* interfaces as the equivalent Web services operations.[53] This can be done automatically by contemporary Java development tools. The third-party developers can now use whatever language and platform they choose to develop their ICDE client tools while sending standard Web services requests to the ICDE API.

There also needed to be a Web services mechanism to notify clients when new events were published. There are actually two questions here: how do clients subscribe to events of interest, and how do they get notified when these events occur. The first of these will eventually be handled by event brokers based on the WS-Eventing standard (or its successors), and the second can be solved by simply using normal SOAP messaging.

For now though, as WS-Eventing is still a long way from being a stable standard, subscription requests were passed as normal SOAP messages to a proxy running inside the ICDE *API Services* code. This proxy subscribes to the JMS server on behalf of its clients. It then receives published events and sends them back to ICDE clients as SOAP messages. The current ICDE *API Client* already performed similar functions on behalf of its Java

---

[53] There's much debate about whether automatically exposing calls to components like EJBs over Web services is a good idea. Java and .NET development tools make this a trivial exercise, so it's very enticing for developers. Put simply, the basic argument against this practice is that most of the time a component's methods are not service-based and hence not suitable for calling over a SOAP messaging infrastructure. This is most certainly true for components with, for example getter and setter methods and which maintain application state. It is however possible to design service-based interfaces and implement these with an EJB or a .NET component. Exposing these over SOAP is not evil in the slightest. In fact it's rather a good idea, and it's one that the ICDE application exploits.

clients, and this solution just replicated this functionality inside the server as well. The resultant architecture can be seen in Fig. 89.

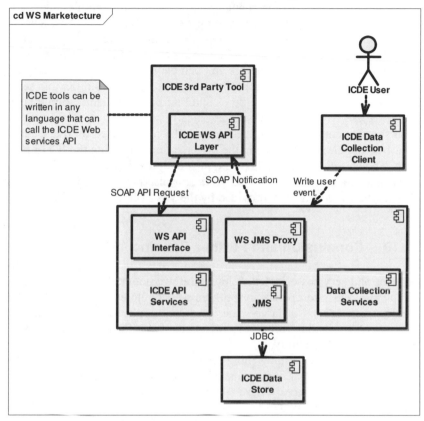

Fig. 89. ICDE API architecture using web services

The second problem the ICDE team needed to solve was to allow remote access to the ICDE platform from Internet-based clients. Our solution had to ensure that requests coming from the Internet were not blocked by firewalls. As we are now accepting requests over an open network, we also had to be sure of the identity of the client systems and protect any sensitive information while it was in transit.

Web services address the accessibility problem caused by firewalls by using the "firewall-friendly" HTTP protocol as its default transport mechanism. Firewalls tend to be configured to allow HTTP traffic through, so our Web services-based ICDE calls can get from clients over the Internet to ICDE servers without being blocked, and without needing special configuration changes to the network and its firewalls.

The ICDE system used usernames and passwords to identify callers and sent all information without protecting it from eavesdroppers. This level of protection is adequate for local access over a trusted network, but something much stronger was going to be needed to accept if we were going to send requests and responses across an open network. Web services address this authentication issue by supporting a range of proven and flexible security technologies, including Kerberos and PKI-based authentication tokens. Both of these solutions are cryptographically strong. This makes either a good security solution, and the choice can be made based on the security infrastructure already in place in the organization deploying the ICDE platform. The chosen security tokens are then included in the ICDE SOAP requests and responses. Sensitive ICDE data is also protected in transit using the encryption mechanisms provided by the WS Security standards.

12.10   Conclusion and Further Reading

Services and services-oriented architectures are pragmatic responses to the complexity and interoperability problems encountered by the builders of previous generations of large-scale integrated applications. Web services are a set of integration technology standards that reflect this need for simplicity and interoperability.

The "really" transforming thing about Web services is that there is (or will be) only one set of common standards that everyone uses when offering or accessing services. These standards are being supported by the entire computing industry and available on every application platform at low cost. The pervasive nature of Web services means that they will become the common and expected technology to use for application integration, certainly for cross-platform large-scale applications and, in many cases, for local integration tasks as well. This ubiquity means that they will take over from existing middleware technologies and protocols for some tasks, and will happily co-exist with them in many other cases.

Service-oriented architectures and Web services are hot topics in today's IT industry. All major software vendors are publishing tutorials and articles on services and how they are supported by their products. There are quite a few good books out there and any number of magazine articles as well. Good starting places are Microsoft's MSDN, IBM's Developer-Works and Sun's developer Web sites, at the following locations:

msdn.microsoft.com
www.ibm.com/developerworks
developers.sun.com/

You'll also find more information on Web services and SOA using Google than you care to imagine. Or just go to your own software vendor and look at what they have to say about how they are supporting services.

Some excellent text books are also emerging. The following are three examples I'd recommend:

O. Zimmermann, M. R Tomlinson, S. Peuser, Perspectives on Web Services Applying SOAP, WSDL and UDDI to Real-World Projects. Springer-Verlag 2004

G. Alonso, F. Casati, H. Kuno, V. Machiraju, *Web Services Concepts, Architectures and Applications*. Springer-Verlag 2004

S. Chatterjee, J. Webber, *Developing Enterprise Web Services: An Architect's Guide*. Prentice-Hall, 2004

13 The Semantic Web

Judi McCuaig

13.1 ICDE and the Semantic Web

In the ICDE application, the platform provides a notification facility allowing third party tools to exchange data. As an example use case for this facility, suppose that an ICDE user is working with a third party tool to analyze the financial transaction records from several organizations. The tool
performs a complex analysis on the transaction records to produce a list of
keywords in various finance-related categories and stores this list in the
ICDE data store. This ICDE user has also authorized other tools to utilize
her ICDE data as input to their own additional analysis. One of these tools
reads the stored keyword list and uses it to perform a search for new, un-
seen information related to the user's financial transaction analysis.

This scenario is only possible if the cooperating tools have the capacity
to effectively share data. This includes a consensus understanding of the
semantics of the data items being shared. Commonly, this consensus is
achieved by creating a data structure that is coupled to each application
sharing the data. The data structure defines the format of the shared data
(e.g. list, table) and the semantics of the data in the data structure (e.g.
document name, document title, document location, document topic, etc).

One way to accomplish a shared understanding with ICDE is to define a
published table structure in the ICDE data store and require the collaborating applications to use the table to share data. However, a fixed table structure is not a flexible solution. The ICDE development team could never
anticipate suitable data structures for every third party tool and every application domain in which ICDE would operate. New tables could be
added of course, but if each third party tool vendor had to negotiate with
the ICDE team to get a suitable data structure defined, agile tool integration would be absolutely impossible.

A more flexible approach would allow any third party tool supplier to
publish data via the ICDE data store using any structure they desired. Sub-

sequently, any other authorized tool should be able to dynamically discover the structure of the data, and understand its content. No prior, hard-coded knowledge of data structures should be needed.

An obvious starting point for this more flexible solution is to use self-describing data structures for formatting all published data. XML documents would suffice in this respect, as any program can dynamically parse an XML document and navigate the data structure. However, raw XML doesn't support "semantic discovery". For example, one third party tool might use the XML tag <location> to indicate the location of some information, whereas another may use <URI>, and another <pathname>. The semantics of these tag names tell a human reader that they all furnish the same information, but there is no way to make that conclusion programmatically using only XML. Forcing all tools to use the same strict tag vocabulary is hardly more flexible than forcing them all to use the same data structure.

What is required is a mechanism to share the semantics of the chosen vocabulary, allowing programmatic discovery of terms that describe similar concepts. Using such a mechanism, a tool can determine that <URI> and <location> are actually the same concept, even when the relationship is not explicitly defined in the software or the published data.

The solution to this problem lies in the set of technologies associated with the Semantic Web. The Semantic Web makes it possible to describe data in ways that make its semantics explicit and hence discoverable automatically in software. One of the key innovations lies in the use of ontologies, which describe the relevant concepts in a domain, and the collection of relationships between those concepts.

This chapter introduces the basic technologies of the Semantic Web. It then shows how domain ontologies can be used in the ICDE platform to support ease of integration for third party tool vendors.

13.2 Adaptive, Automated, and Distributed

The difficulties associated with software integration have plagued software engineers since the early days of the computing industry. Initial efforts at integration (ignoring for now the problems of hardware and storage interoperability) centered on making data accessible to multiple applications, typically through some sort of database management system.

More recently efforts have been made to create interoperable processes using components using technologies like CORBA or J2EE. As explained in the previous chapter, services oriented architectures and Web services technologies are the latest technologies to give software designers the opportunity to create software systems by gluing together services, potentially from a variety of providers, to create a specialized software system designed for a particular business problem.

Of course, there are immense difficulties associated with locating, integrating and maintaining a system composed of autonomous services and components. Some of the major challenges center on the creation, management and utilization of appropriate metadata to facilitate dynamic interaction with the available information, services, and components. It is precisely these problems that the Semantic Web, or rather the technologies that underpin the Semantic Web, is tackling. It provides tools and approaches to metadata management that are generically useful for dynamically integrating software applications.

13.3 The Semantic Web

The purpose of the Semantic Web initiative is to create machine understandable information where the semantics are explicit and usable by algorithms and computer programs. This original goal has expanded to include the goal of creating services, or processes, that are machine understandable and useable by other processes. This shared understanding, whether it be of data or services, is made possible by a rich collection of metadata description and manipulation languages and protocols. For the most part, the Semantic Web exists because of these languages.

The goal of the Semantic Web has been made possible through:

- the formalization of metadata representation
- continued development in knowledge representation
- logic and reasoning techniques that can exploit both the metadata and the represented knowledge.

The key capabilities offered are flexible representation of metadata and relationships, encoded as ontologies, which allow translation between metadata vocabularies and reasoning about the represented metadata entities.

13.3.1 Metadata

The advanced integration capabilities associated with the Semantic Web comes almost entirely on the back of extensive efforts in creating and maintaining metadata. The introduction of the Extensible Markup Language (XML) and the technologies related to it provided a structured, flexible mechanism for describing data that is easily understood by machines (and humans who like angled brackets!).

XML provides the means to label entities and their parts, but provides only weak capabilities for describing the relationships between two entities. For example, consider the XML fragment in Fig. 90. The XML shown describes a *Person* in terms of *Name, Email_Address* and *Phone_Number*, and a *Transaction* in terms of *Type, Client* and *AccountNumber*. The example also shows the use of attributes to create unique identifiers (*id*) for each entity.

```
<example>
    <Person id="123">
        <Name>J Doe</Name>
        <Email_Address>doe@myplace</Email>
        <Phone_Number>123 456 7899</Phone_Number>
    </Person>
    <Transaction transID="567">
        <Downtick>500</Downtick>
        <Client>Josef Doe</Client>
        <AccountNumber>333222111</AccountNumber>
    </Transaction>
</example>
```

Fig. 90. XML example

However, XML is not enough to easily identify relationships between different pieces of information. For example, using only the XML tag metadata, the identification of the email address of the person who conducted a specific transaction is somewhat complex. It relies on the ability to determine that the *Client* field of the transaction represents the name of a person, and that if the *Client* field data matches the *Name* field of a person a relationship can be identified and the person's email address used.

A human can quickly make that determination because a human understands that the tags *Client* and *Name* both signify information about people. A software process unfortunately has no such capability because it does not have any way of representing those semantics.

To address this problem, the Resource Description Framework (RDF) was developed as a machine understandable representation of relationships between entities. It is assumed that each entity and relationship can be identified with a URI. These URIs are used to form an RDF statement of the form {Subject, Predicate, Object}, commonly called a "triple".

Continuing with the previous example, the addition of an RDF relationship *conducted_by* (see RDF example below) between the transaction and the person (using the *id* attributes as the unique identifier) allows a machine to extract the email address of the transaction owner, without requiring replication of information. The RDF statement below indicates that the person referenced by id # 123 conducted the transaction referenced by id # 567.

```
<http://example.net/transaction/id567><http://example.net/con
ducted_by><http://different.example.net/person/id123>
```

The relationship is explicit and easily exploited by automated means once a human identifies and records the relationship. Still, there is still no mechanism that allows automated identification of the relationships or that provides any restrictions on the participants in those relationships. For instance, it is relatively easy for a human to understand that a transaction could be conducted by a person, but that a person cannot be conducted by a transaction! The RDF has no such restrictions however, so the algorithms processing the RDF have no way of verifying the types or expected attributes of the entities in the relationships.

A partial solution to this problem can be found in the schema languages for XML and RDF. The schema languages allow *a priori* definition of entities and relationships to include domains and ranges for attributes and objects. Entities (or relationships) that reference the schema for their definition can then be checked for consistency with the schema. This allows enforcement of range and data type restrictions during data processing without human intervention.

Together RDF, XML and their schema languages provide a robust, usable method for encoding metadata and exploiting it to automatically identify relationships between entities. However, this is only a starting point. Our kitbag of essential technologies for automated metadata understanding also needs the ability to make deductions and inferences about metadata.

Consider again the transaction and client example. The completion of a transaction is usually the result of collaboration between several individuals, including a client, financial consultant and clerk for instance. It would be trivial to modify the XML metadata example given earlier to represent both the consultant and clerk as part of the transaction's metadata, thus explicitly representing the relationship between the transaction and the collaborating individuals.

However, the collaboration between any particular pair of those three entities (consultant, client, clerk) is not explicitly represented in that metadata. So for example, a program that identifies both the client and consultant for a transaction has no mechanism for determining whether specific clients and consultants are known to one another. One way to remedy this problem is to simply add more metadata and explicitly identify the client-consultant relationship, but that solution quickly leads to an explosion in the quantity of metadata. A more general solution is to define logical rules that delineate the possible deductions with the different types of metadata. Those logical rules define the semantics associated with the metadata and are frequently described with the aid of a formal ontology. Ontologies are explained in the next section.

Well defined and ordered metadata is the backbone of the Semantic Web. Metadata is used to dynamically assemble data from a variety of sources, for making informed decisions, and to provide data for planning such things as, for example, vacations and the shipping of goods. While metadata technologies are most frequently used with Web-based information at the moment, they can be used with equal power to identify connections between software services for the purposes of creating any software system.

13.3.2 Semantics

The one feature that distinguishes the Semantic Web from the better understood World Wide Web is the representation and utilization of meaning, or semantics. One common representation for semantics is an ontology. An ontology consists of a set of ideas or concepts and the collection of relationships between those concepts.

An ontology can be used to identify ideas that are related to one another and to provide the structure for a reasoning engine to make inferences about those ideas. An ontology generally models abstraction relationships and frequently models aggregation relationships. More complex ontologies also model domain specific relationships about individuals and classes in the ontology. Ontologies can also provide information about concepts that are equivalent to other concepts, giving them the capacity to act as thesauri. As a result, an ontology can also be used to provide the mapping between different vocabularies used to describe metadata.

For example, consider the ontology fragments represented in Fig. 91. The ontology shows that *Humans* and *Persons* have *Occupations* and that certain kinds of *Occupations* have relationships with other concepts in the ontology. Both *Students* and *Instructors* are concerned with *Courses* and both *Authors* and *Publishers* are concerned with *Publications*. This ontology could be used by an automated system to identify related entities or identify the use of equivalent concepts (such as *Human* and *Person* in this example). The ontology provides logical axioms to a reasoning system which can then make inferences about the information.

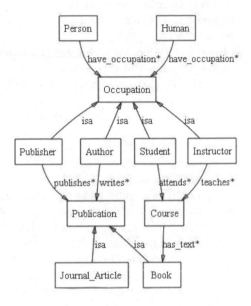

Fig. 91. Ontology example

Within the Semantic Web, the Web Ontology Language (OWL) is a common representation of the axioms and domain concepts.

Consider again the example of the financial transaction. An ontology could provide the logic to automatically identify a relationship between a client and a financial consultant, even when the relationship is not explicitly stated in the available metadata. A reasoning system could deduce that a client and consultant are known to one another if they have collaborated on some specified number of transactions. An additional rule could state that if they have collaborated on more than one type of transaction, they are well known to each other.

With these additions, a knowledge base that consists of information about financial transactions and clients can also be used to identify relationships between humans. Information about client-consultant relationships could be useful to someone analyzing financial transactions for the purpose of identifying sets or groups of people conducting specific classes of transactions (i.e. transactions occurring in a particular time period).

An ontology can also contain rules that constrain relationships. Suppose that the example ontology contains a rule that precludes the same individual from being both client and clerk for a transaction. Using the rule and a reasoning system, the ontology could be used to detect errors in information or to prevent errors in data entry. Ontologies, or similar knowledge representation mechanisms, provide meaning for the metadata that is the backbone of the semantic web.

XML, RDF and OWL are the basic technologies supporting the Semantic Web. One of the first, and most developed, Semantic Web driven information portals, somewhat predictably, supplies information about the Semantic Web (www.mindswap.org). This site uses RDF, OWL and reasoning engines to provide flexible access to a wealth of information about the Semantic Web.

Usage of Semantic Web technologies has increased dramatically in the last two years, to the point where many Semantic Web applications are no longer simple prototypes. For example, NESSTAR[54] is a Semantic Web based application for publishing, protecting and authenticating statistical data. The software enjoys huge success, claiming clients such as Statistics Canada and the Norwegian Institute of Public Health. The software provides Web-based mechanisms for creating tables, subsets and reports using Semantic Web based ontologies and client-provided statistical data. A second example of Semantic Web enabled software is Corese[55], a search engine that uses a domain ontology to support queries across RDF metadata, and that is used in several prototype applications across industry and government in Europe.

13.4 Ontologies in ICDE

The ICDE system could employ ontologies to support information exchange and integration tasks for the third party tools. As hinted in the introduction to this chapter, one application of an ontology to the task of financial transaction analysis is to identify consistent vocabularies. Shown in Fig. 92 is a portion of a financial ontology from Teknowlege.[56] The ontology fragment shows several different kinds of financial transactions arranged in an abstraction hierarchy.

Suppose that this ontology is available in the ICDE system, and an ICDE user was inspecting and analyzing the example data presented in Fig. 90, in which *Downtick* is the XML tag for the transaction ID. The use of *Downtick* as a label in that example could easily prevent other third

---

[54] http://www.nesstar.com/
[55] http://www-sop.inria.fr/acacia/soft/corese/
[56] http://ontology.teknowledge.com/

party ICDE tools from making use of the information about the transaction, because the label may have no meaning to those tools. However, with the ontology and a reasoning engine it is straightforward to determine that *Downtick* is a type of *Financial Transaction* and that the information should be shared with any tools that are interested in data about financial transactions.

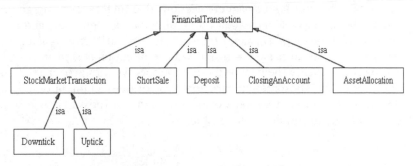

Fig. 92. A simple financial transaction ontology

Ontologies can provide more than just thesaurus services for ICDE tools. An OWL ontology can encode complex rules about the relationships between individuals of particular conceptual types. Reasoning engines can use the rules to make deductions about individual data elements.

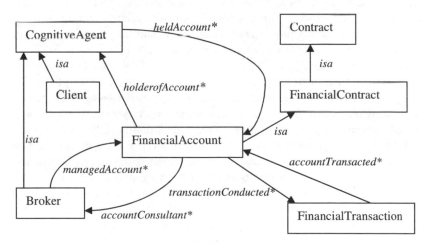

Fig. 93. Rules in an ontology

Consider the ontology fragment shown in Fig. 93. It shows that the ontology contains rules describing the relationships between accounts, account holders, transactions and brokers. A reasoning engine can use these relationships to deduce relationships between a particular client and a broker, or to deduce that a particular broker had a likely involvement with a specific transaction, even when the data being analyzed contained no specific linkage between the two entities.

This kind of shared ontology could allow collaborating third party ICDE tools to help the user notice data connections that might otherwise go unnoticed. For instance, suppose that one tool helped a user select and analyze particular types of financial transactions. Another tool assisted the user to identify social networks of individuals based on shared interest in accounts. Individually, neither of these two tools would uncover relationships between an advisor and a particular type of transaction, but the individual results from the two tools could be combined (possibly by a third tool) to uncover the implicit relationships.

13.5 Semantic Web Services

Web services and service oriented architectures were presented in the previous chapter as a significant step towards a simple solution for the interoperability problems that typically plague middleware applications. Web services also play a part in the Semantic Web. As Semantic Web applications increase in complexity, and as information consumers become more discerning, the focus is turning from semantically addressable information to semantically addressable services that allow automated creation of customized software system, or Semantic Web services.

Current tools provide the capability to describe Web services, but do not have adequate means for categorizing and utilizing those descriptions. The categorizations available, such as WSIndex, (www.wsindex.org) are designed primarily for human use rather than machine. As a result, automated system composition is more a dream than reality right now.

However, unlike most information on the Web, Web services are typically accompanied by adequate metadata, which is the key component of the Semantic Web. The difficulty in using that metadata lies in understanding the semantics. Predictably, there is a substantial amount of research focused on applying ontologies and other tools of the Semantic Web to Web services. Semantic Web services provide a mechanism for creating semantically rich descriptions of services. These can be used to create specifications for composite services, to represent business logic at a more abstract level and to supply knowledge for reasoning systems which can then intelligently assemble software from service descriptions. One of the underlying languages in the development of Semantic Web services is the Ontology Web Language for Services (OWL-S). OWL-S is an ontology language with the goal of enabling automated discovery, incorporation and execution of Web services.

OWL-S breaks the description of a service into three parts, a service profile, a process model and a mapping between the process model and the message passing protocol (called a grounding). The profile is used both to advertise services and to request services. The intention is that the profile is used in service discovery to match appropriate services to requests for services. Profiles consist, in part, of a description of both functional parameters, described as inputs, outputs, preconditions and effects, and non-functional parameters such text fields meant for human consumption or to define quality of service constraints.

The process model uses the OWL-S process ontology to describe the execution of a web service. The process model precisely describes the required flow of control and data to obtain the results specified in the profile and includes three types of processes, namely atomic, simple and composite. Only atomic processes may be executed directly. Finally the grounding provides the binding between the atomic processes and the message format selected. Currently OWL-S has a grounding ontology defined for WDSL that allows for describing the message requirements for atomic processes.

OWL-S is not a complete specification nor is it a stable standard. It is, however, a good start at defining how semantics can be added to Web services. It has been subjected to few real world test cases to date, but experiences with a prototypical use case implementation suggested that OWL-S may be a good start for enterprise integration, but that it currently lacks the capacity to allow fully automated discovery and composition of services. Nonetheless, it seems inevitable that OWL-S or some other similar work, such as the Internet Reasoning Service will result in an automated mechanism for finding and composing services.

13.6 Cautious Optimism

The Semantic Web has enjoyed immense popularity and publicity in the past few years. The effect has been that every researcher interested in anything that could possibly be applied to the Semantic Web has quickly adjusted their research descriptions to reflect that application. Unfortunately, with an increase in claims to be researching (or implementing) the Semantic Web comes a possible dilution of the projects that are actually working on addressing the original and important goals of semantically rich, machine understandable metadata for data and processes.

While many believe in the technologies, a certain wariness seems to prevail. This is possibly because the Semantic Web looks on the surface like a refactoring of the artificial intelligence projects that went out of vogue several years ago. However, it seems that the need for semantic representations in software systems is now widely recognized, and the demand for real solutions is growing. So this time, the timing might just be right.

The Semantic Web also has all the data management issues of any large information system. Who will take the time to provide all the detailed metadata about existing services and information? Who monitors information and services for integrity, authenticity and accuracy? How are privacy laws and concerns addressed when computing is composed from distributed services? Web services providers will spring up as a new category of business, but how will they be monitored and regulated? As systems are built that rely on quality metadata, its maintenance and upkeep become vital operational issues.

Despite the prototypical nature of most of the work so far, the Semantic Web places new techniques, new applications and important experiences in the toolbox of software architects. The Semantic Web is simply a loose conglomeration of cooperating tools and technologies, but precisely because of this loose coupling between technologies, the Semantic Web provides a flexible sandbox for testing new frameworks and ideas.

And, if one looks past the hype, the goals of the Semantic Web community are the same as the goals for distributed software architecture: to create loosely coupled, reliable, efficient software that addresses the needs of users. Through the formally defined mechanisms for reasoning with metadata, the Semantic Web provides the basis for creating software that is truly adaptive to tasks and context.

One of the prime targets for adaptive integration efforts is enterprise integration. The Enterprise Semantic Web is a term used to describe Semantic Web-driven business solutions. The distinguishing feature of the Enterprise Semantic Web is the focus on ontologies and inference as mechanisms for improving data integration, rather than on HTTP and Web services as mechanisms for distributed access. Network Inference (www.networkinference.com/) is a company that creates information management solutions and does enterprise integration based on Semantic Web technologies.

Software developers and researchers are responding quickly to the needs of semantic computing. A 2004 conference on service-oriented computing included plenary sessions on service security and quality of service in addition to more predictable sessions about service-oriented architectures and the design and implementations of services and composed applications. The Semantic Web services architecture identifies message mediation, security, process composition, negotiation and contracting, and message formulation as important aspects of the Semantic Web that warrant immediate exploration and development. Developments such as OWL-S and the Internet Reasoning Service show promise as process description and composition languages. The Semantic Web and software architecture are on paths that are rapidly converging on a new, semantically driven, way of building software.

13.7 Further Reading

Two general books on the Semantic Web are:

G. Antoniou, F. van Harmelen. *A Semantic Web Primer*. MIT Press, 2004
B. Passin. *Explorer's Guide to the Semantic Web*. Manning Publications, 2004

W3C's Web site is a source of great information on the Semantic Web. A good starting point for exploration is http://www.w3.org/2001/sw/.

Specific details of OWL can be found at http://www.w3.org/TR/owl-ref/.

A tool for building ontologies can be freely downloaded from http://protege.stanford.edu/plugins/owl/index.html. It's a good tool for exploring how ontologies can be built and accessed:

Information on OWL-S can be found at http://www.daml.org/services/owl-s/ and http://www.daml.org/services/owl-s/1.0/.

14 Software Agents: An Architectural Perspective

14.1 Agents in the ICDE Environment

During discussions with the third party tool vendors, the ICDE team noticed that the tool developers used the term "agents" pretty frequently. Nearly all the tool vendors claimed that their tools used these things called agents to do various types of really intelligent sounding analysis, collaboration and visualization.

Being from mainstream software engineering backgrounds, the ICDE team was a little puzzled as to what exactly was meant by agents. What differentiated an agent from some other kinds of components? Why were they useful? How does the ICDE application have to cater for integration with all these agent things? These questions were raised with the various tool vendors, but frequently the ICDE team left the meetings more confused than they were when they entered!

It soon became obvious that the team would have to do some investigations of its own to get a deeper understanding of agents and their related technologies. Hence they assigned two team members to do some research into the area. The aim was to be able to characterize exactly what was meant by the terms software agent. And more importantly, they wanted to understand the implications of integrating with agent-based tools for the ICDE design and implementation.

This chapter describes their findings.

14.2 What is an Agent?

The term software agent has gained considerable attention recently in the information technology community. So-called intelligent or autonomous agents are reportedly capable of many advanced forms of behavior. Advocates of agent technologies claim many and varied benefits from their use.

These include better ways to structure applications, improvements in programming language abstractions for complex integrated communications, and a natural metaphor for human-computer interaction.

Software agents and related technology have implications for software architects, as agents represent potential components in an architecture. Agents-based architectures are therefore something an architect might begin to consider as agent technologies continue to transition from the research labs to products.

Agent technologies have emerged from the field of distributed artificial intelligence research. The agents R&D community itself has many definitions of what exactly constitutes an agent system. Franklin[57] points out that many of these are broad and encompass a wide range of software systems, many of which were not conceived or designed as agent systems.

Below is an example of widely cited definitions of agents and their capabilities: [58]

- Agents are situated in some environment
- Agents are capable of flexible autonomous action in order to meet design objectives

The notion of flexibility is further expanded to incorporate:

- **Responsiveness:** agents perceive their environment and respond in a timely fashion to changes that occur in it.
- **Pro-active:** agents should exhibit opportunistic goal-driven behavior.
- **Social:** agents should be able to interact in order to complete their own problems and help others with their activities.

In addition, Michael Wooldridge[59] states that software agents are appropriate for applications in which:

- Data, control, expertise or resources are distributed
- Agents provide a natural metaphor for delivering system functionality

---

[57] S. Franklin, A. Graesser. *Is it an agent, or just a program?*. in Intelligent Agents III, LNAI vol 1193, pp 21-36, Springer-Verlag, Berlin 1997

[58] N. R. Jennings, K. Sycara, M. Wooldridge. *A roadmap of agent research and developmetnt* Autonomous Agents and Multi-Agent Systems, pp 275-306, Kluwer, 1998

[59] M. Wooldridge, N. Jennings. *Software engineering with agents: pitfalls and pratfalls*. IEEE Internet Computing. May/June 1999, pp20-27

- A number of legacy systems must be made to interwork

Taken as a whole, these definitions would seem to encompass a lot of the mainstream IT systems that exist today. Certainly, examining the above from a technical software engineering perspective reveals some interesting issues.

All of the points above describe broad classes of characteristics, or behaviors of agents and agent-based systems. They do not describe from a technological standpoint the competitive benefits of adopting an agent based solution, over, say an object-oriented or component-based technology. This is highly unusual for a software technology. An example will suffice to explain this point.

From a software engineering perspective, autonomy is somewhat difficult to pigeonhole. In agent terms, agents are often differentiated from "passive" objects. This seems to imply an active thread of control for each agent. Cooperative infers that threads representing agents communicate in some way, perhaps across address space boundaries. Reactive infers that threads representing agents receive messages or events from their environment or other agents and somehow process them in a manner that is consistent with their desired autonomous behavior. Pro-active infers some sampling of the environment, perhaps to ensure that environmental state does not become unstable.

Unfortunately, there are multitudes of systems in existence today that are multi-threaded, where threads communicate within and across process and object boundaries, and in which threads react autonomously and pro-actively to handle external stimuli. These systems range from embedded control systems, to graphical user interfaces, to database systems, operating systems and large-scale enterprise applications. Are all these applications agent-based systems? This would probably be news to many of their developers if this were so.

As concrete examples, consider the following. Are these agent-based systems?

- The flight control software of a commercial airliner, including the autopilot.
- Military applications, such as missile control.
- An anti-lock braking management system in an automobile.
- Telecommunications switching network software.
- An enterprise-scale personal information management system such as Lotus Notes or Microsoft Outlook.
- A commercial database management system such as Oracle or DB2

Consequently, a definition of agents-based applications in terms of their external or behavioral characteristics is highly problematic from an engineering perspective. Put simply, such a definition can be used to encompass a significant proportion of software systems that exist today, the vast majority of which are clearly not created using agent approaches and/or technologies.

These definitions also imply that an agent-based system can be identified by external observation of its behavior. Many sources exemplify this by describing agents "that monitor and react to human interactions with a graphical user interface (GUI)", or "crawl web pages looking for information". These descriptions easily capture personal information managers such as Microsoft Outlook, word processors, and Internet search engines like Google. Are these agent-based systems as well? From their external behavioral characteristics, it would appear so.

Let's contrast the above definition of agents with that of a now mature software technology. Object-oriented technology saw many heated debates over what exactly constituted an object-oriented system. As object-orientation grew from a programming language movement, many of these debates revolved around the characteristics that were necessary for a language to be classified as object-oriented. The advocates of pure object-oriented languages such as Smalltalk and Eiffel criticized so-called hybrid languages like C++, and code examples abound demonstrating why a particular language was in some way preferable to others.

Interestingly, never (to my knowledge anyway) were the external characteristics of an application used to define object-oriented systems. The issues revolved around the engineering benefits of object-orientation, such as data hiding, inheritance, polymorphism, improved maintenance and rapid application development. Engineers and management were not heard to request an object-oriented banking system, or an object-oriented GUI. Rather, they discussed a banking system or GUI built using object-oriented technology.

So, it seems that to some in our software world, an agent-based system is simply something that many of us have been building for decades using conventional programming technologies. And the term agent is simply something that the technically minded amongst us might call an active object, a thread or even a process. "Agent" is used here as a label to identify some component of system that has a particular role. Examples like a mail agent, monitoring agent, and transformation agent abound. From an architectural perspective, there's absolutely nothing new here. It's terminology, that's all.

But, there are new and potentially interesting technologies for building agent-based applications. However, with the current widely espoused definitions of agent-based systems, it is unclear what the technical and engineering advantages are of adopting an agent-based approach might be? The definitions are too broad, use anthropomorphism to imbue agents with capabilities that software simply doesn't possess, and have no solid technical basis on which the merits can be objectively assessed.

A deeper insight is obviously needed before the implications of agent technology can be discussed from an architectural and engineering perspective. So pick up a shovel and let's dig deeper.

14.3 Abstraction Revisited

The key role of abstraction is well known in the advancement of software engineering. Abstraction has been responsible for the evolution of programming languages through the adoption of more abstract mechanisms for code construction. Abstract mechanisms are introduced into languages to replace and enforce useful constructs that were only previously possible through hand-coding compositions of multiple basic operations.

Very simplistically, using better abstractions means you have to write less code, make less errors, and can therefore tackle more complex problems in the same time-scale. This pattern has been repeated many times in the software engineering, for example:

- COBOL, a high level language was introduced to provide an English-like abstraction for describing program operations that at the time were written in terms of assembly language operations.
- Object-oriented languages introduced programming constructs for data encapsulation in modules, type extension through inheritance, and polymorphic substitution mechanisms for sub-types. These supported improved structuring and organization of program modules over procedural techniques.
- Distributed technologies such as CORBA provide abstract mechanisms that greatly simplify the construction of type-safe inter-process communications, as compared to using raw network protocols or sockets.

Given this evolution pattern for software technology, it is hardly surprising that agent technologies basically introduce new abstraction mechanisms for application construction. Many technologies for constructing agent-based applications provide extensions to standard programming languages such as Java in order to facilitate new inter-agent communications mechanisms and directly implement agent management policies and semantics.

These new programming language abstractions are the concrete contribution of agent technology to software construction. It therefore becomes vitally important from an architectural perspective to understand the potential advantages of these abstractions, and how their use might make it easier, cheaper or in some way provide a "better" solution than existing conventional technologies.

14.4 An Example Agent Technology

The JACK[60] Intelligent Agents™ technology is a commercially available agent development and deployment system. JACK extends the basic Java language by adding new abstractions for building agent systems. JACK tools convert the Java language extensions into pure Java, and applications are deployed on a standard Java run-time environment. The JACK technology includes an agent language, compilation tools and a run-time engine known as the agent kernel.

The kernel is basically a set of Java classes that support JACK Agent Language programs. The classes are mostly hidden from the programmer, although some act as base classes for the JACK Agent Language extensions, and provide basic interfaces that the new JACK abstractions must support.

JACK software agents directly support an implementation of the BDI (Belief Desire Intention) theoretical model of agent intelligence. Each JACK agent has:

- a set of beliefs about the world (its encapsulated data);
- a set of events that it can respond to;
- a set of goals that it aims to achieve;
- a set of plans that describe how it will behave in response to the goals or events that may arise

The key abstractions in the JACK Agent Language, all of which are strictly typed, are:

- **Agent:** The agent abstraction is used to represent the behavior of an agent in JACK. This includes the capabilities an agent has, the message

---

[60] This description is based on v3.1 of the JACK technology.

types and events it handles and the plans it will execute to achieve its goals.

- **Plan:** Plans define an agent's behavior. They define the logic that the agent follows when it receives events and goals to process.
- **Event:** The event abstraction essentially represents a message that an agent can handle and process.
- **Database:** The database abstraction provides a generic relational database, which has been designed so that it can be queried using "logical members". Logical members follow the rules of logic programming (i.e. Prolog), whereby logical members have an unknown value until a value has been determined. Once determined, the value cannot change. Databases are hence also referred to as knowledge bases. Agents may have "private" databases to hold their beliefs, and "global" databases can be used to share read-only state across agents in the same process. In addition, "agent databases" are read-only and may be shared only by agents of the same type (analogous to class-specific data in object-oriented systems). Read-only databases may not be altered after they are initialized in a constructor call.
- **Capability** – The capability abstraction is a key reuse mechanism in JACK. It allows a set of functional components to be aggregated and packaged in a language entity. A capability consists of plans, events, databases and other capabilities that together serve to define a component of an agent's behavior.

When an agent is instantiated in a JACK system, it waits until it receives a goal to achieve or an event that it can handle. When either occurs, the agent selects a set of actions to pursue by examining its plans to find those that are relevant to the request. If a selected plan encounters problems in execution, the agent can select others that might apply and can continue to try out alternatives until a plan succeeds or all alternatives are exhausted.

If a new goal or event occurs for an agent while it is already executing a plan, the agent can multitask and handle multiple requests simultaneously. JACK agents are therefore multithreaded, with the JACK run-time engine handling the spawning and scheduling of threads implicitly. In fact, native Java threading should not be explicitly used in JACK applications.

Agents are represented by first class abstractions in JACK. The outline of an agent is given below, with the JACK-specific keywords in bold:

```
agent AgentType extends Agent
{
    // Knowledge bases used by the agent…
    #private database DbType db_name(arg_list);
```

```
    #private data DataType data_name(arg_list);
    // Events handled and sent by the agent...
    #handles event EventType;
    #posts event EventType reference;
    #sends event EventType reference;
    // Plans used by the agent...
    #uses plan PlanType;
    // Capabilities that the agent has...
    #has capability CapabilityType reference;
    // other Data Member and Method definitions
}
```

The JACK Agent Language provides the *Agent* base class. It implements the base methods that provide an agent's core functionality. Within an agent, both JACK-specific abstractions as well as normal Java code can be declared.

Agents use JACK databases to store their private beliefs (data), or get access to shared beliefs in agent or global databases. Each JACK database type defines a relation that has both unique (key) fields and value fields, and an associated query method. Private database relations are unique to an agent. The agent may query its private database relations using the database's query method, and modify the tuples in the relation using the *assert()* and *retract()* methods provided by the database base class. Agents may also store their beliefs in agent data members using the data declaration to create named Java objects. Like databases, agent data members can have private, agent or global scope.

JACK agents communicate by exchanging messages. Agents are obligated to specify which message types they can accept, and which they will send. The *#handles event* statement specifies a type of event that the agent can accept. If an agent is sent a message type that it cannot handle, a runtime warning message is generated and the event discarded. There are various *Event* classes defined in JACK that can be extended by the programmer to handle various circumstances.

The *#posts* and *#sends* event statements declare the event types an agent emits. When an agent posts an event, it is in effect sending the event to itself to process in one of its plans. When an agent sends an event using the *send()* operation, it essentially transfers a message to another agent to handle. The send operation specifies the unique name of the agent that is to receive the message. Send operations are one way. If the receiving agent wishes to provide a response, it must use a *reply()* operation in the processing of the message.

Events may also be sent to agents that reside in another JACK process, essentially another JVM. In this case the send operation must specify the process and host name that the target agent resides in. Denoting one JACK process as an agent name server supports inter-process communications.

JACK agents are basically idle until they receive an event to process. By default, an agent will process the events it receives one at a time. If an agent receives multiple simultaneous events, they are placed in a queue associated with the agent. When an agent completes processing one event (or it enters a blocking state), it moves on the next event in queue. Agents may also specify that they want to time-share their processing amongst multiple events. In this case the JACK run-time provides a round-robin task manager that accepts a programmer-defined time-slice for multi-tasking.

Plans define how agents handle events. An agent should specify that it uses one or more plans that are capable of handling the events it accepts. Each JACK plan is associated with a single event type as illustrated below in the skeleton plan code below:

```
plan PlanType extends Plan {
    #handles event EventType reference;

    static boolean relevant ( EventType reference)
    {...}
    context()
    {...}
    #posts event Event1 handle1;
    #sends event MessageEvent1 messagehandle1;
    #reads database Relation1 relation_name1;
    #modifies database Relation2 relation_name2;

    #reasoning method methodName ( parameters )
    {...}
    body()
    {
    // Main reasoning method that executes when an
    // agent runs an instance of this plan
    }
}
```

When an agent receives an event to process, it first determines which plans can handle the event. For each plan, a series of filters are applied that test whether a plan is suitable for handling the event. The *relevant()* method for a plan is the first such filter. This typically contains Java code that tests the parameter values associated with an event to see if they are suitable for processing by this plan. If not, the method returns false and the plan is discarded as a candidate for processing this event. If the *relevant()* method is not declared or returns true, the next plan filter, the *context()* method, is applied.

The *context()* method is designed to execute a logical expression to see if this plan is applicable to the current event. The logical expression is a JACK agent language statement that attempts to bind values from the agent's set of beliefs to logical members, in the style of unification in logic programming. For each possible value that matches the logical expression, an instance of the plan is generated and the agent runtime selects one for execution. When a selected plan is successfully completed, the agent is deemed to have processed the event. This execution mechanism supports agents that are designed to explore different approaches to respond to external stimuli.

Once a plan instance is selected, execution starts with the first statement in the plan's *body()* method. The *body()* method is known as a "reasoning method", and has additional semantics associated with its execution. Essentially each statement in the method is executed as a logical expression, which returns true or false. If any of the statements in the *body()* method returns false, then the plan execution is deemed to have failed and is immediately terminated.

Reasoning methods can also include some JACK agent language specific statements, which syntactically are differentiated by starting with an "@" character. These reasoning method statements provide abstractions over a set of common behaviors required to express agent behavior. Reasoning method statements fit into two broad categories:

- **Communications:** *@send*, *@post* and *@reply* statements enable the agent executing the plan to send events to other agents. The JACK runtime takes responsibility for message delivery, and ensuring for example that a *@reply* statement is called in an appropriate context.
- **Conditional Tests:** These statements allow an agent executing a plan to test some logical condition and react accordingly. For example, *@wait_for* delays plan execution until a specified condition becomes true, or a time-out occurs. *@test* evaluates a logical condition, and if the value is unknown, it posts an event that triggers further processing in the agent to try to resolve the value of the condition. *@achieve* specifies a condition that the agent must attempt to make true. If the condition is not true, plan execution is suspended and a specified event is posted to the agent. This event triggers a plan execution, and the *@achieve* statement succeeds or fails based on the outcome of this plan.

JACK also supports a class of events known as BDI events, which introduce a feature known as meta-level reasoning into plan behavior. The arrival of a BDI event at an agent triggers the normal event handling mechanisms described earlier. However, when more than one plan is a candidate for execution, the JACK run-time posts a *planChoice()* event to the agent. The process of handling this event is called meta-level reasoning in JACK. It gives the agent the opportunity to override default plan selection behavior and select a plan to handle from the set of possible plans. Plan selection is based on the BDI event and the current set of beliefs held by the agent.

Agents must consequently include one or more plans to handle *plan-Choice()* events. This is done as follows:

```
#handles event PlanChoice event_handle;
#chooses for event event1 event2;
```

Once a JACK plan is selected, it is executed following standard JACK mechanisms. If the selected plan succeeds, processing of the BDI event is complete.

If the plan fails, there are two possibilities. By default for BDI events derived from either *BDIFactEvent*, *BDIMessageEvent* and *BDITraced-MessageEvent*, plan failure results in overall failure to handle the event. However, for events derived from the *BDIGoalEvent* class, failure of the initially selected plan results in the BDI event being reposted to the agent. Upon receiving the reposted event, the agent can either choose another plan from the original set, or re-evaluate the applicable plans (the initial plan or another concurrent plan execution may have caused a change in the agent's beliefs) to generate a new plan set to choose from. This process continues until the agent finds a plan that succeeds, or all possible plans fail.

Consequently, the relatively sophisticated built-in JACK mechanisms for handling events of type *BDIGoalEvent* support goal-driven behavior in an agent. An agent can try all the alternative plans it has available to achieve the goal, and can take into account changes of state that occur while it is trying alternatives.

This is an excellent example of the power of agent technology. A JACK agent is simply an abstraction that has a set of available behaviors, which are represented as reusable plans. The application of these behaviors to processing events and goals is flexible and adaptable, in that they can be applied and tried in various orders that reflect the current state of the system. Importantly, nowhere in the code is the order of plan application hard-coded, and the programmer does not have to resort to arcane coding methods to implement flexible plan application. The language and underlying runtime framework provide the necessary abstractions and mechanisms to support this sophisticated behavior.

This discussion of the JACK technology is by no means complete, nor does it attempt to cover the many other abstraction mechanisms used in agent systems. Agent communication languages like KQML and agent mobility mechanisms as in Aglets are issues that add to the growing tapestry of agent technologies.

The key issue is that these abstractions and technologies characterize and define agents and an agent-oriented approach to problem solving. The abstractions and mechanisms make it easier to build complex decision-making software. Agents in this context are much more than conventional active objects and communicating distributed components, which, with sufficient development skill and guile, could happily acquire all the behavioral characteristics of agents. It will just take more effort.

14.5 Architectural Implications

In many cases, agent technologies extend existing object-oriented languages like Java or C++. Hence, many if not all of the design principles of object-orientation, will apply equally to agent-based systems. In addition, the concurrent and often distributed nature of agent systems bring into play other issues that, while not new, are worth restating and examining in an agent technology context.

14.5.1 Concurrency

In order to realize their aims of collaboration and autonomy, agents systems are necessarily concurrent. Concurrent systems are well known as being considerably harder to build than pure sequential applications. This means that the code must take adequate measures to protect shared resources from concurrent update attempts.

In addition, agents are responsible for enforcing any desired ordering of events through explicit synchronization. JACK, for example, supports dealing with concurrency through statements that are guaranteed to execute atomically, and statements such as @*wait* to aid with synchronization. It however remains incumbent upon the software engineer to thoroughly understand these issues, and provide correct implementations.

14.5.2 Scalability

There are a number of aspects to scalability that are relevant to agent systems. First, consider thread usage. It is well known that highly threaded application architectures can suffer performance degradation as the number of threads begins to exceed available system (CPU, memory) resources. Such systems are consequently not scalable. This kind of behavior is typically seen in applications that continually spawn new threads without due regard for their resource usage. As agents are often referred to as active objects, this potential exists in any agent technology that dedicates an individual thread to each agent. Undisciplined agent creation and management is likely to lead to non-scalable application behavior.

Second, agents often exist in and communicate across different processes on different machines. This means that inter-process communications costs between agents are considerably higher than those between co-located agents. In applications in which agent communities exchange frequent messages, these communications costs may become non-negliable. Agent architectures that employ a centralized broker style architecture can exacerbate this situation. If a broker is responsible for handling all incoming and outgoing messages for a collection of agents, the message latency introduced by the broker may become significant, especially under peak traffic loads. In general, agent applications that do not pay sufficient attention to communications costs across process and machine boundaries are unlikely to scale well.

Finally, the whole intent of some agent applications raises questions of scalability. Agents are often touted as intelligent web crawlers, acting as background personal assistants and constantly trawling the Internet for new and relevant information. While this is an enviable aim, it raises questions about what would happen if every user had a personal agent that continuously "roams" the Internet, accessing Web pages and digesting information.

For example, a study of traffic patterns at a major e-commerce site[61] indicates that a significant percentage of all site accesses are currently from software robots extracting information such as pricing and availability. It is not hard to imagine the load problems on Web sites that would occur if there were a sudden mass deployment of personal Web crawlers across the many millions of Internet users worldwide. This is unlikely to be a scalable situation, and could cause chaos by overwhelming the available software and hardware infrastructure of the Internet. Hence it may be that the whole notion of personal Web assistants may need rethinking, or regulating in some way before this style of application becomes feasible.

---

[61] M. Arlitt, D. Krishnamurthy, J. Rolia. *Characterizing the scalability of a large web-based shopping system*. ACM Transactions on Internet Technology, vol 1, no 1, August 2001, pp 44-69

14.5.3 Mobility

The ability for software agents to move from machine to machine to fulfill their goals is a potentially attractive proposition. Probably the best known technology is Aglets, which extends Java to handle agent migration. Aglets provide a comprehensive infrastructure for "weak" agent migration. This involves transferring an agent's code from one machine to another, and starting the code in the target execution environment. The Aglet infrastructure manages agent migration and communications with traveling agents.

Two of the main motivations for mobile agents are both performance related. By migrating to a remote location, an agent can more quickly access the local resources at that node. It can then efficiently send back its answer across the network, minimizing bandwidth utilization. Of course, these gains are only realized if the benefits of migrating an agent are greater than the actual costs of migration.

Efficient evaluation of this cost function is a problem with no known general solution. This is because it is not normally possible to have a priori knowledge of the amount of work an agent will perform when it reaches a remote execution site. Even if it were, the current CPU or memory usage on the receiving machine may be so high as to negate the performance benefits once the migration has taken place. The whole problem is further exacerbated by "strong" migration mechanisms, which also migrate an agent's current state. This is because the agent's state and threads stack contents vary in size as the agent executes, and hence affect the cost of migration.

Agent migration must also be concerned with issues of security, including authentication and authorization before migration occurs. In addition, the dangers of hostile code migrating to a machine are too high for many applications. Hostility may be in the form of damaging local resources, or for example entering an infinite loop and stealing available CPU cycles.

Straightforward mobile code applications would seem to be the most compelling applications of mobile technology. For example, once a mobile application infrastructure is in place, new components can be created and sent to remote hosts to provide them with updated and new functionality. This obviates the need for distribution of new functionality manually. It would also extend to limited resource domains such as PDAs, in which mobile applications could be used on demand and then flushed from the execution environment to create more resources for other applications. However, in many cases, ignoring the allure of mobility and settling on a more conventional static client-server or peer-to-peer distributed architecture will likely lead to simpler, more secure and higher performance applications.

14.6 Agent Technologies

The agent technology landscape comprises a number of commercial products and several more experimental technologies from research labs and academic institutions. The market place can be characterized as relatively fractured and mostly immature. There are a number of small development organizations (e.g. Reticular Systems, Agent Oriented Software, CHI Systems) with proprietary agent products (AgentBuilder, JACK, IGEN), along with efforts from major multinational research labs that typically offer open source technology (e.g. Aglets from IBM Japan, ZEUS from BT Labs).

In its current state, it is difficult at this moment in time to predict the directions the market will take, and which products and technologies will be sustainable. This situation exacerbates the risk of adopting a particular product as a strategic platform for an organization's development.

The agent community is aware of this issue, and in 1996 the Foundation of Intelligent Physical Agents (FIPA – www.fipa.org) was formed to define standards for agent technologies. In its 2001 definition of the FIPA Abstract Architecture (//www.fipa.org/specs/fipa00001/), a foundation platform is described that can potentially provide interoperability between FIPA-compliant products. Achieving a high level of interoperability between different vendor platforms is a significant step forward for agent technologies, as it would obviate to some extent the issues of vendor lock-in. It remains to be seen how many influential FIPA becomes, and how quickly products begin to adhere to the core FIPA specifications. Equally importantly will be the steps that are put in place to ensure and test FIPA interoperability.

14.7 Conclusions

The ICDE team concluded that agent technologies represent a highly promising new approach for a number of classes of applications. This particularly includes systems in which adaptable, flexible software behavior is required in complex distributed environments. Agents are certainly much more than the well understood and widely deployed paradigm of collaborating, distributed, active objects. They represent the merging of abstractions and problem-solving techniques from the realm of artificial intelligence with proven software engineering mechanisms for building distributed systems. To build an agent-based system, skills and knowledge in artificial intelligence and distributed, concurrent systems are a pre-requisite for using agent technologies and toolkits in the way their makers intended.

Despite the very significant interest in the potential for intelligent agents-based applications, the technology is still in an early stage of development. Much more work is needed by the leading academic and industrial research labs, standards bodies and product vendors to progress this state towards a set of mature, well-supported interoperable products with well-understood methods for design and engineering. Fortunately, the signs are encouraging. Still, in an area as dynamic and diverse as software technology, only time will tell precisely which tools and technologies will emerge as the pervasive foundations for intelligent agent systems.

In terms of the ICDE development, what does all this mean? Basically, the third party tool developers were welcome to use agent technologies in their solutions. This had no impact as far as the ICDE platform was concerned. The tools may use ICDE as a form of blackboard system for sharing data and sending notifications. The data can also be stored in the ICDE data store in any format convenient for agent communications. As long as it is self-describing and backed up by ontologies, the tools can happily communicate. In this respect, it looks like the ICDE's simple data storage and notification architecture had achieved its requirements for flexibility and modifiability.

14.8 Further Reading

If you're looking for a broad and accessible description of the basis for software agents from AI, a good place to start is the following:

J. Bradshaw (Editor). *Software Agents.* AAAI/MIT Press 1997

Another interesting collection of writing on agents with a software engineering focus is:

V. Plekhanova (editor), *Intelligent Agent Software Engineering*, Idea Group Publishing, 2002

An excellent Internet resource on all things concerning agents is at http://agents.umbc.edu/. The specific pages covering agent technologies and applications are:

http://agents.umbc.edu/Applications_and_Software/Software/index.sht
ml

An interesting agent and relatively mature open source agent technology
is Cougaar. It's a technology that's grown out of the logistics domain, and
has some sophisticated features for building multi-agent applications. The
best source of knowledge is:

www.cougaar.org

15 Concluding Thoughts

15.1 Challenges

In roughly fifteen years, the profession of software architect has progressed a very long way. There's now an established body of professional knowledge, design tools, supporting middleware technologies and professional societies. There's an active and productive R&D community that spans industrial practice and academic research groups. The latter is extremely encouraging, as it promises to evolve the discipline in pragmatic ways, grounding advances in what actually works in practice.

So while there's much to be optimistic about, there's still a lot that we as architects don't do very well at all. Amongst all these areas for improvement, many of which are covered in the previous chapters, there are two which I confront regularly and find particularly challenging. So I'll conclude this book with a brief description of these, to whet your appetite for what lies ahead.

15.1.1 Architecture Knowledge Management

A recent incident emphasizes the importance of this area. An ex-colleague of mine, working in a large IT operation in a major financial organization, told me of the disaster that ensued when their Chief Architect suddenly resigned (destined for more lucrative pastures). The architect was by all accounts a remarkably talented designer and engineer, and in many cases was absolutely fundamental in getting projects operational within deadlines.

By the time the architect unexpectedly resigned, much of the knowledge about how and why the organizations' systems integrated resided only in his head. As all the IT projects operated in a high pressure environment, there had been little time to capture, document and disseminate the design decisions and knowledge that had shaped the organization's complex IT environment. Delivering functionality to clients was what mattered, and design rational capture had a low priority. When he resigned, this knowledge went with him, leaving the organization in disarray. In fact, six months later, projects are still being delivered consistently late and over-budget, while the reconstruction of this design information gradually takes place. It's is not a happy place to work, I hear.

There's nothing new in this "Super Hero" syndrome. But when so much of the critical information behind the design and integration of core business systems lives only in a single person's head, albeit a super person's head, this is a disaster waiting to happen. It's amazing that this situation prevails so commonly in IT departments around the globe.

It's easy to take an "ivory tower" position on this problem. If organizations estimated and budgeted better, then time and costs would be allocated to capturing key design decisions in documents and repositories that can be revisited and reused. But reality is different, and ever-increasing business pressures and shrinking IT budgets are simply not going to allow this to happen.

So a breakthrough in this problem area requires the confluence of two solutions. First, we need to understand how to capture, organize and reuse architecture design knowledge. This is more than documenting architecture designs in the UML or some equivalent notations. It requires the rationales for design decisions to be recorded, so that the fundamental reasons behind a decision can be understood. As systems evolve, this information can be digested by engineers other than the ones who made the original decisions. It makes it possible to understand the design alternatives considered and the ultimate trade-offs that were made.

Second, and just as important, we need to create ways in which we can capture this architecture design knowledge as a by-product of the architecture design process itself. Requiring additional steps in the design process to document decisions plainly doesn't work in tightly budgeted projects in high pressure IT environments. We need design tools that make this information capture process an integral part of the design itself. Then we'll have a solution that will work in practice.

I don't know of any serious solutions to these problems that are emerging, but there are definitely some promising approaches.[62] When we know how to efficiently capture and exploit our architecture design knowledge, project risks and costs are likely to be greatly reduced.

---

[62] We've been trialing this approach, with promising results, as described in this paper: T. Al-Naeem, I. Gorton, M. Ali Baba, F. Rahbi, B. Boualem , *A Quality-Driven Systematic Approach for Architecting Distributed Software Applications*, International Conference on Software Engineering (ICSE) 2005, St Loius, USA, IEEE Computer Society

15.1.2 Adaptive Architectures

Once an application's requirements, environment and constraints are fully understood, as a profession we're pretty good at building software that works. We don't always do it as cheaply or as quickly as estimated, but the plethora of business critical applications that we all use every day demonstrate what we're capable of.

In many cases, the occasions when software systems start to have problems are when something unexpected changes in the environment. Perhaps the concurrent user load exceeds the estimates for peak loads, or a network link saturates or fails, or some data in a new format arrives that we hadn't anticipated. These issues cause problems because most of the architectures we design are "static" in that they are not designed to handle many unexpected occurrences. There are good reasons for this. It costs a lot more to build a system that can adapt to various changes in its environment. And it's more difficult too, as predicting the unexpected is always a tricky business!

The solution to building robust applications that adapt to their environment is to utilize "adaptive" architectures. It's simply too difficult and expensive to build custom adaptive logic into every application. Just like existing middleware embodies design patterns that help us solve complex problems, we need a new generation of middleware that provides the core mechanisms for creating adaptive software systems. Adaptive middleware will contain components that monitor their environment (e.g. CPU usage, network capacity, and platform and application resource usage) and provide communications and management mechanisms to respond to changes. It'll also supply a programming framework so designers can plug in their own components to respond to changes that they wish to intercept.

To their great credit, IBM is helping drive the R&D agenda in this area through their autonomic systems initiative.[63] Microsoft's Dynamic Systems Initiative[64] is similar in nature. Both are focusing on technologies for self-managing systems, to significantly reduce the ever-growing administrative burden associated with large enterprise applications.

Adaptive middleware technologies are a key part of this autonomic vision. Current R&D efforts are still investigating and trialing possible approaches, but the strong business imperatives for such technologies will dictate their emergence in the not-too-distant future. Still, this is a challenging area of R&D and technology, and all the problems will not be

---

[63] http://www-03.ibm.com/autonomic/
http://www.research.ibm.com/autonomic/
[64] http://www.microsoft.com/windowsserversystem/dsi/default.mspx

solved in my lifetime. But even incremental advances in middleware technologies should make it possible for us to start building dynamic architectures that can support levels of robustness and performance that we can't cost-effectively achieve today.

It all promises to be a fascinating future.

Glossary

ACID The ACID properties of transactions, namely atomic, consistent, isolated and durable.

ADL Architecture Description Languages are a body of research comprising graphical and textual languages for formally or semi-formally describing software architectures.

AOP Aspect-Oriented Programming, as supported by programming languages such as AspectJ.

AOSD Aspect-Oriented Software Development comprises AOP as well as analysis and design methods to support AOP.

API An Application Programming Interface is a programmatic interface to a technology such as a component, database, middleware or communications system.

ATAM The Architecture Tradeoff and Analysis Method is an approach to architecture evaluation devised at the SEI.

BMP Bean-Managed Persistence entity beans are managed by a container, but contain programmer-supplied code to access an associated persistent store such as a database.

BPO Business Process Orchestration is used to manage long-running business processes or workflows that typically span multiple back-end systems.

CCB A Change Control Board is an organizational mechanism used to control changes to a software product line.

CCM The CORBA Component Model is an Object Management Group standard for components in a CORBA environment. At the time of writing, it has not been widely implemented.

CI A Configuration Identification is a name used to identify a specific configuration (version) in a software product line.

CIM In MDA, the Computation Independent Model captures the business model of the system. It is typically developed by a business analyst.

CMP Container-Managed Persistence entity beans are managed by a container, and use information in the bean's deployment descriptor to generate the code needed to access an associated database. A technology known as an Object-

	Relational Mapper (ORM) is used to implement CMP.
CORBA	A standard for multi-language distributed object systems that is widely supported by multiple vendors.
COTS	Commercial-Off-The-Shelf components can be any part of a system that is acquired rather than built. The term is typically used rather loosely, ranging from simple components such as widgets in a GUI, to complex technologies like Oracle.
CTW	Compile-Time Weaving is used in AOP to weave aspects in to the application's code at compile-time.
EAI	Enterprise Application Integration is a name for a set of technologies and methods for integrating the existing stand-alone applications that an enterprise has built and/or purchased.
EJB	The Enterprise JavaBean component model is part of the J2EE platform. EJBs are server-side components for implementing business logic and accessing databases.
ERP	Enterprise Resource Planning systems are packaged applications like SAP and PeopleSoft. Enterprises purchase and tailor them to implement their core business processes.
IDL	Interface Description Languages are used in technologies like CORBA to define the programmatic interface that a component or object supports.
J2EE	The Java 2 Enterprise Edition is a Java platform for server application development in an N-tiered environment.
JDBC	Java Database Connectivity is a Java API for accessing data stores, usually relational databases.
JMS	The Java Messaging Service is a part of the J2EE platform that defines the API for Java-based messaging and publish-subscribe.
JSP	Java Server Pages are part of the J2EE platform aimed at handling Web interactions.
LOD	A Line of Development is an identifiable component of a product line that evolves independently.
LTW	Load-Time Weaving in AOP is when aspects are weaved in to an application as the application is loaded.
MDA	Model-Driven Architecture is an approach to building applications from high-level models. The models are input in to code generators that produce the final application code. MDA is an Object Management Group initiative and Trademark.
MOF	The Meta-Object Facility is a meta-modeling language that

must be used to describe the models used in MDA. The MOF can be used to define the elements of any modeling language.

MOM   Message-Oriented Middleware provides queue-based, asynchronous communication channels between two applications.

NFR   Non-Functional Requirements are the constraints (such as cost/schedule) and quality attributes (such as reliability and scalability) that a design for a system should satisfy.

OWL   The Web Ontology Language is a markup language for publishing and sharing data using ontologies. It is a key part of the Semantic Web technologies.

OWL-S   OWL-S is an OWL-based ontology for Web services. It supplies Web service providers with a markup language for describing the properties and capabilities of their Web services in a dynamically interpretable form.

PIM   In MDA, the Platform Independent Model is a model of an application's functionality.

PKI   Public Key Infrastructure is a security technology that can be used to verify and authenticate the validity of each party involved in a distributed interaction.

PLA   A Product Line Architecture is an approach for designing families of software systems that exploits large-scale reuse of design and development artifacts.

PSM   In MDA, the Platform Specific Model captures the implementation of an application's PIM for a specific technology platform.

RDF   The Resource Description Framework is a framework for describing and interchanging metadata.

RTW   Run-Time Weaving in AOP allows the definition of aspects to be weaved dynamically as an application executes.

RUP   The Rational Unified Process is an adaptable software process framework for iterative software development.

SCM   Software Configuration Management is the discipline of managing and evolving different versions of software applications.

SEI   The Software Engineering Institute in based at Carnegie-Mellon University in Pittsburgh. The SEI's Architecture group has been fundamental to the progress of thinking in the software architecture discipline.

SOA   A Service Oriented Architecture is an approach to building software systems from independent applications that communicate only by accessing the business-level services that each application provides.

SOAP   SOAP (not an acronym) is an XML-based messaging protocol used in Web services. A SOAP message comprises three parts, namely (1) an envelope describing what is in a message and how to process it, (2) a set of encoding rules for expressing instances of application-defined datatypes, and (3) a convention for representing remote procedure calls and responses.

UDDI   Universal Description, Discovery and Integration is an XML-based standard for a Web services distributed directory (registry) for businesses to advertise their services and discover services of interest.

UML   The Unified Modeling Language is the Object Management Group standard for modeling software systems. The UML 2.0 is the latest version and is a significant upgrade over versions 1.x.

WS-*   A set of Web services standard definition including WS-Addressing, WS-Eventing, WS-Security and several others.

WSDL   The Web Services Description Language (WSDL) is an XML-based standard for describing a Web service. WSDL describes how to access a service and where a service is located.

XMI   The XML Metadata Interchange is used for interchange of metadata between UML modeling tools and between tools and MOF-based metadata repositories.

XML   The Extensible Markup Language is a general-purpose markup language for describing different kinds of structured data. One of its main uses is to facilitate the sharing of data between different business applications.

Index

Gustavo Alonso, ETH Zentrum,
Zürich, Switzerland;
Fabio Casati, Harumi Kuno, Vijay Machiraju
Hewlett-Packard, Palo Alto, CA, USA

Web Services

Concepts, Architectures and Applications

XX, 354 p. Hardcover
ISBN 3-540-44008-9

Like many other incipient technologies, Web services are still surrounded by a tremendous level of noise. This noise results from the always dangerous combination of wishful thinking on the part of research and industry and of a lack of clear understanding of how Web services came to be. On the one hand, multiple contradictory interpretations are created by the many attempts to realign existing technology and strategies with Web services. On the other hand, the emphasis on what could be done with Web services in the future often makes us lose track of what can be really done with Web services today and in the short term. These factors make it extremely difficult to get a coherent picture of what Web services are, what they contribute, and where they will be applied. Alonso and his co-authors deliberately take a step back. Based on their academic and industrial experience with middleware and enterprise application integration systems, they describe the fundamental concepts behind the notion of Web services and present them as the natural evolution of conventional middleware, necessary to meet the challenges of the Web and of B2B application integration. Rather than providing a reference guide or a "how to write your first Web service" kind of book, they discuss the main objectives of Web services, the challenges that must be faced to achieve them, and the opportunities that this novel technology provides. Established, as well as recently proposed, standards and techniques (e.g., WSDL, UDDI, SOAP, WS-Coordination, WS-Transactions, and BPEL), are then examined in the context of this discussion in order to emphasize their scope, benefits, and shortcomings. Thus, the book is ideally suited both for professionals considering the development of application integration solutions and for research and students interesting in understanding and contributing to the evolution of enterprise application technologies.

Contents: Part I: Conventional Middleware 1) Distributed Information Systems 2) Middleware 3) Enterprise Application Integration 4) Web Technologies Part II: Web Services 5) Web Services 6) Basic Web Services Technologies 7) Service Coordination Protocols 8) Service Composition 9) Outlook Bibliography; Index